PLEASURE FROM PLANTS

Novels

The Grapevine in England
From the Waste Land
Soil and Civilization
Prophecy of Famine (*with H. J. Massingham*)
Vineyards in England
The Speaking Garden
The Orchard and Fruit Garden (*with A. A. Jackson*)
The Last of the Incas (*with George Ordish*)
The New Statesman. The History of the First Fifty Years 1913-1963
The English Garden
Dionysus
The Wings of the Morning
A Time to Cast Away
To Sea in a Bowl
William Medium
Bloodmoney
Not in our Stars
The Astrologer
Sylvester
Gentian Violet
Stories and Cream
The Slaughterhouse Informer
Into the Dream
Taking it Easy
All we Possess
A Perfect Stranger
The Last Poor Man

Pleasure from Plants

Edward Hyams

LONGMANS

LONGMANS, GREEN AND CO LTD
48 Grosvenor Street, London W1

Associated companies, branches and representatives throughout the world

First published 1966

Printed in Great Britain by
The Camelot Press Ltd., London and Southampton

Author's Note

In an effort, probably futile, to avoid rebuke from experts, I should explain that I have done my best to name the plants in this book correctly. Almost certainly, however, I can be faulted in one respect: the names of what botanists call cultivars—varieties known only in cultivation—should be printed in Roman letters and put into single quotation marks; whereas the names of varieties found in nature are printed in italics following the word var., meaning variety. The difficulty, using reference books and catalogues which are not all up to date in this respect, is to know which plants are cultivars and which not. For practical purposes it does not matter, since the name is there. But if I have inadvertently broken the rules sometimes, I apologise.

The decorations in this book—I do not call them illustrations for they do not always match the text—express a part of my pleasure in plants as I could not do it in words. They have been deliberately chosen from Besler's *Hortus Eystettensis* (with the help and kind permission of the Lindley Library of the Royal Horticultural Society), because, by a measure of stylisation, they emphasise the element of pattern which is one of the great beauties of plant forms. We are obliged, nowadays, to use photography to illustrate plants and the method has its merits: but they are not equal to the merits of a good drawing and few modern artists have the courage, when drawing plants, to use stylisation without losing botanical accuracy.

E. H.

Acknowledgement

This book is based upon articles contributed by the author to *The Illustrated London News* in recent years. The author and publishers wish to thank *The Illustrated London News* for their co-operation and courtesy in connection with the publication of this book.

The illustrations are taken from the two volumes of Besler, *Hortus Eystettensis*, by courtesy of the Lindley Library, Royal Horticultural Society.

Contents

IIII.

Viola martia flore albo.

Chapter 1

Introduction

The object of a preface is to persuade the reader to approach what he is about to read in a particular spirit, the spirit which suits the author; though without, of course, appearing to do so.

Reading about another man's garden is like visiting it; I have no doubt whatever about the spirit in which I like my garden to be visited—and therefore read about. It is clearly set out in a short piece which I wrote for *The Illustrated London News* some years ago and which, since it serves my introductory purpose, I reproduce here.

There is an extreme opinion that no garden is large enough for more than one person. My own view, for what it is worth, is that gardening is best done in the company of one person; but the two gardeners must be very fond of each other, so used to each other that they communicate almost without words. On the whole they will work at opposite ends of the garden; they will come together for periods of rest and to admire or deplore the results of their past efforts. I was meditating on these matters and it occurred to me to try to define the perfect garden visitor, the man or woman whose arrival in the middle of a job you have long been looking forward to doing is an uncovenanted pleasure.

This visitor will be someone you know, but not very well, so that there is no need to waste time exchanging enquiries about families. The moment he gets out of his car in front of the house he looks around him, an expression of amazement comes over his agreeable face, and he exclaims in accents of deep sincerity, 'How extraordinarily well all your plants are looking! No, really, I have seen nothing like them this year.' He does not remark on the weather; he ignores it, he is as capable as you are of remaining outside in conditions which would reduce any non-gardener to shivering misery. Just before coming into the house he turns again to his car and takes out a pot which he puts down beside the door, saying, 'I expect you have it already, but one always has room for a plant. It's not much, I'm afraid.' You take it up to look at it while you thank him: it is a rarity of astonishing beauty which you have been looking for for ten years and which even Hillier of Winchester has been unable to provide.

Later, as you go slowly round the garden with your visitor looking at every single plant and discussing it, his interest and admiration never flag for a moment. When he says 'cupresso*s*yparis' and you pronounce it 'cupresso*k*yparis' he defers at once to your botanical 'Latin', laughingly confessing that he never knows how to pronounce the names of plants, so that when you yourself stumble you are not mortified. You mention that so-and-so, a well-known expert and nurseryman, pointed out when he called last week that you have all your hydrangeas wrongly named; your visitor at once says, 'O, that fellow. My dear chap, he does exactly the same thing at Kew and Wisley.'

Your visitor knows, of course, where you can get the fine old York stone paving slabs you have given up all idea of, for a song, although when you tried to buy them they were priced at the value of half a dozen whole operas. His reactions to your name-dropping are exactly what they should be. When you explain that such and such a plant was given you by Archie Gibson, or begin with 'Heathcoat-Amory was telling me . . .' or 'Dorrien-Smith is of opinion that . . .' your visitor looks at you with respectful admiration, for these are names of power in gardening; he never makes the mistake of asking you whether you actually know these great men, which you hardly do, but assumes that you are, of course, not only on terms of horticultural intimacy, but deserve to be. Nor does he try to trump your court cards with some casual reference to a conversation he had with Lord Aberconway at the last council meeting of the R.H.S.

Whenever you come to some plant which is supposed to be difficult and with which, for some reason which has more to do with luck than skill, you have succeeded in growing, your visitor shakes his head ruefully and admits that he for his part has repeatedly failed with it. And the rooted cutting you offer from your cold-frame is accepted as if it were made of solid platinum set with emeralds.

Although he ignores the actual weather, except to remark once that it will clear up in a minute, he is perfectly willing to discuss the weather of the past several months; his memory of it coincides exactly with yours and he takes the opportunity of this discussion to say that he is even more astonished at your results when he considers the difficulties with which you have had to cope. In his garden, on the other hand, the weather was more favourable, yet he can show nothing equal to yours. He has read and can discuss the same garden books as have come your way and he listens with respect to your criticism of them and comments in such terms as make it abundantly clear that all these books would have been much improved had you been given the opportunity to correct them in manuscript for the authors who would no doubt have been very glad to have you do it.

Does this paragon exist? Hardly, although I know gardeners, and in every case they are very good gardeners indeed, who have such beautiful visiting manners that their calls, nicely spaced out and always timed to be welcome, are hardly less gratifying. But life being what it is (yes, I know this is sententious but after all, it *is*), there is another kind of visitor; in fact, several other kinds. There are those who have really called because they have nothing better to do and who don't know a paeony from a pernettya: the proper way with them is to say emphatically, 'You don't want to see the garden', and give them another gin and french. The only even tolerable garden visitor must be a gardener himself. But even with that condition fulfilled, there is always the possibility of encountering a man, rarely a woman, whose gardenmanship is better than your own.

This character has you completely beaten from the start. It is not that he ever directly criticises your plants: one way he goes about getting you down is to stand looking at a group of, say, shrubs, and then remarking, 'Of course, your soil's all wrong for them, I quite see your difficulty'. You come to some rhododendron or camellia which, you thought, was not to be had from mere nurseries and which is a rare and lovely thing: you are about to embark on the enjoyable explanation of how you got it, when he says, 'How wise of you to grow really well-tried old favourites'. As to the plants in his own garden, with which he repeatedly compares your own with implications which do yours no credit, he has a wonderful technique. *He has no plants with mere names.* 'Of course,' he says, 'you know Farrer's 5793?' Or it is, 'Yes, I have something like it, but with more distinction in the form of the corolla. Kingdon-Ward's 7682. Two or three of us had the seeds direct from Tibet.' You know, dismally, that you cannot compete with this sort of thing nor with his opinion that, with the marvellous climate your garden enjoys, you should be able to grow absolutely anything.

I have cast doubts on whether the first, the paragon visitor, exists. As to the other one—well, does he? Life being what it is, yes. But I do not want to give the impression that I dislike him. He is a plant snob and of all the products of an English garden not the least delightful, to my taste, is the plant-snob. If Mr Stephen Potter ever wants to add a volume to his learned treatise on Lifemanship, he might do worse than turn his attention to Plantmanship.

There is, of course, a legitimate and useful branch of this craft whose greatest living exponent is, in my view, Mr Will Ingwersen. His is the plant erudition of the real professional and he expounds his deep knowledge for us gardeners, without pretentiousness, with simplicity and, what is rare, with wit and style. This is admirable and it has nothing whatever to do with that plantsmanship which is a branch of one-up-man-ship, and of which I have made a study during years of garden visiting.

Plantsmanship of the latter order flourishes chiefly on acid soils, but it is not a calcifuge, for I have found it occasionally on the chalk, and growing very rankly too. Surrey and Sussex produce the finest specimens, but I have found good ones as far north as Yorkshire. Outside of England, it is extremely rare. The amateur of this singular cultigen should see it in the kind of 'garden' which is no more a garden than the sort of house so stuffed with objects of vertu that it looks like a museum, is a home. Such gardens are really collections; and since collectors can never have enough, the specimens crowd so thickly one upon another that none flourish and all are hard to see. And as the collector shows you round, mercilessly pouring out the history of every wretched plant in the place, he slowly forces on you—this is his aim—a realisation of your own horticultural ignorance.

Halting before a debilitated and straggling rose creeping its half-hearted way through the branches of a blighted mauve-leaved hazel which turns out to be *Hamamelis atro-purpurea*, grown from a slip stolen by a Jesuit from the Dalai Lama's garden in Lhasa, the collector says, 'Now, this will interest you. You recognise it, of course?' He knows perfectly well that you don't and when you shake your head raises his eyebrows and goes on, 'I'm told Hidcote have it, but I must say *I* couldn't find it there. I had it from Meyer in Strasbourg, just before he died. It's the original "Cuisse de nymphe épouvantée". Lovely colour, isn't it?' The colour is that of very old frozen meat, but you admire it, for the man is your host. You have hardly recovered from the effort of doing so before he is making you kneel in the wet and ill-mown grass to peer at a small, chlorotic-looking plant, something between a primula and a funkia in appearance, but with flowers like uncooked kidneys. To expose the thing, the collector has to disinter it from beneath the collapsed stems of a hideous green-flowered centaurea briefly dismissed as, '. . . the *viridiflorus* which only occurs in the east moat of the Hospitallers' castle on Ischia'. 'This,' he says, '—but, of course, you know it—is the hosta Banks collected near Tsarong-Ipi. My own view is that it's identical with Delavay's *Hosta quinquedentata*, var. *anarcardium*. What's your opinion?'

You have none; your face reveals the fact. One corner of his mouth turns up in silent comment. He looks at you with the expectant air of a man about to say something outrageous and goes on, 'I'll tell you my opinion for what it's worth and I warn you you won't find a man at the Linnaean Society to agree with me. It may have crossed your own mind, though . . .' He steps nearer and breathing hard in your face says, with ponderous emphasis, 'My dear fellow, it's obvious; Delavay had *never really read* the *Pen ts'ao*'. The collector steps back to observe your amazement at this outrageous—presumably it is outrageous—statement. 'Consider,' he continues, 'what Čen Tsiao says in his *T'un Ci*. And it's no good telling me that when it comes to the Sung Dynasty, Laufer is apt to misread . . .'

You interrupt to confess that you have never heard of the *Pen ts'ao*, nor of Čen Tsiao, nor, even, of Laufer. This is a mistake he has been waiting for, and he promptly offers to lend you his copy of the *Pen ts'ao*, adding, 'But you will take great care of it, won't you? Vonderaa of Shanghai took eight years finding me a copy. It's very *scarce* . . .' [This is bookmanship; in the trade books are never *rare*, they are *scarce*.] '. . . Of course, it's insured, but only for five hundred.'

By this time he has you in such a state that when you admit that your knowledge of classical Chinese is poor you feel as if you are confessing to an unusual and shameful illiteracy. The collector replies that he supposes, at least, that you read German and will lend you Bretschneider's translation, 'Though, mind you, it's full of mistakes'.

And so it goes on: a botrytis-stricken verbascum with very small flowers of a peculiarly repulsive shade of khaki was 'collected' by your host on the lower slopes of Aconcagua and is the 'Heaven-aspiring angel's hair' of the Quetchua poet Huayna. At last you come to something which you can contrive to admire with some show of sincerity; it is a pale blue daisy almost as nice as an aster. You ask what kind of aster it is, only to be told that it's the so-called tree-mesembryanthemum of eastern Asia: '*M. arbusulum coeruleum.* Not really a garden plant at all. Rex sent me the seeds from Kamchatka last August, when he was staying with the Yellow Hat monks of . . . of course, you know Rex, however?' No; you do not even know Rex, who, it transpires, is the seventh duke of Wessex and who has the finest collection of exotic dog's mercuries in the world, 'Apart from the herbarium at the Massachusetts Technical Institute, of course'.

You are getting near to the end of your ordeal. Determined to show that you are not an utter ignoramus, you search the crammed borders for something you know beyond question, find it at last, and pointing carelessly, say, 'Rather an unusual form of *Rhus continus*, surely?' The plant in question is fighting a losing battle against a lush growth of what look to you like giant dead-nettles with flowers whose livid colour could best be described as *mal-de-mer*. You host glances at the shrub and, as you wait in something like desperation to hear that Farrer sent the seed to him from the Shogun's garden at Hacijo Shima, he shrugs and says, 'One of those strokes of luck, you know. My wife planted it as variety *atro-purpurea* and it turns out to be an orange-leaved sport. Half the nurserymen in England have been after me for it. I'm thinking of showing it at the R.H.S. for an Award of Merit.'

Does this read as if I am excusing my own horticultural ignorance by mocking the learned? I am not: in 1959, after twelve years of gardening in Kent and two years before we moved to Devonshire, I wrote an essay for *The Illustrated London News* on the pleasures of ignorance in a garden, and what I wrote is still true.

ON NOT KNOWING IT ALL

I believe that if you were to ask me what, in my years of turning acres of waste land into garden, had given me most pleasure, I should reply: 'My own ignorance.' The man born to the work, or trained to it from boyhood, very rarely has the incomparable pleasure of astonishment. I shall never forget my delight when my first graft 'took'; even today I am capable of pleased surprise on finding a crop of potatoes under the haulms. But the peak of excitement until now was due to finding that a whole seed-box full of lily seeds had, after nearly two years, germinated. Of course one knows—in the way one knows that the earth goes round the sun—that lilies, like any other plants, grow from seed. But to get them to do so oneself was quite another matter.

And had I not been ignorant I should never even have started with those seeds. For they were seeds of *Lilium martagon*, the capsule taken from plants which grow wild in a wood not a thousand miles from our house. The status of martagon lilies in the English flora is uncertain: most authorities give it as 'naturalised', a few as native. But what I did not know was that it takes between five and seven years to get a flower from a martagon seed.

By no means all lilies take so long: I was given a pinch of *L. formosanum* seed by a friend. Following his instructions. I sowed them in heat early in February, five to an eight inch pot, thinned the seedlings to three, and by October had a dozen pots of magnificent white trumpet lilies, fragrant and graceful, on three foot stalks. The bulbs under them were subsequently planted out into the garden: here, the unhappier side of ignorance came into the story; I lost most of the bulbs—wrong soil, wrong site, wrong depth of planting. Enough survived, however, to establish themselves—and maintain my enthusiasm. I became a reader of lily books, and while thus dispelling some of my ignorance, also paralysed my new lily mania, and that for years—the reason being that I could not afford to grow lilies in our garden as it seemed to me they should be grown, to wit, as woodland plants under light shade and some sun, and with an undercover of azaleas. This obstacle out of the way, however, a real start has at last been made. Part of our garden consisted of a large hole in the ground caused, according to local tradition, by the jettisoning of a Zeppelin's bomb load in 1916 or 1917. A more probable explanation is: excavation for brick-earth in about 1800. At all events, self-sown trees—ash, elm and a hawthorn—had grown to a fine size round and in this hole by the time we bought the property. Our soil was chalky and we could grow no calcifuges. But by having this hole filled with lime-free loam, we made ourselves a tiny piece of woodland capable of growing rhododendrons. Here, then, I am working vast quantities of peat, leaf-mould and sand into an area to be protected by an artificial bank, which I am building up at the same time. Bank, and the place it protects, will be planted with dwarf evergreen azaleas and perhaps some other shrubs; among them will go the lily bulbs.

I shall buy a few flowering-size bulbs, just to keep up my courage; but meanwhile, our small—and only—range of cucumber frames has been filled with J.I. No. 2 compost and made over to raising lily bulbs for at least four years. The seeds of fifteen species have been sown, the bulb scales of one (*L. martagon*) and the leaf-axil bulbils of one (*L. tigrinum*). Seven, including the bulbils, have germinated already. One, at least, will not germinate until the spring of 1961. I hope, from time to time, to give news of the lily garden.

I have just had the pleasure of yet another surprise due to ignorance. Spending a week in Devonshire to get up strength for the 1959 vintage, and to get away from the spectacle of wasps consuming our supply of wine for 1961 while it is still on the vines, I noticed, in the hotel lounge, a vase of very attractive pink and red flowers, unknown to me, and which looked a little like an epipactis, a little like a small, coloured chincherinchee, a little like a miniature gladiolus, and a little like a certain small, white asphodels which grow in the Touraine. They were locally grown and I sought out the nurseryman-florist in question. He had a large plantation of these flowers. The only name he had for them was 'Kaffir lilies', *ergo*, they are South African. I cannot say anything more about them until I am back among my reference books: but if, as the nurseryman assured me, they were once commonly grown here, are perfectly hardy, rapidly increase—being bulbous or rhizomatous—and flower steadily from September until Christmas, then it is time they were widely reintroduced. Even if they are not as hardy as all that, they could be cloched to provide flowers for the house in early winter.

It may be that in treating of Kaffir lilies as a 'discovery' I am exposing myself to ridicule. Well, if half the nation grows them, all I can say is, I have never seen them in a garden before and I have the love of plants which makes me a fairly keen observer in other people's gardens as well as my own. My nurseryman-informant says that his stock of these plants survived the terrible winter of 1947–48, and has given me a 'clump' of each colour. We shall see how they do in east Kent.

I.
Auricula Ursi flore
albo.

Chapter 2

Ericas

I have learned a lot since my first experiences with lilies described in the previous chapter. The range of plants which one can grow in Devonshire is much wider than in Kent and in growing them one learns them just as one learns a language by reading it. And one gathers preferences and prejudices. The pleasure which I have had and still have from plants is much greater from some families of plants than from others; from certain genera within those families than from their congeners; and from a few species within those genera than from the rest.

There is a family of plants, the *Ericaceae*, about which I learned very little in Kent for neither our soil nor our climate were suitable for them, whereas in Devonshire, when we moved there, we found them ideal. The family includes some of the most beautiful plants in the world: *Arbutus*, *Rhododendron*, *Kalmia*, among many others, belong here; and so, of course, do *Calluna*, and the ericas themselves, the heaths and heathers.

WINTER HEATHERS

Probably the hardiest winter-flowering plants one can grow are the varieties of *Erica carnea*. Mr Fred J. Chapple, who knows more about heaths and heather than anyone else and whose book *The Heather Garden* (Collingridge, 25*s*) is the best on its subject for the amateur or professional gardener, has this to say about the hardiness of *carneas*:

> Without wishing to be dogmatic I think I am right in saying that no hardier plant exists in the wide field of garden cultivation: one could grow *carneas* to flower perfectly on the slopes of Ben Nevis or on the summit of Snowdon.

This fact, combined with the fact that they are perfectly tolerant of lime provided the soil at the time of planting is helped with a little good loam or some peat, makes the *carneas* universal plants, as it were; there is nowhere in the British Isles, and probably nowhere within the Temperate Zone where they will not do well, and for all I know they would be equally useful in the sub-tropics, if watered.

The variety 'Winter Beauty' begins to flower in November, is invariably in good flower at Christmas, is at its brilliant best throughout January, and is often still flowering away in March. It forms a slowly increasing prostrate 'rug' of good foliage, very dense, never tall, and a plant may ultimately cover four square feet of surface which, in January, is a sheet of deep pink bells. This seems to be the earliest *carnea* I have grown yet, but 'Eileen Porter' is earlier; it is also a better colour. In the south-west it will probably be in flower late in October, and at its best in mid-winter, going off towards February; in the north it will not flower until early December and will last in flower until March, or even April. This variety should, apparently, be chosen now in preference to the older, equally early variety 'Queen Mary', for whereas the new one is reliable in any garden, or so I am told, the old one is not and there are gardens where it has been for years without flowering.

The earliest white-flowered *carnea* of merit—and it is a good idea to break up the mass of pinks and carmines and rosy-purples with some white—is 'Cecilia M. Beale'. It is a very dwarf but spreading plant, its flowers are quite large and it is usually in flower by the middle of January and continues throughout February and just into March. With it plant 'Springwood White', which is beginning to flower as the other is at the height of its season, and which is at its best when the 'Cecilia M. Beale' is going over. 'Springwood' flowers into April and is judged by specialists to be the best white and one of the half-dozen best heathers in cultivation. Its foliage is bright, indeed a vivid green, and it always looks young and fresh. The flowers are large; the chocolate brown anthers act as an accent on the white, softening the whole effect to cream. A single plant will, fairly soon, for the variety is a quick grower, cover a square yard. There is a pink form of this *carnea* which should also be planted; and I have heard of, but never seen, a crimson form.

Another winter-flowering *carnea* variety is, by reason of its name, apt to lead to verbal tangling: it is *Erica carnea* var. *carnea.*

This again, has particularly bright green foliage; its flowers are pink and of good size and substance. It is commonly in full flower in January and it continues flowering until the end of March. The same is true of 'Mrs Sam Doncaster', a strong-growing rather taller plant, dense enough in habit to suppress all weeds except, I find, certain grasses. The flowers are large, and a rather pale pink, not one of the best for colour. For a really deep red the best early I have grown, though I find it has apparently vanished from our planting, is the variety *praecox rubra*. But I would rather see this one planted by itself or among plants of some other genus, for it is an open, non-carpeter, of lighter habit altogether, and when it is planted among other *carneas* it is apt to look leggy, as if there was something slightly wrong with it.

With one or two, or all, of these, you can have heather colour until March. There are many very good *carneas* to follow these, beginning their season in March, but these are obviously spring-, not winter-flowering. However, one must be mentioned, for it received the R.H.S. Award of Merit: it is 'King George', and its distinctions are fine foliage, good form, and flowers of a deep rose-crimson in abundance. It flowers in March.

There are a number of heaths which are hybrids between one or other variety of the winter-flowering *carneas* and *E. mediterranea* which, by the way, is not a Mediterranean plant, but one which grows 'in the midst of the land', i.e. *away* from the sea. These hybrids are called *E. darleyensis* after the nursery where the first appeared. *E. darleyensis* is tolerant of lime where the soil is otherwise suitable and attains about eighteen inches in height and is fairly compact, and bushy. Its flowers, which are very plentiful, are rose-purple, the classic heath colour, and in warm gardens they first appear in December, although in most gardens this plant blooms in January. The *darleyensis* variety 'Arthur Johnson' is a cross between the *carnea* 'Ruby Glow' and *E. mediterranea* var. *glauca*. This flowers from January to March inclusive with extraordinarily long sprays of dark pink flowers. With this can be planted what is virtually a white version, although of different provenance, 'Norman Webster'.

I shall presently have something to say about the tree heaths, favourites of mine, but although in the mountains between Portugal and Spain I have seen some of them brilliantly in flower in February, with the flowers shining under a film of melting snow, in Britain they do not flower until March, and cannot therefore be considered as winter-flowering. I think the earliest of the group is *E. arborea* which may produce its myriads of pale cream, fragrant flowers in late February here, in mild winters. In Ireland, and in Portugal, I have seen this fifteen feet tall or perhaps rather more, and with stout enough timber to make a small table, or a chair. There are some very big ones in Cornish gardens, too.

I have propagated winter-flowering *carneas* in two different ways, both easy. First the taking of very tiny cuttings when the plant is growing vigorously and rooting these in pure peat or in peat and sand. The only disadvantage of this method, if it is one, is the smallness of the plant you have to start with. The other method gives bigger plants from the beginning, and I tried it after first reading Mr Chapple's book. What you do is dig up a plant, choosing a fairly young one so that it is not unwieldy to handle, and replant it several inches deeper, deep enough to bury part of the stems. When the replanting is finished the plant should have its growing tips showing, of course, but otherwise be up to the neck, so to speak, in soil; when doing this, add a few handfuls or spadefuls of peat to the soil and pack it tight. About six months later you can dig it up again, when you will find that almost every stem has made a system of roots, and you can then cut them off and plant them out. You can get dozens, even scores, from a single parent plant in this way.

When layering heathers by this or other means, remember that old, hard wood will not root, and the part of the stem brought in contact with and covered by soil should be of young wood, in fact as far as my experience goes, the younger the better. A very simple method is this: choose some stems which are near the soil and growing horizontally; at the point where the younger growth begins, place a fairly heavy flat stone; now bend the growing tip gently upwards until it is vertical and place another stone to hold it there. Roots will form at the bend and in a year's time a good new plant can be separated from the parent and planted out.

1.
Sambucus arbor rosea.

Chapter 3

Tree Heaths

If anyone who reads this is planning a motoring holiday in the Iberian peninsula during February, March or April, and has not yet settled on a route, here is a suggestion: cross the French frontier at Hendaye—you can stay at St Jean de Luz the night before—and go through San Sebastian, Vitoria, Valladolid and Salamanca, thence to Ciudad Rodrigo and there turn right for the Portuguese frontier, crossing it on the Guarda road; there is an excellent hotel at Guarda in the mountains, where you can have your lunch. These mountains are very well worth exploring, for gardeners and botanists; the acacias, on the road into the very pleasant university town of Coimbra, are magnificent. I shall always think of Coimbra with pleasure and admiration: in my first walk through the town I saw, in the window of the best bookshop, two works in English prominently displayed side by side: one was the *Works of Shakespeare*, the other was my last novel. I felt that the shopkeeper could hardly say fairer than that. However, what really enchanted us in these mountains were the flowers: lithospermums, acacias, here and there the most beautiful of the narcissi, *N. triandrus*, the Angel's Tears daffodil; and the tree heaths. I think there were two species of these, *Erica australis* and *E. lusitanica*, but they are both variable and perhaps all we saw were varieties of one. I am fairly sure of *E. australis*, however, because the colour of the rather large flowers is so much richer than in any other tree heath I have seen. Here, too, we saw a great deal of *Daboecia cantabrica*, mostly purplish-rose, but one or two whites.

Erica australis is not the biggest of the tree heaths. It is, I believe, capable of growing to nine or ten feet but I do not think I ever saw one, either in the wild or in an English garden, more than six or seven feet and it is often not so tall. It is not perfectly hardy; probably it should only be planted in the south and west and near the sea elsewhere. The habit is neat and erect and the half-inch bell flowers are a deep, rich red. It is not difficult to propagate by cuttings but it is not one of the heaths which will tolerate much lime; I am not even sure that it will grow in neutral soil; what it likes is acid peat and leaf-mould over gravel. There is a very beautiful and very rare (in the wild) white variety which was discovered by Lieutenant Robert Williams after an arduous ten-day search and by him introduced to the family garden of Caerhays. He was killed near Loos in October 1915 and Bean gave this white tree heath the name by which its discoverer was known in the Caerhays household, 'Mr Robert'.

A species which made a great impression on me when I was in Ireland recently, because of the enormous specimens one sees there was *E. arborea.* At Mount Usher, in the gardens of Old Conna, and in the garden of the house where we stayed in Wicklow, these heaths were very neat and sturdy, upright trees to almost twenty feet, with trunks a foot and more in diameter, stout erect branches and the general shape of a good juniper, that is, a spire. The heath will attain its maximum height in the south and west, but elsewhere it is usually a smaller plant, a little upright tree about six feet tall. The pine-like foliage is neat and pleasing, the terminal flowers, produced in enormous numbers in late winter and early spring, are a curious greyish-white and they are fragrant. This heath is fairly hardy; Mr Fred Chapple, the great heath and heather gardener, has grown it in the Pennines. It may be damaged but will not usually be killed by a severe winter. For the coldest part of Britain, however, there is a hardy variety of this tree-heather, *E. a.* var. *alpina.* It is not a tree but a many spired bush. Its taller spires may attain four or five feet; the flowers and the scent are the same as those of the type. This variety is hardy anywhere in Britain. It is probably not tolerant of much lime, but I have seen a big healthy specimen in a garden which is death to most rhododendrons.

E. mediterranea, like its near relation *E. carnea* and its hybrid offspring *E* × *darleyensis*, *is* lime tolerant. Whether it will actually grow in chalk I cannot say; it will certainly flourish on limestone or grow where there is lime in the soil and real calcifuges curl up and die.

Perhaps I should not call *E. mediterranea* a tree heath; it should grow at least six feet and, in favourable situations, up to ten. In fact, however, and possibly because there has been a failure to sort out strains and varieties, it is quite apt not to grow more than three feet. It is not, as I have said, a Mediterranean plant but what I may call a Biscayan plant, native to both the French and Spanish Biscay provinces and to Galway in Ireland. It makes a dense and bushy plant of bright, healthy-looking foliage, in habit fastigiate when young, spreading a little later and when in flower. Flowers are borne in the leaf axils of the previous season's wood; they are about a quarter of an inch long and across, a rich purplish-red, and very sweetly scented. The species is supposed not to be perfectly hardy anywhere in Britain, but with care in the choice of site, and the sort of protection it would normally have in a small or medium enclosed garden, or a town garden, it will survive our winters. *E. mediterranea* will certainly survive twenty degrees Fahrenheit of frost and probably more. It has several varieties: *alba* is a small round bush with white flowers; the Galway native, var. *hibernica*, is glaucous and attains about four feet, and it is a plant of the peat bogs which makes its lime-tolerance extremely odd.

E. lusitanica comes, as its name implies, from Portugal, but also Spain, attains about ten feet where it is happy, six elsewhere, flowers in February in warm gardens and elsewhere in March or April. It has, says Mr Chapple in *The Heather Garden*, a better chance of not being killed outright by a savage winter than *australis*. The flowers are white with a tinge of pink and so cover the plant in a good year that foliage and flowers together give the whole a curious and very attractive smoky look. The largest plant of this species I have ever seen grows in the garden of the hotel Palacio de Setiais near Cintra; as I recall it, it must have been well over fifteen feet tall, very full in habit, and with a massive trunk.

E. caniculata is for the mildest districts only, for it is a Cape heath. In my experience it will survive about twelve degrees of frost, possibly more. It is not strictly speaking a tree heath because it forms a small thicket of stems, not a trunk; at least, never as I have seen it. However, it may be very tall, perhaps well over twelve feet. It is, for my taste, the loveliest of the tree heaths in flower, because the flowers, at first white with a very faint tinge of pink, have prominent chocolate-coloured anthers which make them very pretty; as they age they turn pink—the corollas, not the anthers—and again at this stage this light and feathery heath is very pleasing. It is quite intolerant of lime, like most Cape plants.

The Corsican heath, *E. stricta*, is not confined to the island of strong wine and feuds; it is also native to Sardinia, to parts of Italy, and to south Spain. I found it wild, very common, in the mountains north-west of Genoa. It is an erect plant of several spires, the foliage dense and a medium, bright green excepting the young growth over six feet in the warmest gardens and elsewhere about four. The flowers are a soft, pale rose and generously borne.

There are a couple more tree heaths; one, *E. scoparia*, has no garden merit whatever: it sprawls untidily and although it has nice leaves the flowers are barely visible, being very small, light green, and giving the impression of aborted buds.

It will occur to most readers that with so many tree heaths to work with it is a wonder we do not have some remarkable hybrids. There is, in fact, only one that I know, and that was the outcome of an accidental, natural cross and not of deliberate plant-breeding. *Erica* × 'Veitchii' appeared as a seedling in Veitch's nursery at Exeter about 1900 and it turned out to be a cross between *E. arborea* and *E. lusitanica*. There is apparently no doubt about this, but the odd fact remains that it does not grow more than six feet tall, that is, despite 'hybrid vigour' it is not nearly as tree-like a plant as either parent. It has white flowers and they are very strongly and sweetly scented. It has, in my opinion, rather an untidy habit. Still, it is well worth planting where it can be sheltered from the worst of the east and north-east winds. I do rather wonder, though, why little or nothing has been done in the way of deliberate hybridisation of these plants: perhaps there are genetic difficulties; or practical ones. *Arborea* crossed with *australis* might give us a real tree heather with the stature of *arborea* and the magnificent flower colour of the Spanish Heath.

Until we came to Devon we were confined to the lime-tolerant ericas. But in Devon the case was different, and we were soon trying others. Two varieties of *Erica vagans*, the Cornish Heath, have given us great delight: the variety 'Alba superba darleyensis' is the best white heather I know; only it is not white, it is cream. The other is the pink-flowered 'Mrs Maxwell'. These two grow to about eighteen inches. Of the very many cultivated *Callunas*, we have found 'Alportii praecox', blooming in July; the white *erecta*; and 'C. W. Nix' to be very fine. There are rather fewer good garden forms of *Erica ciliaris*; two good ones which flower in July are *globosa* and 'Stoborough'.

In front of these relatively tall varieties in a heather border should go those which do not normally exceed about a foot in height. There are, to begin with, scores of *Callunas*; the winter-flowering *hyemalis* and, to lead up to it with its October blooming, *hibernica*, which hides its foliage in the exuberance of its flowering and spreads widely while never attaining more than seven or eight inches in height at the most. There are even more suitable short varieties in the species *E. cinerea*: 'Lilacina' bears its almost lavender flowers in June and July; 'Apple Blossom' its pink ones in August; 'atrorubens' its deep, crimson bells likewise in August. This species is, in fact, very useful for its summer habit, flowering at a time when the spring and early summer glories are past. There are many more varieties with much the same kind of growth. But for the very front of the border there is the plant which is, I suppose, the dwarfest of all heathers, *E. c.* var. *coccinea*, bearing its red flowers in July at about two inches from the top of the soil.

I have said nothing of the magnificent Cape Heaths from South Africa. In the first place they are inclined to be tender, although they might find the South Devon climate congenial; in the second place I have no personal experience of them, with the single exception of *E. canaliculata*, a shrub heather which, according to the books, can attain something like twenty feet, but which when I tried to grow it, seemed reluctant to exceed twenty inches. It is, however, among the Cape Heaths that flowers other than purples, pinks and crimsons are to be found, as in the orange and yellow-flowered *E. macowanii*, and in the tear-shaped, green-tipped orange blooms of *E. blenna*. You may not be able to grow these yourself; but you can see them in flower in an English garden, Tresco Abbey, in the Scilly Isles.

1\. Buxus.

Chapter 4

Rhododendrons

Here is an ericaceous genus which has given me great delight and it occurs to me to describe my discovery of it, for in an important sense it was a discovery, by reproducing some of the articles I have written about it over a period of several years. I began by knowing nothing whatever about them; I now know a little; but only a little. For there are approximately a thousand species and several hundred hybrids in cultivation: the smallest is a shrublet eight inches tall, with leaves not much more than two or three millimetres in area; the largest is a forest tree attaining eighty feet of stature and other tree forms have leaves two and a half feet long and a foot wide. There are rhododendrons which are among the most ruggedly hardy of plants, others, from the tropics, which are too tender to be grown anywhere out-of-doors in Britain. Most of them are evergreens but many are deciduous; there is one which is a small climbing plant. Flower size varies from a tiny bell half an inch long, to a huge trumpet six inches across the mouth. Clearly, real knowledge of this protean genus is the acquisition of a lifetime's study.

I grow, or have grown, about forty of the species and a score of hybrids. I have visited and have been generously entertained and instructed by the great rhododendron gardeners of south-west Scotland which is the home from home of the genus in Britain by reason of its wet climate, its mildness and its acid soil. I have seen the famous rhododendron gardens of Cornwall, and notably Caerhays where so many of the species introduced from the Himalayas and from China were grown in Europe for the first time. I have immensely enjoyed not only the plants themselves but also my glimpses of that, as it were, higher gardening which is at its most refined among the great rhododendron men who, shrugging off the flamboyant hybrids, rejoice in the smallest variations of form and colour among the botanical species and their natural varieties. How pleasant it has been to stand respectfully and watchfully silent while four famous Scottish gardeners argued over a group of plants gorgeously in flower to decide whether, to the name they bore, *Rhododendron cinnabarinum* var. *roylei*, should, by virtue of certain superiorities in this form, be added the epithet *magnificum*.

It is, of course, impossible to live in Britain and not know a rhododendron when you see one. One species has become a weed of forests on the acid soils, *R. ponticum*. But to most people the name implies those rather coarse-leaved bushes with huge spherical heads of flower in flaming colours—those rhododendrons which one might fairly refer to the Surrey butler-belt and which make such a spectacle at the Chelsea Flower Show. Only when you get among the real specialists in this genus do you realise how little credit these hybrids do it.

My own introduction, as gardener, to rhododendrons, could not have been more fortunate; for my mentor was Sir James Horlick who had, by then, already turned the island of Gigha into a garden and than whom no man living has a better practical knowledge of these plants.

A PRESENT FROM SCOTLAND

July 2, 1960

My real subject here I owe to a gardener who, in the kindness of his heart, sent me, from the Scottish island where he has the good fortune, or good sense, to live, three species of rhododendrons which were not known to me, for it is really difficult to be a rhododendron man in East Kent, and from which I have had so much pleasure that I am anxious to communicate it. As the species are dwarfs, we did not plant them in the rhododendron-azalea-lily garden we are trying to make, but in what we call 'the bath'. It always causes some surprise to strangers when, replying to a question about how we have managed to grow this or that notorious calcifuge, we say, 'Oh, we grow them in the bath'. 'The bath' is, in fact, two old baths bought in a builder's yard, sunk in the ground, surrounded with brick walls, provided with drainage, and filled with acid peat and leaf-mould. Chalky water cannot possibly infiltrate such a bed. The death of some gentians and a heather in the bath, then, made room for my present from Scotland: the three plants are *Rhododendron mucronatum*, *R. calostrotum* and *R.*

impeditum, and to anyone who has a suitable place and conditions for them, such as an acid soil rock garden, they are to be recommended with enthusiasm.

Of the three, my favourite is *R. impeditum.* It is an evergreen, prostrate, very dense little shrub about two inches tall, but it will, apparently, grow to twelve inches. My specimen is about eight inches in diameter and I do not know how much, if at all, if will spread outwards. It has tiny leaves, barely half an inch long, of a very bright dark green. I do not know why I did not expect it to flower in this, its first season, here: but it surprised me by doing so within a few weeks of being planted. It was because I had not expected flowers and had therefore not been watching it closely, that it delighted me by suddenly, one morning, being decorated all over its small flattish dome of minute foliage with single, purple flowers on half-inch stalks, these flowers being a little more than three-quarters of an inch long. One of the most charming miniature plants I have ever grown, if I can be said to have grown it after having it only a few weeks. I find, on looking it up, that it came to us from China in 1911. But unless I have been blind to it hitherto, three decades have not sufficed to make it very well known.

As to *R. mucronatum*, it may have been a mistake to plant it in the bath, since it is capable of growing to four or five feet. If it proves vigorous it will have to be moved, but in our climate, so unpropitious to the ericaceous family, I do not expect it to grow as it would off the west coast of Scotland. It is an evergreen with wide, bright green leaves and white flowers not in singles like *impeditum*, but in pairs or threes. These flowers are reputed to be fragrant; I confess that I can detect no scent, but I have an unreliable nose, there are times, when I cannot even smell honeysuckle, others when the faintest fragrance, the subtle perfume of grape-flowers or the strange scent of tea-roses, seems strong and all pervading. *R. mucronatum*, although it is given specific rank, is not known in the wild. It originated as a sport on a pink-flowered azalea in southern Japan. It is not a novelty, having been introduced nearly a century and a half ago, but it was new to me.

R. calostrotum, although not such a pygmy as *impeditum*, does not exceed a foot in height, so it should be happy in the bath. This is the only one of the three which did not flower. I hope to see it do so next May, and meanwhile have seen the flowers in a west country garden visited a few weeks ago. These flowers were in pairs, their colour was crimson and they were unusually wide open, looking almost flat. The very small leaves of my young specimens are a peculiarly agreeable shade of sage green, in sharp contrast with those of their neighbour. *Calostrotum* comes from Burma and has been in cultivation here for forty years.

I began, then, with these dwarfs; my second discovery within this genus was of the giants, the rhododendrons which one never even sees in the east of Britain but which are the glory of many extreme south-western English, south-western Scottish, and Irish gardens.

PRIMITIVES
August 4, 1962

When we come across a living creature which has survived unchanged for millions of years, we become very excited. There was that fish, the coelacanth, which was caught off the coast of South Africa if I remember rightly: the thing must have received more attention in the Press than any Prime Minister or royal baby. I wonder why? Perhaps I have a blind spot about this kind of thing, just as I am unable to be anything but bored stiff by the remnants of ancient cities unless they happen to be beautiful. But when we come to plants the primitives, the relatively few survivors from a time in the world's history when not even the most unpromising of man's first ancestors in the long chain of evolution had put in an appearance, the case is different, for the majority of these plants are magnificent.

In a sense, of course, many of our garden and farm plants are ancients. The populations of today's vineyards are not all that different from the vines of the Tertiary epoch; still, they have evolved. Whereas the plants I call primitives have not; having reached a satisfactory arrangement with their environment, as it were, they simply stopped changing millions or tens of millions of years ago. This argues, I suppose, a very stable environment. And it is a fact that the most interesting of these old plants comes from that part of Asia which was not affected by the last ice age. The southward spread of the ice must have wiped out a whole flora in other parts of the world, and where the ice did this the survivors were on the whole rather lowly plants, although there were some very fine ferns among them.

I have planted a number of the primitives in my garden, then, not because their diehard conservatism makes any special appeal to me—as a radical anarchist I disapprove of that—but because they are good plants on their own merits, and they are not particularly difficult to grow.

By far the most exciting of these survivors of the remote past is *Rhododendron sinogrande* and other rhododendrons of the *grande* series. Devonshire, at least our bit of it, is not ideal country for this noble plant; our rainfall is not really high enough and there is even some small risk of one or two winters in a man's lifetime when the thermometer may fall to a point at which this rhododendron suffers damage. It is, however, not one of the tenderest rhododendrons, for although it comes from the Yunnan forests, it is found at great altitudes, up to 14,000 feet I believe. Its R.H.S. hardiness rating is C, which stands for 'Hardy along the seaboard and in sheltered inland gardens'. The species succeeds best in south-west Scotland, parts of Ireland, and Cornwall, but that is as much a matter of high rainfall and humidity as of temperature.

R. sinogrande is a small tree, up to about thirty feet tall or a little more. It is never free-flowering and it does not flower at all in its extreme youth, although I saw a specimen in the Dartington Hall gardens coming into flower this year when not, I think, more than six feet tall or thereabouts. However, this is not important, for beautiful and impressive though the huge flowers are, the glory of this tree is its foliage. On my young plants of this and on a hybrid between it and *R. macabeanum*, the stiff, thick, leathery leaves are something like eighteen inches in length or a bit less, and six or seven inches wide. But on established plants the leaves can be much larger. Where the soil and the climate really please *R. sinogrande*, and in the western world it is said not to reach its highest perfection excepting perhaps in the fog belt of the United States Pacific Coast, in the neighbourhood of San Francisco, the leaves may be three feet long and a foot wide, and the gigantic rosettes in which they are ranged round the massive stalks, may thus measure two yards across. The pleasure this rhododendron, young though it is in our garden, has given us this year, has been by means of its young foliage. The whole process of growth is fascinating to watch.

The buds are at first, in winter, round or stubby, but when growth begins they elongate and show up a bright red. This red outer cover unwinds, as it were, and falls away to reveal the tightly-packed young leaves; as these open to the light they are not green but silver, for they are densely covered in silvery-white indumentum. The old leaves of the rosette below the buds are held pointing downwards if the plant is at all short of water or when it is not in growth; but in growth they rise to a horizontal, or higher plane. The opening rosette is held pointing upwards, slowly sinking towards the horizontal as the leaves grow. From across the garden their shining silvery colour makes them look like some strange flower. As rain or irrigation water washes away the indumentum, the young, but already enormous, leaves emerge bright medium green to darken later. The flowers, when they come, are creamy or yellow, twenty or thirty, thick, waxy bell-shaped flowers to a truss, arranged in neat layers.

Even the beautiful young growth of *sinogrande* is not to be compared, for colour, with that of another primitive, *R. macabeanum*. I have been sitting for ten minutes trying to think how to describe this colour for those who have never seen this species when it opens its growth buds in the spring; let us say a bronze plate with a patina of verdigris and the surface lightly dusted with flour. Like all the *grande* series these two rhododendrons need a deep acid soil very rich in leaf-mould or peat, shade from the sun provided by taller trees, preferably oaks or conifers, protection from wind, and a rainfall of at least forty inches and preferably much more.

By 1963 I was much more familiar with these giants and by then too I had—although for posterity so far as flowering goes unless I live to be ninety—planted *R. falconeri* with its great leathery leaves lined with cinnamon-red indumentum; *magnificum* for its name as much as anything; *sinogrande* and *grande* and *macabeanum*; and even *giganteum* with its immense leaves and its potential eighty feet of stature. I also had in the garden by then young plants of certain hybrids within this group sent to me as a present by Mr Archibald Gibson of Glenarn, one of the dozen greatest rhododendron gardens in the world, distinguished by a specimen of *R. falconeri* over a century old. By then, moreover, I had developed an attitude, a state of mind, towards the whole genus.

BOTANICAL SPECIES OR HARDY HYBRIDS?

March 9, 1963

The genus rhododendron exercises an especial and powerful influence over gardeners: there is, among a large number of gardeners, a state of mind in which rhododendrons render all other genera almost invisible. The genus has given rise to a vast and often recondite literature and this is not to be wondered at since it includes such an immense diversity of plants within its limits. There are perhaps a thousand species and I do not know how many garden varieties. The species vary in stature from shrublets two or three inches tall with leaves a couple of millimetres in diameter, to forest trees eighty feet tall, and others with leaves having a surface area of three hundred square inches per leaf; rhododendrons may be evergreen or deciduous, very hardy or very tender, may have scaly leaves or be free from scales, may be downy, hairy, or quite glabrous. The colour range of the flowers includes the whole spectrum short of a true, pure blue. Most species grow in soil, yet there are many which are epiphytes upon rotting wood or upon other trees. How is the gardener to find his way among this embarrassment of riches? He can, by spending twenty or thirty pounds on acquiring the principal treatises on the subject and undertaking a serious course of study, try to master the whole subject. Few will take that course. There is an alternative, and that is to follow the advice of a single authority; but which authority? Nurserymen give sound advice; so does the R.H.S. Or you can buy, for 7*s* 6*d*, the smallest, cheapest and in some ways the best book on rhododendrons ever published, *Rhododendrons*, by that very great plant collector to whom we owe many of the species we now cultivate, the late F. Kingdon-Ward (first published in 1949, reprinted Macdonald, 1963).

When, as a result of Hooker's work in 1849–51, and subsequently of Wilson's collecting, Asiatic rhododendrons began pouring into Britain, nurserymen and amateurs and head gardeners started to hybridise them. This process of plant breeding was continued as the stream of new introductions swelled to a torrent as Forrest and later Kingdon-Ward joined in the hunt for new species. The result was the production of a very large number of garden rhododendrons which are ruggedly hardy, many of them quite capable of withstanding long periods at zero Fahrenheit, which have enormous trusses of large and often flamboyant flowers in almost all the colours of the rainbow, and which are of very easy cultivation given the basic conditions for the genus, a soil fairly free from lime and an adequate rainfall. This being so, why should anyone bother with the botanical species? They are more difficult, and sometimes very difficult, to grow; you have to know something about them for they vary in hardiness from absolutely hardy to hopelessly tender; they are fussier about soil, measure of shade, aspect.

The fact is that the plant breeders inevitably lost something when they gave us the oversize flowers, the hardiness and manageability of the garden rhododendrons; what they lost was first that indescribable quality for which we use words like *distinction*, *breeding*: the botanical species are aristocrats and look it; the 'hardy hybrids' are worthy burgesses. However, there is at least one more tangible attribute one can point to: the botanical species have, in very many cases, great beauty of foliage, there is much diversity of shape, size, colour: some are very glaucous, many have the underside of the leaves coated with tomentum varying in colour from white to a rich ginger. In the case of the better known and more commonly planted 'hardy hybrid' rhododendrons, this is quite lost, and their foliage really is very dull.

In some nursery catalogues the distinction is clearly made. Taking Hillier of Winchester by way of example, the general catalogue gives first a list of botanical species; then the hybrids, but in two sections: one section is entirely devoted to the 'hardy hybrids' for general planting; the other is a list of hybrids, usually more recently produced, which retain much of the distinction and often the fine foliage of the botanical species but which, also, retain many of their defects as 'good garden plants'. I believe that it is safe to say that any gardener of taste who has seen one of the gardens in which the botanical species and the better hybrids flourish, will become very dissatisfied with his 'hardy hybrids'.

One problem has at least been solved for everyone in advance. The R.H.S. classification of species in six classes for hardiness, or the American Rhododendron Society's similar classification, enable the gardener to choose species which are hardy in his region. The classification is very conservative, and bold rhododendron lovers often ignore it with success: careful choice of a sheltered site makes it possible to grow a desirable species out of its zone. But for the less bold and less expert, it is best to stick to the classification. The R.H.S. one ranges from A, species which can be grown anywhere in the British Isles, down to F, species which must have greenhouse protection. (Since this was written the system has been changed and hardiness is now indicated by H and a digit, as in the U.S.A.) The American classification is a little more precise. Each species is marked in lists with an H followed by a number and that number relates to the lowest mean winter temperature which plants of this kind will stand. Not as many species and varieties have, however, been classified in America as in Britain.

From letters which I receive on the subject of species rhododendrons, I have extracted one or two questions which seem to occur most often. What is the 'bluest' species? *R. augustinii*, but it is a very variable shrub and certain gardens pride themselves on having nearest-to-true-blue forms. In this respect I would give the prize to Bodnant, where the *R. augustinii*, especially those in the deepest shade, flower—and how abundantly!—as near true blue as no matter. There is also a good blue form at Dartington Hall. This species has been used in the breeding of several very pretty, small-leaved, densely shrubby hybrids with more or less blue flowers, notably 'Blue Boy', 'Blue Tit' and 'Blue Diamond'. These, too, vary from garden to garden and season to season in degree of blueness.

Are there any perfectly hardy *tree* rhododendrons? No. But although the west, and especially the south-west, is the tree rhododendron country where old specimens of *R. arboreum* are often fifty feet tall or more, it is a fact that one does occasionally see this or some other tree species, or that fine old winter-flowering hybrid *R. nobleanum*, in parts of the country where, in theory, they ought to have died of cold.

Are large-leaved rhododendrons confined to the south and west, and to south-west Scotland, by tenderness? Not absolutely, I think: that gloriously exotic looking giant shrub, with its immense leaves and colossal flower-trusses, *R. falconeri*, is surprisingly hardy if given shelter from wind. So is *R. macabeanum*. But there is another thing to consider: rainfall. These mighty and primitive plants will not grow unless they are in a permanently moist atmosphere and thus present a great difficulty on the eastern side of Britain. But as to sheer hardiness, I have noted with admiration during this atrocious winter with what perfect equanimity even *R. sinogrande* whose leaves may measure thirty inches long, has withstood bitter east winds which have simply shrivelled lesser plants.

Once we had rhododendron species in the garden it was, of course, easier for me to write about them. But I had to be careful and to exercise restraint: there is no more catching mental disorder in horticulture than rhododendron-mania. Readers of my *Illustrated London News* page live all over the world, many of them on limestone soils and they would soon complain if I gave too much space to writing about plants they could not grow. I say 'could not grow' but I should add, now, a qualification and make that, 'could not grow without taking special steps'. For here there has been a very interesting change: the production, by the Geighy Company of Switzerland, of an iron chelate called, and marketed as, 138 Fe, has changed the whole picture and I should say something about it here.

Limestone soil, and even chalk, its most 'extreme' form in Britain, is not positively poisonous to rhododendrons and other calcifuge plants; on the contrary, like all green plants they need some calcium. But if lime is present in the soil at such a level that it gives that soil an alkaline or neutral, instead of an acid, reaction it inhibits the intake of iron salts by certain plants, including the rhododendrons, which do not seem very good at capturing the iron they need from the soil. Lime does this by combining with iron so quickly and in such a way as to deny it to the plants. The consequence of this is a deficiency disease called chlorosis: chlorophyll is not produced in sufficient quantity; the leaves turn yellow; in time the plant dies. But supposing that despite the chalk or other limestone, some method of getting iron into the plant can be devised? In that case, the plant will flourish for the lime has no direct deleterious effect on it. The feeding of the plant with even massive quantities of iron salts in their ordinary form never worked, because the calcium immediately combined with the iron and locked it up away from the plant. But chelated iron salts are so constituted that the iron is held so firmly in combination with some other element that the lime cannot get it away, and the salt is stable in the soil and available to the plant. The first chelates were not stable enough, and it was not until we had what was first called 'Sequestrene iron' and is now known as 138 Fe that we had a chelate so massively stable that the calcium could not get at the iron. Thus calcifuge plants can now be grown in calcium-rich soils if they are given an annual dose of this chelated iron. The stuff is very dear but only a small quantity is needed.

Most gardeners, however, refuse, and rightly, to grow things 'unnaturally' in their gardens. They want a garden, not a plant hospital. So that I had to be careful not to let myself be carried away by my interest in rhododendrons and it was nearly a year before I returned to the subject, excepting in brief asides.

HYBRID SELECTION
January 4, 1964

Greatly to our delight, rhododendrons prove to be, at least till now, very much at home in this garden. Their rate of growth and the healthy colour of the foliage, and their readiness to flower, have vindicated the methods we used to make the soil more suitable for them, methods which were recommended by the Royal Horticultural Society's experts after an analysis of the soil. For the most part we have planted species because, as I have said before, they have a grace which only the finest of the hybrids aspire to. I have yet to see a 'blue' flowered hybrid, although there are some good and easy dwarfs in that category, which compare with a good form of *R. augustinii*; and such delights as the minute *R. impeditum*, the strange flower colour and form of *R. campylogynum*, the grandeur of *R. sinogrande* are not to be found among the hybrids. But some hybrids we have planted.

It seems to be universally agreed that the most spectacular group of hybrids is that series of forms collectively known as *R. loderi*. The parents of this group are *R. griffithianum*, a rather tender Himalayan small tree which attains to twenty feet in favourable climates and has the largest flowers of all species; they are white, fragrant, and sometimes flushed with rose-pink; and *R. fortunei*, a large Chinese shrub with very fragrant, pale rose flowers, quite large, borne in loose trusses; it is much hardier than *griffithianum*. The offspring, *loderi*, is not one but several, because seedlings of this cross while they all have much the same mighty stature and tremendous vigour, good foliage and colossal flowers, vary in colour, which has given rise to a score or more named varieties. The hardiness rating which they receive from the R.H.S. is C, which means 'hardy along the sea-board and in warm gardens inland'. It is worth while for any gardener, even in the cold belts of these islands, who can offer a sheltered site and has the right kind of soil, to try a specimen; for the R.H.S. ratings are, very properly, on the cautious side, and of late years rhododendrons tried by the ordeal of harsh winters, have on the whole proved hardier than they are supposed to be. *R. loderi* requires a lot of room; I think that a circle with a diameter of twelve feet would be by no means too much where the plant grows well. The flowers are each about five inches in diameter, and they are borne in trusses of many, so that the trusses are enormous. Perhaps the biggest are those of the variety 'King George' and these are pure white with a green flash or blotch at the base. In 'Pink Coral' the flowers are pink with a puce flash; 'Venus' and 'Fairy Queen' are pink without a blotch or flash; 'Julie' has very large white flowers with a suffusion of pale yellow. There are many more.

Of an entirely different sort is another hybrid we have planted here, and had to replant once for this requires a really sheltered spot and it is difficult on our hill and despite our trees, to place touchy shrubs out of the wind. 'Lady Chamberlain' is the offspring of *R. cinnabarinum* and the orange form of a hybrid called 'Royal Flush', itself bred from *R. cinnabarinum* and another aristocrat, *R. maddenii*. 'Lady Chamberlain' is erect and rather stiff in bearing, about five feet tall but covering six or seven feet of surface when well grown in a really warm corner; the leaves are small, oval and rather glaucous. The flowers are extremely numerous, and they are hanging, rather long, narrow tubular bells which have the look of being made of fine wax. Colour varies with form or variety, the commonest being what is called 'mandarin' red in the tube, fading to a sort of reddish buff in the lobes. Colour variation is by no means great, but the fastidious gardener will do well to choose his specimen in flower in the nursery if he can. Although this lovely hybrid rhododendron is rated C, it does not seem to me to be as hardy as *R. loderi*; but we may have been unwise in our placing of our first specimen, and we were certainly unlucky with our first two winters of its life in our garden. Rhododendrons which are rated much more tender survived when it was killed, another reason for thinking that not cold alone was to blame.

Another hybrid of the kind which can compete with the species for elegance, and which we have planted here in both its excellent forms, is 'Penjerrick'. Again, this is rated C for hardiness; it does very well in woodland conditions and is worth planting in all but notoriously cold and exposed gardens. Its parents are *griffithianum* again, and *R. campylocarpum* var. *elatum*. This is a hardy, erect Himalayan shrub with good yellow flowers; but I read that when the *elatum* variety of it is used in breeding, then it 'throws' both pink and cream flowers. At all events, the two 'Penjerricks', named after the great Cornish garden of their origin, are graceful, fairly open shrubs of fine stature, but not enormous, with very attractive oval leaves, rather glaucous than not, and they are vigorous in growth. The flowers are ravishing: huge, broad, open bells, three, four or five to a loose truss, pendent, and with a kind of translucence which seems to intensify the light which shines on and through them. People who have the pink form hold it to be the better and are annoyed by visitors who say, 'Ah, but I have the cream form . . .' The thing to do is to plant both, of course. Specialists have no doubt whatever that the cream is superior.

Going, again, away from the stately and magnificent, to the pretty and charming, a very good hybrid of great distinction in its kind is 'Yellow Hammer'. This is a small, stiffish, hardy shrub bred from *R. sulphureum*, a tender Chinese dwarf with rich yellow flowers, and *flavidum*, another dwarf, also Chinese, but very hardy indeed, and also bearing yellow flowers. 'Yellow Hammer' usually flowers twice a year, in this garden. The narrow tubular bell-shaped flowers are not borne in trusses but in pairs and not only from the top of the twig but from the upper leaf axils as well. This hybrid will stand full exposure to sun and it should be near the front of the border.

I have written more than once in the past of the merits of the early-flowering hybrid *R.* × *praecox* and will not do so again; I mention it only by way of a reminder that it is one of the gardens' heralds of spring.

Of the rather straggling, richly fragrant, white-flowered *edgeworthii* series, none is rated hardy even among the hybrids, but a fine old hybrid (*edgeworthii* × *formosum*) called *fragrantissimum* is worth trying in south-western and perhaps other coastal gardens where protection is available. Its F rating makes it 'usually a greenhouse shrub', but in my garden a young specimen did not show any damage after suffering last winter out of doors; it is true that we covered it at night with a tea chest, but the temperature inside that chest must have fallen to many degrees below freezing more than once. Other hybrids of this kind are 'Princess Alice' and 'Lady Alice Fitzwilliam', the latter being in my experience the most deliciously fragrant of the whole genus: it is an awkward-looking plant, with very long, thin stems topped with tufts of leaves which are dark, pointed, not large, deeply marked with veins. The buds of all this group are very pretty, the scales being red edged with white, or brown-red edged with white. They are often planted to walls, but I never saw one looking anything but miserable as a wall plant.

A fine little hybrid for small gardens is 'Elizabeth'. Its parents are *R. repens* and *R. griersonianum*, and it is hardy almost anywhere. It forms a low, quite dense bush of good foliage, and the cluster of five or six trumpet-shaped flowers are *not* 'light blood-red' as described in the supplement to the R.H.S. *Dictionary*, but a 'rich dark red' as described by Hilliers in their list. I find that it grows fast here, and that, moreover, like its *repens* parent, it flowers in the autumn as well as in the spring.

From what I wrote then it seems clear that I had already referred at some time to the hybrid rhododendron *R.* × *praecox*. But a couple of months later, once more impressed by the sight of it in flower in my own garden, I reverted to the subject in an article on a number of early-flowering shrubs entitled, predictably, 'Harbingers'.

R. × *praecox*
March 21, 1965

Some gardeners maintain that there is no point in using valuable garden space to plant things which flower in winter. There is something in this: we are lucky enough to have plenty of room, about three acres, and as I find that in most winters there are very many days when the garden looks fine in low-angle sunshine, I would not be without the winter-flowering species and above all the evergreens which take off something of that dead-season look imparted to any garden-scape by the leafless twigs of deciduous plants. But whatever may be the case against December and January-flowering plants, the case for February is different, because the bulbs and the shrubs which flower then are heralds of what is to come in March. It is perfectly true that, for example, a hamamelis, in flower in mid-winter, must be enjoyed for its own sake: there is still a lot of winter ahead. But when the garden is lively with drifts of snowdrops, touched with the gold of aconites, and of crocus, with crocus blues as well, and the sky-blue stars of omphalodes, the case is very different: we are on the upgrade out of the winter slough and there will be a swifter and more numerous burgeoning now, with no more long, barren pauses.

I noted on February 20 that the innumerable flower-buds of *Rhododendron* × *praecox* were showing slits of rich colour, at the moment when another of this genus, *R. mucronulatum*, not to be confused with the azalea, *R. mucronatum*, was going over. For the benefit of those who have room for shrubs which are truly winter-blossoming, *R. mucronulatum*, still a small specimen here, is worth noticing: it is deciduous and has an erect, narrow habit of growth; and it will attain, in time, about six feet. The flowers are always borne on leafless stems since they open from about Christmas until about the end of February. At the tip of each stem is a cluster of flower buds; but these open one at a time, so that for weeks each stem is decorated with a small, wide open, rosy-purple flower. They look particularly lovely above a cover of snow. They will stand a few degrees of frost; a sharp frost withers them, but then another bud opens as soon as it gets warmer again. However, like hamamelis, this rhododendron is not a herald of spring. The next one, *R.* × *praecox*, a shrub very suitable for small as well as large gardens, certainly is.

The parents of this rhododendron are *R. dauricum*, a Siberian species which has been grown in Britain for about two centuries; and *R. ciliatum*, a Sikkimese species introduced just over a century ago. In our garden the largest specimen is about four feet tall and wide, but it may grow rather bigger than that. However, it is never a really large shrub. As one of its parents is an evergreen and the other more or less deciduous, this one should be something between the two. It is evergreen here; in very cold weather it sheds some leaves and looks a bit thin, but it very soon replaces them and becomes well-furnished and bushy as ever. Its flowering potential is fabulous: last year, held back by the bitter weather until well into March, our three bushes of it were one complete mass of colour. The flowers open almost plum colour, but when fully open the general effect is between rose-pink and purple.

There are plenty of gardens in which this very pretty little bush is of no use for the reason that, as it opens its flowers in February, they are caught and turned into an ugly, sodden brown mess by frost. But there are also very many gardens where this is not the case, or rarely, and in them it would be difficult to think of a better early-flowering shrub.

By the time I wrote that I had discovered that it was possible to have rhododendrons in flower every month of the year—by a knowing choice of species—only October depending on the second-flowering of certain hybrids whose real season was May. Because most people are familiar with rhododendrons in the shape of the hardy hybrids with their limited season, not many know this, however, so that a common criticism of the rhododendron garden is that, once May/June are over, the garden is left flowerless.

RHODODENDRONS AT KILLERTON

September 5, 1964

Visitors seeing how heavily we lean on rhododendrons in this garden are apt to say, 'Yes, it must be lovely in May; but the trouble is they are all over so early in the season'. It is true that one thinks of rhododendrons as spring-flowering shrubs. But in fact there are several which are not at their best until mid-summer and a very few which flower as late as August or even September. Oddly enough one sees them rather rarely in gardens; but there are exceptions. I paid a visit to the gardens of Killerton in Devon, on July 9 this year; the garden is now under the National Trust and so can be visited any day in the spring or summer. I will digress for a moment to say that anyone who is interested in fine trees, in exotic conifers particularly, should visit this garden; and that, apart from the rhododendrons which I shall come to in a moment, I saw one of the best specimens of *Cornus kousa*, probably in the variety *chinensis*, that I have ever seen, in full flower or perhaps one should say 'in full bract'; and that I also had the great pleasure of seeing a specimen of *Desfontainea spinosa* covered with orange-and-yellow flowers and with its foliage in perfect condition, which is unusual in my experience. Another visitor who was engaged in making a colour photograph of the bush remarked in a friendly way that he had never seen a holly bush flower like that, a perfectly reasonable mistake to make. The garden also has some very fine hydrangeas and a double hedge of the dwarf, dark-blue Hidcote lavender which looked magnificent.

But to the rhododendrons: one part of this fine garden is a steep bank climbed by zig-zag paths and well wooded with fine trees. Among the trees on one part of the bank stands a group of bushes and small trees of *Rhododendron discolor*, or one of its hybrids; I think it was the species; the labelling in this garden is good on the whole but there are some omissions and it was raining too hard for me to go fossicking in the undergrowth seeking a hidden label. *R. discolor*, according to the *Rhododendron Handbook* of the R.H.S. (1963; 15*s* from the R.H.S., and a great improvement on the earlier edition), is 'a robust shrub up to 20 feet or more', flowering June–July and with flowers 'in a loose truss of about 10, up to 3½ inches long and 4 inches across the mouth, funnel-shaped, white, or white faintly flushed with pink, or pale pink, seven-lobed, fragrant'. The hardiness rating, by the new system, is H3, which means 'hardy in the south and west and along the seaboard and in sheltered gardens inland'. The species is very variable; there are forms with flowers which are among the finest of the genus, others not so good. I doubt whether the Killerton form would receive the top rating of F4 for its flowers, but the many bushes, some with one trunk and a round head, others true shrubs, all covered in the big flowers, were a very fine spectacle. I have a specimen of this species but it has not yet flowered.

Farther along and lower down on the same bank at Killerton is a magnificent tall, rather narrow and open bush which, on July 9, was flaming with crimson-scarlet, shining trusses of flower, the colour gleaming among the surrounding greenery in a most effective way. Again, there happened to be no label that I could find, but I think that this plant was either *R. facetum* or a hybrid of that parentage. I had seen a number of bushes of *R. facetum* in flower at Heligan some days before, but this was an altogether better plant, or perhaps only better cared for. For lateness it is even better, if only you can get the really late forms, than *R. discolor*, for it can be at its best late in July, and will sometimes produce flowers in August, September, and even as late as November. At maturity it may reach a height of thirty feet, although none I have seen is so large, about fifteen to twenty feet seems average. The flowers, of the tubular-campanulate form which I think the most beautiful of the several forms taken by rhododendron flowers, receive the rating F3 from the R.H.S., I would give these at Killerton F4. Most unfortunately the hardiness rating is only H2, that is to say 'requires protection even in the most sheltered gardens'. I can only add to that, that this fine plant at Killerton must have survived the bitter winter of 1962/3 when the temperatures at Killerton must have been frequently down as low as 10°F, and when the cold winds persisted for many weeks. But as the *Handbook* points out, the variability, in hardiness as in other attributes, of this genus is becoming more and more apparent, and it may well, be that there are forms of *R. facetum* hardier than the norm.

There are no hardiness worries in the case of *R. auriculatum*, a fine rhododendron which flowers in late July and August. It is a tree-shaped plant, or at least mine is, very erect and with stiff, horizontal or nearly horizontal branches. It may attain to twenty feet or more. It has lanceolate leaves and its flowers, in loose trusses, are large, funnel-shaped, white (rarely pale pink), 'splashed greenish at base', and very sweet-scented. This plant is hardy anywhere in Britain. It does not even begin its seasonal growth until July; its foliage seems to me better than the F2 rating which the R.H.S. give it; but there is a note to the effect that 'many plants in cultivation have an unhealthy yellowish-green look'. I don't think mine does. I think it likes rather heavy shade. By the way, it does not flower when young, and you will have to be patient if you plant it.

All these rhododendrons have hybrid offspring with at least some of the lateness of one parent; notable among the *auriculatum* derivatives is the hybrid 'Polar Bear', of which there is a magnificent July-flowering specimen in Mr Lionel Fortescue's Buckland Monachorum garden. But these are often very big plants, like the three species just discussed. There are smaller late-flowering species. *R. brachyanthum*, for example, which flowers in early July, does not exceed three feet though it spreads rather wider than that; it has trusses of small pale yellow flowers of varying merit according to the form. It is hardy. On the other hand *R. brachysiphon*, about six feet tall and with lovely pale pink and very sweet-scented flowers, I have seen only under glass and it is, apparently, very tender. I do not know *R. brachycarpum*; I have just seen it in the *Handbook*; apparently that flowers in July too; it grows to ten feet, however. The *Handbook*, again, gives *R. crassum* as flowering into July, but that surprises me; my own is always over by mid-June. The rare dwarf *R. lowndsii*, a relatively new introduction, bears carmine-spotted yellow flowers in July, and grows only about one foot tall. But I think it is rather difficult to get this plant. *R. maximum* is an American woodland plant of the *ponticum* series, bearing its pink flowers in July; it is perfectly hardy and like *ponticum* itself will grow in deep shade; it can be very large at maturity, but is not unmanageably so as a rule.

Whether for species or hybrids, the best way to choose late-flowering rhododendrons for your garden is to visit one of the great rhododendron nurseries, or one of the best rhododendron gardens (Bodnant, *par excellence*), in July and see for yourself what is in flower. From a little experience and a great deal of observation of this genus, I would say that shade or partial shade is more important to the late-flowering rhododendrons, even to such tough hybrids as 'Romany Chal' which carries its vivid crimson-scarlet flowers well into July here, than to spring ones, if only because, if there happens to be fine weather in mid-summer, the sun will be very hot indeed and the flowers will not enjoy that at all.

While it remains true that the real rhododendron season is April to June, it is also the case that at least in theory it is possible to have a rhododendron in flower every month of the year; and fairly easy, in milder parts of Britain, to have some rhododendrons flower showing in ten months out of the twelve.

Pœonia rubra flore sim-
plici.

Chapter 5

Lime-lovers

Some writers on gardening almost give one the impression that it is such a terrible misfortune for any gardener to live on a chalk or limestone soil that he had better either move or curse God and die. What these Job's comforters really mean is that on chalk you cannot grow rhododendrons. So what? Not only is the natural chalk flora very rich indeed, but so is the flora of the chalk garden. Fifty or sixty years ago this fact was not realised and the feeling that gardening on chalk is a hopeless waste of time is a relic of that ignorance. We know better, much better, now; and there exists, happily, a magnificent demonstration of our knowledge created by the man who sought and found it for us. That demonstration is the garden called Highdown: I visited it, not for the first time of course, late in 1964; was shown round it and given lunch by its makers, Sir Frederick and Lady Stern; and thereafter wrote a brief account of what I had seen and been told.

THE GARDEN AT HIGHDOWN

January 2, 1965

Were I asked to name the greatest 'creative' English gardener of our lifetime I should answer without hesitation, Sir Frederick Stern. In 1909 he and his wife bought a handsome, flint-built house overlooking the Channel between Worthing and Angmering. There was no garden, only two lawns, some fine evergreen oaks which screened the place against the prevailing south-west winds, a paddock and the big chalk-pit created by the digging of chalk for liming the local farms. Gardening was considered virtually impossible on chalk, but certain knowledgeable friends, principally Sir Arthur Hill, later a director of Kew, were in favour of trying what could be done; Hill insisted that this trial should be a real experiment, that no new soil should be imported, but all planting made into the very chalk itself. To cut short a long and interesting story, it was soon found that when shrubs were planted into holes cut in the undisturbed chalk, they did not flourish, the roots behaved as though they were in an impenetrable pot; but in one corner, by the pit, a cliff fall provided a large heap of mixed chalk and thin top-soil and the shrubs, trees and other plants put into this behaved very differently; they flourished magnificently. This lesson was taken to heart and as the garden grew with Stern's appetite for gardening, the chalk was laboriously broken up first to a depth of thirty inches. Once that had been done, then shrubs and trees and herbs and bulbs which were not positively calcifuge, grew as well as, or better than, in most gardens.

There is so much to say in a small space about Sir Frederick's work with plants, that of the garden design I shall say almost nothing: it is on a slope, is served by broad grass paths which separate the mixed shrub and herb and bulb plantings; and its focus is the chalk-pit garden backed by cliffs which, though very steep, are also planted, and overhung by fine trees. But go and see it for yourselves. (Southern Region B.R. railway station, Goring-by-Sea, is within sight of the house.)

The problem facing the Sterns was to discover what plants would grow in the chalk, a thing hardly known at that time. Various methods were adopted: some were scientific, such as the study of geological maps of all parts of the world in order to choose and obtain limestone genera; others were hit-and-miss, such as the buying in, at Veitch's great Coombe Wood sale in 1912, of Chinese plants collected by E. H. Wilson. And another method lay between these two; that of taking shares in first the collecting expedition of Reginald Farrer, and later in other similar enterprises, notably those of Kingdon-Ward. By these means, and over the course of many decades, it was established for the subsequent profit of chalk gardeners, that a far greater range of plants would grow very well on broken chalk than had ever been thought possible: and how they have grown! The enormous size of some of the cotoneasters, for example, of the *Hydrangea villosa* specimens which, by the way, flower blue, not pink; and, above all, of the tree-paeonies, is quite startling. Moreover, all these plants, now often past their half-century, have grown together to make the garden into an integral work with its own unity and its own tranquil and mature atmosphere.

As most experienced gardeners know, Sir Frederick Stern is a world authority on paeonies and I asked him how this came about: for if he is and long has been a learned botanist and cytologist, it is because he made himself into one; he did not study the subjects until he had become a gardener. It was Elwes who suggested to him that since paeonies were lime lovers, and since the nomenclature of the genus was in a shocking muddle, Stern should grow, from seed collected all over the world, all the species of *Paeonia*, and then study his plants and put the genus in order. This immense task was undertaken about 1924 and it was not finished until after the second world war. In the course of this work, with La Cour and Darlington as his mentors (Sir Frederick later served as R.H.S. member of the Council of the John Innes Institution), he made himself into a geneticist. 'But I had', he told me, 'been interested in genetics, although there was no such word at the time, as a very young man. My approach to it was, I suppose, unusual: I approached plant genetics by way of a study of the hound and horse studbooks.' Stern was certainly the first amateur phytologist to set up a laboratory and make his own chromosome counts; his results enabled him to arrange the whole genus *Paeonia* in comprehensible order and the work culminated in his magnificent *A Study of the Genus Paeonia*, published by the R.H.S., with very beautiful plates by Miss Snelling. The book, alas, is out of print now and when a copy does change hands it is at a very great price. But turning himself into a scientist in the service of horticulture did not make Sir Frederick overlook the garden itself, and his paeonies, notably some of his moutans, are the finest in the country; one plant of *P. suffruticosa*, Rock's variety, annually carries several hundred of what are, perhaps, the most beautiful flowers borne by any shrub or tree.

A twenty-year study in depth of an important genus would be enough for most men. But his great paeony book is not Sir Frederick's only contribution to the standard literature of garden plants. A study was also made of the genus *Galanthus* and on it based what is still the best book you can read and refer to if you are interested in the snowdrops—Stern's *Snowdrops and Snowflakes*, another R.H.S. publication, but this one is still obtainable from the Society. Snowdrops were, I should add, already flowering at Highdown when I was there, on the day after the first sharp frost of the winter, November 30. The species is *Galanthus caucasicus* and snowdrops will be in flower at Highdown now until the end of March and into April, the late ones mingling with the glorious show of anemones for which the garden is also remarkable.

Another genus in which Stern took a keen interest was *Lilium*. He was away fighting in the first world war when seeds sent from China by Farrer, and raised by the head gardener, turned out to be *L. duchartrei* and *L. leucanthum* var. *centifolium*. These did so well at Highdown that after the war it was decided to set about discovering which lily species would grow on chalk. At the same time a programme of breeding lime-tolerant lilies was undertaken. This was far from being the only Highdown attempt to create new garden plants: work of the same kind was successfully done with daffodils, germanica irises, paeonies and roses. I asked Sir Frederick what his chief aim in hybridising plants had been. In the case of the lilies, it was to make lime-tolerant garden plants, but, as he says in his own book (*A Chalk Garden*, Nelson, 30*s*), 'We have been raising hybrids . . . with the object of producing an improvement on the wild species, but retaining the grace and charm of the wild forms . . .'

Sir Frederick's work in the service of the English garden from 1909 to 1965 has not been confined—though 'confined' is hardly the word—to the creation of a very beautiful garden with an immensely wide range of plants, many of which were not even thought of as garden plants until he made them so; to the discovery of how to work chalk and what to plant in it; to the trial, study and ordering of the genera paeonia and galanthus; to fruitful co-operation, decade after decade, with all the great botanist gardeners of his time; to the discovery and proof of, for example, which magnolias, lilies, hydrangeas will grow in chalk; to his contribution to plant genetics; to his writing of *A Chalk Garden*, by far the best thing in its field that I have read. He has also been for many years a public servant of horticulture—by serving on the Council of the R.H.S.; by his work on the Council of the John Innes Institution; and by his continuing Vice-Presidency, in his eightieth year, of the R.H.S. No living gardener has done more new, original and endearing work for the English garden and the gardens of those other lands with great masses of chalk or limestone in their geological composition.

I had, of course, been interested in lime-loving plants before that, and especially in the paeonies. I first consciously distinguished tree-paeonies as they are absurdly called, at Sissinghurst where the late Lady Nicolson, Victoria Sackville-West, grew them with a north exposure. But the first time I was really taken with them was when I saw Rock's form of the true 'moutan', *Paeonia suffruticosa*, in Wye College garden, which is one of the best medium-sized gardens in Europe. I had grown the herbaceous paeonies for some time before I ever planted any of the shrubby ones; and I first wrote an account of the genus as I knew and rejoiced in it in gardens, in 1962.

TREE-PAEONIES OR MOUTANS
June 16, 1962

The season of paeony flowering is about two months, May and June. The May paeonies are of two main classes: the so-called tree-paeonies, that is those which are woody shrubs; and those herbaceous paeonies which are not of the *P. lactiflora* group which appears to include all those formerly classed under *P. sinensis* or *P. albiflora*.

The great specialist in paeonies is, of course, Sir Frederick Stern, and it is a shameful thing that his unique treatise on the genus is out of print and I have failed time and again to buy a copy. Some years ago a collection of his tree-paeonies from Highdown was offered, in very small number, by Messrs Notcutt, and I treated myself to a dozen of these splendid shrubs. But there are many others which are outstandingly beautiful. As chalk-lovers they are of particular value in those parts of Britain where rhododendrons and azaleas cannot be grown without great trouble.

Although lumped together as tree-paeonies, with sometimes a reference to them as *P. suffruticosa*, *arborea*, *moutan*, or what have you, there are at least three distinctly different kinds of shrubby paeonies. There is a group of low (three or four feet), sprawling, fully clad paeonies which make neat mounds of fine foliage in a corner or against a wall, and which I think of as 'moutan' paeonies; the typical flower is a large, single white with a deep maroon centre, and I am not sure that it is not the most beautiful paeony of all. There are other colours, notably pink and maroon, in this group and when you have a chance to collect seeds from any of them it is well worth while to take and plant them, for all the seedlings will probably be good plants.

Secondly, there is the group which has long, unclad woody stems, rising to five or six feet, or even, sometimes, more, topped with a head of fine foliage. Typical is the species, *P. delavayi*, but this has relatively small, single, mahogany-red flowers; it is, nevertheless, a fine plant and well worth growing. I suppose that there is *delavayi* sap in all the garden varieties, which have this tall and, it must be admitted, rather ungainly habit. The flowers of these varieties may be single, semi-double or double, and they vary in colour from white, through all the pinks, to deep red. They are enormous and very magnificent, and a good healthy shrub of this group carrying a large number of flowers is a sight to take the breath away. The list of named varieties is now a long one and I am not going to suggest a 'short list' because the only way to choose tree-paeonies is to go and see them in flower at the nursery and to make sure, from the nurseryman, of the height and habit of the ones you like before buying them.

Finally, the third group is that of the hybrid yellow-flowered tree-paeonies. These, too, vary much in stature; they are, I believe, mostly, and perhaps all, crosses of *P. suffruticosa* varieties with *P. lutea*, and they range in colour from primrose-yellow to deep gold and even salmon. One or two of them are strongly fragrant. But in addition to these hybrids is what I think is a species, *P. lutea* var. *ludlowii*, or just plain *P. ludlowii*, which makes a beautiful shrub about five feet tall, with very fine bright green foliage and clusters of relatively small, golden flowers. In all my tree paeonies but this one, which is green from spring to autumn, the spring colour of the young foliage is one of the greatest beauties, the leaves being soft bronze reds, golds, glaucous bluey-greens, and only slowly assuming the summer green.

Most of the tree-paeonies you buy from a nursery are grafted on to a herbaceous paeony root. They should be planted with the graft junction well below the level of the soil, so that the scion soon forms its own roots. In due course the stock root will die, leaving the shrub firmly established on its own roots. As to soil, the genus is not fussy, but it will do well in loam and sandy loam rather than heavy clay; bone meal is a good fertiliser for tree paeonies, and they like leaf-mould. One is warned not to use animal manures, but compost which has been made with farmyard manure and is so well rotted and mature as to be almost humus, can do nothing but good. Tree-paeonies like lime but can manage very well without any.

The second class of May-flowering paeonies is one of herbaceous perennials. They are for the most part singles, and they are either white, pure red, rose pink, or yellow. The yellow species of this group is, for form and distinction, by far the best, a paeony of outstanding merit. This is the unpronounceable *P. mloklosewitchii.* The leaflets of its foliage tend to be kidney-shaped, the leaves are very firm and substantial and of a fine green shot with bronze. The numerous flowers are cup-shaped, with substantial bright yellow petals and a dense centre of coral-red stamens. Best of all, the plant grows into a low, very neat, almost stylised form; two or three together make a most lovely object in a border or in front of a shrubbery. This species can be, and generally is, grown from seed. *P. anomala,* flowering late in April is bright crimson; and the best white of this group is *P. officinalis* var. *alba plena.*

The June-flowering paeonies offer an enormous embarrassment of choice, and again I shall name none, for the only way to buy is to see them in flower. To the best of my belief, Kelway, of Langport, has the finest collection. Here, too, again there are sub-groups. Single-flowered paeonies vary in colour from flesh-pink to very deep carmine; I do not know a good, single white though there perhaps is one. In height they may be as low as two feet and as tall as four feet. This is also true of the doubles, but in them there is not only a very great variety of colour—it is this that makes recommending paeonies by name quite useless otherwise than as an indication of one's own taste—but also of form. In some the flower is formally double; in others it is an untidy mass of petals in which the arrangement seems to have gone wrong. The double paeony of purest form is by many considered to be 'Kelway's Glorious', which is an exceptionally fine white. One should remember, when buying paeonies, that some of them are now fragrant.

A third sub-group of herbaceous paeonies are 'double' in a different way. Instead of the rose-like (or, come to that, cabbage-like) fullness being produced by a number of corollas of petals one within the other, in this group there is an outer cup of stout petals crammed with a mass of petaloids in a contrasting colour. Of this group I suppose that the two which have made the greatest name for themselves are 'Bowl of Beauty', which, as I recall, was the sensation of one Chelsea Show; and 'Globe of Light'. 'Bowl of Beauty' has pink petals and cream petaloids. It is a very beautiful flower, there is no doubt about that, yet for a peculiar reason I do not want it in my garden: the reason is that the juxtaposition of just those two colours happens to suggest to me vanilla and strawberry ice-cream, and I dislike gooey comestibles. 'Globe of Light' has rosy petals and golden petaloids and it is, therefore, for me, a better flower not suggestive of any kind of confectionery. Several of this group of paeonies are so late that they carry the paeony season into a third month, or even a fourth, since at least one single begins in April.

Paeonies are valuable not only for flower but for their foliage during the rest of the season; for this purpose none of the hybrids can compare with the species; the old deep crimson *officinalis flore pleno*, if that is the right name for it; the small-flowered and exceptionally neat *P. anemonae* 'Flora rubra', a great favourite of mine; the miniature of the old *officinalis* which I have seen only at Haddon Hall and have never identified by name; and, of course, *mloklosewitchii*—these, after flowering, leave one with fine mounds of beautiful leaves which are an ornament until cut down by frost. Too many of the hybrids are too tall and floppy to have this admirable quality.

A few points: herbaceous paeonies benefit from bone meal and from very mature compost; they are gross feeders. They like full sun, will stand a little intermittent shade, hate being moved or disturbed in any way. Tree-paeonies and the shrubby moutans burgeon so early in the spring that the young foliage is exposed to frost; this will not matter provided it is not *also* exposed to the early morning sun; a slow thaw before the sun strikes the shoots leaves them unharmed, a fast thaw from direct sunshine will kill them. It is a matter of careful siting. Finally, I have found that in their first year in light soils, and sometimes even in their second year, tree paeonies quickly wilt in a drought; watering, then mulching with leaf-mould or grass cuttings, prevents this.

My complaint that Sir Frederick Stern's treatise on the paeony was out of print and unobtainable did not result in a reprint. But early in 1963 Constable published, at a guinea, Mr Michael Haworth-Booth's *The Moutan or Tree-paeony*, a very useful handbook full of information which one wanted. It was interesting to find so great an exponent, designer and maker of rhododendron gardens emphasising the superiorities of the moutan—its rugged hardiness, for example, and tolerance of almost any kind of soil.

The book opens with a short history of the tree-paeonies which I found very interesting. It is fun to realise that during the decade of the sixth century when Augustine was busy converting the English, garden writers in China were writing about the origins of the tree-paeony in the wild, and that the art of cultivating the already numerous varieties was old and sophisticated. The author provides what must surely be the longest list of cultivars in this genus yet to be printed; I confess to being astounded at the number, I had thought that this was one of the kinds of shrubs where choice is easy because there are few to choose from. Nothing of the kind; Mr Haworth-Booth lists (I have not counted) at least 400, but as he also provides, in his appreciations of the habits of these plants, an excellent guide to making the right choice, this is all to the good. He is also honest about the fact that although moutans are tolerant of hard conditions in the matter of climate and soil, they are relatively exacting in the amount of attention they require from the gardener. But really all this amounts to is that moutans must be gardened, not just admired, and no real gardener minds that. Propagation is discussed and it is nice to know that if you start off with good varieties—and I must say that a really old bushy moutan, beautifully covering some scores of square feet of ground with a great mound of handsome foliage dotted with glorious great flowers, is among the most beautiful objects in any garden—raising plants from their seeds which are freely set is well worth while and the chances are in favour of the seedlings being themselves good garden plants. I suggest that not only those whose soil prevents them from growing camellias and rhododendrons should get and read this admirable handbook; the rhododendron grower might well consider diversifying his shrub borders with moutans, for they will grow equally well in acid or alkaline soils.

It seems to be some sort of rule with me as a gardener that I start off with the garden varieties of a genus, through them discover the botanical species, try them, prefer them and in due course find myself growing them rather than the more spectacular man-made plants. It was so with paeonies, with the following result:

PAEONY SPECIES

March 2, 1963

For centuries before we were interested in gardening, or for that matter in a state to practise this most civilised of the arts, the Chinese and later the Japanese were busy producing garden varieties of paeonies, so that this is one of the genera which we were ultimately able to import ready-made for our gardens. But the genus was attractive to nurserymen and to plant-breeders, so that as well as the Far Eastern garden kinds we have a very large number of hybrid paeony varieties, short and tall, single and double and semi-double, scented and scentless, and in every colour excepting blue. I have nothing but admiration for many of these splendid garden plants and in the long paeony-flower season it sometimes seems to me that if, for some reason, I was not allowed to cultivate any other genus, I could still be content. But in the case of paeonies as in the case of, for example, rhododendrons and roses, in producing hybrids with new colours, larger flowers, and more vigorous habits of growth, something possessed by the botanical species is inevitably lost. There is no word for this quality, just as there is no word, really, to describe the same quality in certain kinds of human beings: race, blood, distinction, gentry . . . something of the kind. There is, in the paeony species, a fineness of line, a restraint of design, a subtlety of colour, a firmness and, as it were, self-control in the habit of growth, which are pleasing in a way very few hybrid paeonies can equal.

The species paeonies which I describe below can be grown in ordinary flower borders, although in one case care must be taken to choose a sheltered corner. But better still they can be planted among shrubs, preferably several plants of a single kind together to form small masses. They can be raised from seed, taking about three years to reach flowering size. Do not be impatient with the seeds, which may take rather a long time to germinate, for the *testa*, the outer coat of the seed, is extremely hard: there are ways of 'chipping' this *testa* which will result in quicker germination, but want of skill in using these methods may kill the seed. The *testa* can be carefully thinned by use of an abrasive such as fine sandpaper or a nail-file; it can be literally chipped with a sharp penknife; the seed can be exposed to frost, for example in a refrigerator, and then to heat; in the case of some very hard seeds, those of certain acacias for example, scalding with boiling water is resorted to, but I do not know whether paeony seeds would stand this. Very fresh seed germinates more quickly than stored seed, so that if you collect your own the results will be better: but if you have more than one species in your garden you must not count on the seedlings 'coming true', for paeonies cross-breed very readily. Yet even this can be turned to account, since if you have the three below within easy range of each other, you may get some very beautiful first-cross hybrids of your own.

Paeonia cambessedesii is a native of the Balearic Islands and it was introduced to cultivation in Britain about sixty-five years ago. It has remained rare in gardens, largely because it is not as hardy as it might be and because the measure of horticultural sophistication which results in the rejection of garden hybrids in favour of the botanical species (and the kind of gardening which makes this possible and desirable), is something fairly new. The plant is wide and flat, growing only about eighteen inches tall. The leaves are pinnate (to be precise one should, apparently, say that they are 'ternately pinnatisect'); anyway, they are composed of several leaflets growing from a central leaf-stalk; these leaflets are about four inches long, so that the whole leaf is a large one. In the seedlings, and in the young foliage of mature plants, they are very beautiful indeed, being glaucous blue-green shot with pale carmine. But the ordinary mature leaf is a rich deep green above, and a rich purple on the underside. The flowers open in late April or in early May, varying a good deal with the season. They are single, and very beautiful, with that perfection of design which distinguishes the best of the paeonies and to which it was very natural that a people with such exquisite taste as the Chinese should turn. They are cups which may be as little as two inches across but are, in a well-grown and mature plant, nearer to four inches, the colour of the petals being deep rose-pink. The filaments of the stamens are red, and these are surmounted by bright yellow anthers. After the flower fades the seed vessels develop. There may be as many as eight; they are a smooth, rich purple. In due course they open to display the seeds, for this plant is decorative throughout the active seasons. This is the moment to collect and sow the seed for fairly quick germination, but in that case it must, of course, be done under glass. The seedlings will then be growing out of season, since the plant is a herbaceous perennial; however, they do not seem to mind and will grow slowly, in the greenhouse, throughout the winter. Do not be in too great a hurry to plant them out; pot them on into larger pots and wait until you have a plant of reasonable size, and during the first winter in the open ground it may be as well to cover the plants with cloches, but not until they have entered their period of dormancy. This paeony is not perfectly hardy and the site chosen for a group should be protected from north and east winds. Like other species paeonies, it will stand some shade but should receive sunshine for part of the day.

The next species is very commonly grown in half-shade, so that it too is admirable for shrubberies, but it should be grown under leggier shrubs, or farther back than *cambessedesii*, or, in a border, placed in the second rank, for it grows three feet tall. This is *P. peregrina*, and it comes from the Balkans, presumably from a fairly high altitude because it is hardy. Its leaves are deeply divided into many segments and the segments themselves may be divided again, the whole leaf being large and handsome, deep, shining green above, glaucous on the underside. The flowers, single of course, are of particularly beautiful form for the marked concavity of the petals makes them into firm cups with the rim turned inwards: they are up to four or more inches across, smaller in some cases and on immature plants. The colour of both petals and stamens is red and the carpels are hairy. As a rule, in a normal season, this species is in full flower when *cambessedesii* is going over, but sometimes they flower more or less together, for example, when the winter has been severe and is followed by a warm spring with everything rushing into flower.

P. mlokosewitschii is as lovely as its name is hard to pronounce, one of the most beautiful of perennial herbs. This glorious paeony was discovered in the Caucasus by Mr Mloklosewitsch, and first came to the attention of British botanists in 1908 when it was pictured in the *Botanical Magazine*. It was more than twenty years before it received its well deserved Award of Merit, at the Chelsea Show in 1929. Ten years later enough had been propagated by nurseries for the plant to appear in the catalogues at 5*s*. Flowering-size plants now cost between 10*s* and 15*s*, and by no means all nurseries have them; there is quite a waiting list for plants at the larger nurseries.

P. mloklosewitschii can be grown in almost any good garden soil, but it does not flourish in very light soils, whereas it does like quite heavy clay. In four or five years it forms a clump about three feet across and may be expected to bear between twenty and thirty flowers in season. Like *P. cambessedesii* this paeony grows about eighteen inches tall and you can look down into the cup of the flowers. The petals are concave so that the flower shape is like that of *P. peregrina*, but the flowers are often larger, being between four and five inches across. They are pure yellow, on the pale side, but rather variable, beautifully held against the background of ternate, darkly glaucous leaves. But the beauty of this plant is by no means finished for the season when the flowers go over. Three hairy carpels develop and when these are ripe they split open to reveal very dark blue-black seeds about the size of coffee-beans, held in a brilliant pink pulp or whatever the tissue should be called. This display is so handsome that one is reluctant to collect the seeds.

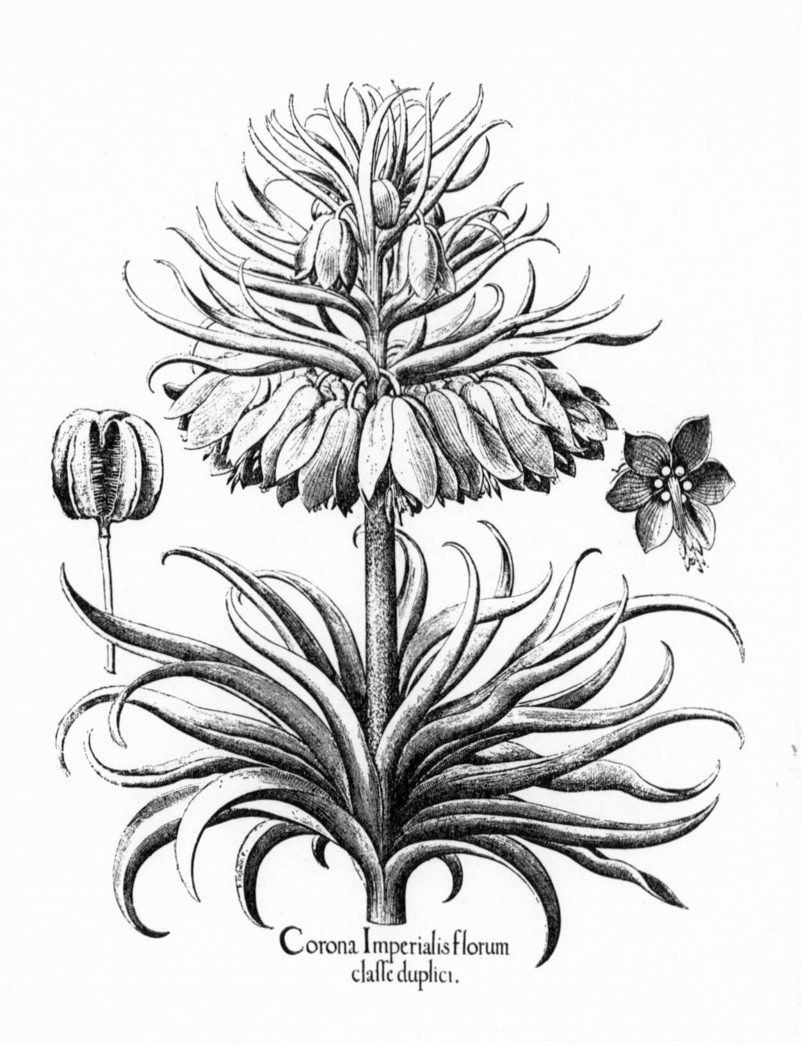

Corona Imperialis florum classe duplici.

Chapter 6

Flowering Evergreens

A striking difference between the east and west sides of Britain, which made an impression on me when we moved from Kent to Devon, is that the winter in the west, whatever the temperature and however gloomy the sky, does not look so wintry, is not so spare and bony. The reason is the greater wealth, in both woods and gardens, of evergreens: In the half-wild, the cherry laurels and the wild rhododendrons are examples, not to mention the great range of exotic conifers. The first evergreen genus in which I took a real interest, while we were still in Kent, was *Myrtus*; but at that time—until anyway 1959—I was familiar with only one species, the Sweet Myrtle, so long beloved of English gardeners despite the difficulties of growing it in a country of hard winters.

THE SWEET MYRTLE
September 12, 1959

Of the shrubs growing in my garden it is the myrtles which are at once the most troublesome and the source of the greatest pleasure. There are four of them, three being young plants grown from cuttings taken from the fourth, which was given to me in a pot, by a friend. Although the original myrtle is now seven years old, it is still only five feet tall, for it has twice been almost killed by frost. Two of the others will not, we hope, be subject to the same risk, for they have been planted against walls in the warmest corners we can find. There is nothing spectacular about the small, pointed leaves: they stay bright green, have a good gloss on them, and are pleasant to see at all seasons. But when the shrub flowers, it becomes very beautiful, for the small, starry white flowers have extraordinary distinction. And their scent, spicy, balsamic, is incomparable, an aura of fragrance which, on warm evenings as the dew begins to fall, fills the shrubbery.

But there is something more: the merits by which we judge a plant must surely include that plant's history, its significance in the history of civilisation, as well as its form, colour and habit. It is perhaps impossible to know when and how myrtle was introduced to England; nor does it matter, for the shrub is part of the fabric of our culture, like the grape-vine, the sonnet form, symphonic music, the wheat plant. Myrtle was Apollo's tree, and since it had to be planted round the shrines of that god, its diffusion westward from some Asiatic Greek centre was ensured by the spread of Apollo's cult. That centre was probably Lydia. It is written that in the city of Temnos in that country, on the left bank of the River Hermos, was a figure of Aphrodite 'carved from the living myrtle by Pelops the son of Tantalus to obtain the favour of the goddess in his wooing of Hippodamia'. What does 'carved in the living myrtle' mean? If the figure was of myrtle-wood, it was small. Can it be perhaps a case of very early, and sacerdotal or ritual, topiary? At all events, myrtle is as closely entwined with the old religions of Europe, especially that part of Europe which gave birth to our civilisation, as the grape-vine. In Cyprus, Astarte's parish, it was into a myrtle that the king's daughter Myrrha was changed to save her from the persecutions of her incestuous father. It was myrtle which formed the wreath carried in procession at the festival called Hellotia, in honour of the goddess Europa, held annually in Crete and in Corinth. The Arabian myrtle is *smyrna*; the town was called after Myrina, whose tomb, as I am reminded by Victor Heyn in his *Wanderings of Plants and Animals*, is mentioned in the *Iliad*. This priestess was in the service of the Lydian moon-goddess, whom it is difficult to distinguish from Europa. It would be possible to fill many pages with such instances.

The point is that from the near-neighbourhood of the shrines where it was planted in European Greece, the myrtle colonised the rocky coasts of that country. And since religion was the core of civilisation, the shrub must soon have come to be associated with a polished and humane way of living, rather than with a specific and originally barbarous and even orgiastic cult. We do not know at what date the shrub came from Greece to Italy; presumably it was taken there for its religious significance and use by colonists from Greece. Nor can one know to what extent it was still associated with Apollo and Aphrodite as it moved north into Gaul. No doubt, by the time it reached England, its religious associations had been quite forgotten by all but scholars. I feel sure that it came to us, however, not strictly on its botanical or horticultural merits, but as one of those symbols which, throughout English history, proclaim the radiant energy of the classical civilisation, its attraction for the northern peoples, and its influence on them. It is customary to seek evidence for this in such stony artefacts as Doric columns or Corinthian capitals; or in the influence of Greek thought and feeling on English religious and secular ideas. But for those who have eyes for such things, it is quite as apparent in garden plants, and notably in myrtle. I have said that my own has twice been cut down by frost; the symbol, then, is a complete one, for how many Mediterranean ideas, introduced, beloved and fostered, have failed to survive the climate of a land which lies on the periphery of two different kinds of culture?

The preservation of our myrtle during our sometimes very cold winters presents a problem, for it does not seem 'right' to bundle up an evergreen in straw and sacking, as one can very well do with deciduous shrubs. One winter we made an even worse mistake: we built a jury-rigged tent over the shrub, with bamboos and polythene, making it a temporary greenhouse to itself. But these transparent plastic films, while they have their uses in summer, are worse than useless in winter. By the time we had discovered that temperatures under polythene are sometimes *lower* than over it, the damage was done. The most one can do is to plant myrtle where walls and other, hardier, shrubs protect it; erect a temporary screen against the coldest winds in winter; and hope for the best.

A year later I reverted to the subject, approaching it from a slightly different angle.

A CHILEAN MYRTLE

August 20, 1960

One of the major formative influences in the history and culture of the English people has been the fact that, turning and at times straining towards that great source of civilisations, the Mediterranean, her people are not quite Mediterranean in their feelings and manners. Yet that turning towards the south rather than the north, that bond, however, slight, with Rome and with Hellenism, has made a visible impression upon the English garden. For century after century Englishmen have brought back from the south seeds and shrubs and trees as if, like colonists in a strange land, they wanted to create about them a landscape planted with a flora grateful to them and in which they felt at home. And many, very many, plants of Mediterranean origin have, in fact, been acclimatised here: it has been possible because our climate is milder than the latitude of our country entitles us to expect, a boon we owe to the sea around us. All the same, it has not always been easy, and in any county but Cornwall many of these exotics need careful winter nursing. The vine, it is true, is happy here because, although one thinks of it as Mediterranean, its original home lies much farther north and in a land where winters are extremely harsh. The fig, too, is an ancient element of the English garden scene: my own seven trees in five varieties are all heavily laden with fruit this year, which I attribute to the beneficent effect of the sun on the wood during 1959. Attempts have occasionally been made to establish the olive in the south-west and I know of one such which has been started this year: olive trees will stand four or five degrees of frost, perhaps a little more, and there must be many favoured sites near the sea where they could safely be planted. They suffer, however, from the damp of our climate rather than the cold; and this, I fancy, is true of many other plants, not to mention people.

To another group of plants which Englishmen have always sought to establish in their gardens belong the shrubs and trees which have an important place in myth, legend and religion and which reinforce this claim to our affection by their own native qualities. Daphnes are perhaps the most popular but, and I have said this more than once, none of them can compare, in my opinion with the myrtles. Not even the bay is as beautiful, for although it, too has handsome foliage and a delicious, spicy fragrance, it does not have the myrtle's beauty of flower.

I do not know when myrtles were first introduced into England; I daresay some of the Roman 'occupiers' planted them by their villas, but if so they would subsequently have been lost. Alicia Amhurst, in her *History of Gardening in England*, quotes the following letter from Lord Burghley, written in 1561 or 1562, to Thomas Windebank who was in Paris: '. . . I pray you procure for me a lemon, a pomegranate and a myrte (*sic*) tree . . . and beforehand send me in writing a perfect declaration how they ought to be used, kept and ordered.' I very much like Mr Windebank's answer: 'Sir, according to your commandment I have sent unto you by Mr Caro's man, with his master's trees, a lemon tree and two myrte (*sic*) trees, in two pots which cost me both a crown, and the lemon tree fifteen crowns, wherein, sir, if I have (done) more than perhaps you will at first like, yet it is the best cheap we could get it, and better-cheap than other noble men in France have bought of the same man, having paid for six trees 120 crowns. . . . Well, I think that this good may ensure by your buying it, that if the tree prosper . . . you will not think your money lost. If it do not prosper it shall take away your desire of losing any more money in like sort. My Lord Ambassador and Mr Caro were the chosers of it.'

I started with one very small myrtle cutting; we now have four myrtles in various ages and sizes, for the genus is very readily propagated by cuttings of half-ripe wood in late summer, or ripe wood under glass in winter. All these shrubs are flowering well this year—another legacy of last summer no doubt. But my reason for reverting to a subject which I have touched on before is a letter from Mr Alec Day, of Cork in Ireland, enclosing photographs of a myrtle *tree* about which we had had some correspondence in the past, and which must, I think, be one of the most remarkable, perhaps the most remarkable, in Europe.

Recently Mr Day sent me foliage from the tree so that I could make quite sure that it was, indeed, a myrtle; as far as I could tell, the tree is of the species *Myrtus communis*. Comparing the foliage sent to me with that of my own myrtles, I found that the only difference was that Mr Day's tree has leaves very slightly broader. It is possible to distinguish *M. communis* from *M. luma* by the difference between their flowers, since the latter's have four petals, the former's five. Unfortunately all the flowers received from Cork had come to pieces in the post. Mr Day also sent me some bark from his tree and it was the handsome cinnamon colour which characterises *M. luma*. On the other hand, a very similar colour appears on the trunk of my own largest *M. communis*. *M. communis* is described in the R.H.S. *Dictionary of Gardening* as a shrub ten to fifteen feet tall. I will suppose Mr Day's identification and my own to be wrong. Even so, none of the species described in the same work of reference is given as taller than twenty-five feet, the tallest being *M. luma* which may not be a true myrtle at all, and is not one of the classical myrtles, by the way, since it comes from Chile.

Mr Day estimates the height of his tree at between forty and fifty feet. One of its main trunks has a curious look of being a eucalypt, but as I have never seen a myrtle nearly as big as this one, and as its age is no doubt very great, I have no means of comparing it with others. The tree would be much taller if it had not to be topped on more than one occasion. It has another peculiarity which makes me wonder about its identity: it flowers twice a year, the first time in July and again in September. The bulk of its timber is as remarkable as its height: the circumferences of the four principal trunks are 24 in, 37 in, 50 in and 55 in, 166 inches in all. I estimate that there must be something like 500 cubic feet of good myrtle timber.

My hope, in publishing an account of this mighty myrtle, is that some botanist will tell us whether there is some species which might have got itself planted in Cork and which is more likely to have attained such noble proportions than *M. communis*. My own guess is that it is, in fact, *M. luma*, despite its enormous size.

The tree in question is in fact a specimen of *Myrtus luma*, a species we became familiar with and which I myself planted once we had moved to the West Country where it flourishes, although it does not seem to reach the great size, in England, that it sometimes attains in Irish gardens where it is favoured by the milder winters and heavier rainfall. Nor was that the only species I planted: by 1964 I knew rather more about myrtles, in fact.

CHARACTERISTICS OF MYRTLE SPECIES

February 8, 1964

From the country of Lydia, of which Croesus to whom Solon the law-giver of Athens said that he should call no man happy until he was dead (gloomy old party), we had the cultivated grape-vines of ancient Asia; but that is not all, for we probably owe the Sweet Myrtle to the same land, or by way of that land, to Iran. When Pelops the son of Tantalus needed the help of the goddess in his wooing of Hippodamia, we are told that he carved a figure of Aphrodite in living myrtle. Can he have been a topiarist? For if the tree was living he can hardly have cut the image of the goddess into its timber without killing it. The fact that this lovely evergreen is so common in Greece and all those countries which formerly composed Magna Graecia has led many to suppose it native there: it is, rather, naturalised, but its planting about shrines and temples and in sacred groves is of such enormous antiquity that we can certainly call it native now.

Of the hundred or so species of the genus this Asiatic and Hellenic tree is perhaps the most beautiful; I cannot pretend to have seen, indeed, more than a dozen species, but if there was one which surpassed it we should have heard of it. A shapely, well-grown bush of myrtle covered with its starry flowers, their clusters of stamens just creamy yellow enough to contrast with the white petals, and the whole plant richly aromatic, takes a great deal of beating. But what of its tenderness? From my own experience with several specimens in different places, I would say this: if you cannot give it very thorough protection from the north and east winds, don't plant it. But if you can give it the shelter of a wall exposed to the south or the west; or of a yard protected by buildings; or of a planting of dense, evergreen conifers, the myrtle or stand of myrtles being planted into a suitably contrived niche among them, then your myrtles will stand fairly severe frost without taking much harm. As a matter of fact myrtles are rather rarely killed outright even by very severe frost; but where they are repeatedly cut back every winter by the cold, they will never be either shapely or floriferous, and are not worth growing.

I was given, by a fellow-gardener, a young plant, in a pot, labelled *Myrtus obcordata*: I think, however, that it is, rather, *M. bullata*; it is true that the leaves are more nearly inversely heart-shaped than they are ovate, but they are not green, there is, at least in its present stage, no green at all in this striking little shrub, the colour being a reddish brown in general effect, made up on closer inspection of reds and buffs. *M. bullata* should, it is true, have blistered leaves, but my plant may be too young to show any. Both shrubs are from New Zealand. Mine will go out in the coming spring, in a place on the lee side of a fairly dense windbreak of thuja where half-tender shrubs do better than elsewhere in this garden since the east-wind cannot get at them. I class this myrtle with such shrubs as *Pittosporum barretii,** *Pseudowintera* (or *Drimys*) *colorata* and one or two others whose foliage is far more important than their flowers and is itself strikingly colourful.

Two Chilean myrtles, again, tend to confuse themselves in my mind: *M. ugni* is a neat, narrow shrub about six feet as I have seen it (my own are about six inches), with very glossy evergreen foliage much like that of Sweet Myrtle, but flowers much inferior. However, it becomes a most attractive sight when the fruit is ripe, for there is often a great deal of it; the berries are rather larger than red currants, and they are black shot with reddish lights. Now last autumn I saw a very fine specimen of what I took for this myrtle, well covered with fruit, on Garinish Island. But this plant turned out to be *M. lechleriana.* I tasted the fruit and found it to be quite as agreeable as that of *M. ugni*, which is much pleasanter than, for example, black currant, and which makes good jam. If you plant this myrtle, or *lechleriana*, give it protection from the east and north, and while the plant is young, and so small, cover it in winter with a cloche. By that means you can get it through two hard winters before it becomes too big for cover; by that time it will be better able to resist cold. I should say that it is not a whit more tender than Sweet Myrtle, and possibly slightly hardier.

It is a curious fact that whereas I have not come across a single instance of the Sweet Myrtle, I mean common myrtle, which does at least belong to our own hemisphere and our own temperature zone, self-seeding in any English garden, another and very handsome Chilean species does, so freely in some gardens that seedlings come up all over the place, even some way from the parent trees: This is *M. luma.* In favourable conditions this plant is by no means the 'shrub' which it is called by the R.H.S. *Dictionary* and by Bean: I have seen it up to forty feet, and very definitely a tree; and even as a small plant, say twenty feet, it has the true form of a tree. Indeed, if this were not the case it would lose half its merit, the very lovely cinnamon-red bark which, where a stand of these trees has been well placed to catch the sun, is positively fiery. This beauty, however, is a work of time, it is not apparent in young

* I have had difficulty in ascertaining the correct name of this rare plant. I shall use this form but it may really be *Pittosporum tenuifolium* var. *garretii* or *P.t.* 'Garretii'.

trees. As to the hardiness or otherwise of the species, several in my garden, all young and therefore extra tender, in fact all seedlings a year or two old, received the same damage as young *M. communis* plants in the winter of 1962/3, and thereafter recovered. In short, eight weeks of frost and frosts as severe as 20° F will not kill *M. luma* outright. Even so, do not plant it where it is exposed to frost winds every winter, for it will never be able to grow away and form a shapely bush, let alone tree.

A myrtle which I should very much like to try here, which I saw many years ago in a garden near Richmond, Virginia, and have not seen since, is *M. nummularia*. So will any reader of this page who happens to live near the Straits of Magellan be kind enough to send me some seeds? (As far as I can be sure the only people which does not have gardeners who write to me is the Eskimo.) This myrtle is a dense, ground-hugging prostrate evergreen, and as well as growing near the Straits of Magellan it is native to the Falkland Islands and to Tierra del Fuego where, according to Bean, Darwin collected it while he was making the famous voyage of the *Beagle*. It ought, I imagine, to be relatively hardy; and apart from its value in the rock garden and elsewhere where there are stones or stony banks to cover, it would be very interesting to try and cross this myrtle with some of the tall-growing and less hardy ones. It is a curious fact that no chance crossing of myrtles has yet occurred, even in the great Irish and West Country gardens where several species are represented by fine, floriferous, freely seeding plants; and that, to the best of my knowledge, no deliberate crosses have been made, or at least have succeeded. I did not see this plant in flower on my only meeting with it, but the flowers are apparently more like those of *luma* than of *communis*. On the other hand, the fruit, quite large berries, are apparently bright pink.

There is no difficulty about propagating myrtles. The seeds when you can get them fresh germinate readily. Cuttings root quite quickly: a fairly sure way of making these is to take quite young, but really very soft, shoots in late spring or early summer, and put them into pure silver sand in a propagating case. *M. communis* produces small, twiggy shoots round the base, not true suckers I think, but which, springing from below the soil surface, are often found to have formed roots; these can be cut off below the ground surface and then grown-on under glass.

The myrtle of which I was in some doubt when I wrote that was, in fact, *M. obcordata*, a pretty and very delicate little tree which has grown rather well in a very sheltered place but which, I know, will be lost one winter sooner or later, for it really is tender. As for *M. nummularia*, my appeal brought me seeds and I now have this very attractive and quite hardy evergreen, alpine, prostrate shrub growing over some stones: it has tiny leaves, quarter-inch cupped flowers which look up at you, twisting branches which hug the ground and root themselves as they grow, and red fruits.

So much for the myrtles: another evergreen genus of which I knew only a single species while we still remained in Kent, is *Mahonia*. At one time classed with *Berberis*, this genus has become something of a mania with me, the only one which I not only plant but am in some danger of 'collecting'.

MAHONIAS
December 30, 1962

Among the plants which flower in the winter and early spring my favourites are the mahonias. At one time they were included with the barberries and in a few catalogues they are still to be found there; but they now form a distinct genus; their distinctions from berberis are several; they are invariably evergreen, they have few or no spines and the foliage is simply pinnate. I believe that there are something like fifty species, but of these a much more limited number are good garden plants; those that are good, however, are very good indeed.

I suppose that the most commonly planted of the genus is *Mahonia aquifolium*; it is a north-western American shrub which is usually about three or four feet tall in English gardens, spreading by underground suckers so that it is very easily propagated by division and also readily forms a thicket or hedge. The clusters of flower racemes begin to open in February and continue to do so into the spring, reaching a zenith in late April. The flowers are small, vividly yellow, and they give way in due course to berries which are actually black but do not look it as they are covered with a pale violet bloom. The leaves, normally dark, glossy green, turn colour in autumn, going through a number of shades but ending up a sort of winey purple. This species is hardy anywhere in Britain, which many of the mahonias are not, but it is not really one of the best and where space is limited I don't think I would plant it.

Much more spectacular and likewise more graceful is *M. japonica*; it is, moreover, an encouraging shrub, for, despite what is written about its reluctance to transplant, it grows away very fast after first planting in any good loamy soil, delighting the gardener's heart by the inches it adds to its stature in a very short time. It may attain a height of ten feet. Its foliage is very handsome indeed, each leaf a foot or more long and composed of an uneven number of leaflets each two or three inches long, very stiff and hard and polished, and contrasting with the light green of the young stems. Compared with the very small flowers of *M. aquifolium*, those of *M. japonica* are magnificent, the racemes being eight or nine inches long, fountaining out from the terminal buds of the stalks, and smelling strongly of lily-of-the-valley. The flowers give way to large, oval, purple berries.

M. japonica is not, apparently, perfectly hardy everywhere and it may be that the gardener should make careful enquiries in his own neighbourhood before planting it; but for my part I know nobody who has failed with it because of cold. Hardier than the type is *M. j. bealei* and it is, perhaps, the better of the two in other respects, with a deeper colour to the flowers, and larger, rounder, leaflets; moreover, it is said to be more vigorous. The difficulty is to make quite sure that you are in fact getting this variety; either nurseries are not certain which is which or there is a lot of the type being sold as *bealei*. This difficulty can be avoided by the simple device of dealing with one of the great nurserymen with as much interest in plantsmanship as in profits. Any experienced gardener can sense this spirit in a very few minutes and will know exactly what I mean.

There is, I find, a notion abroad that these mahonias can, or even should, be planted in shade, that they are shade-lovers. I do not believe it. At best they are more or less tolerant of shade, but anyone who has had the chance to compare specimens growing in shade with specimens receiving a good deal of sun will be in no doubt about it: these two mahonias like at least some sunshine and are twice as good if they get it. I do not know what kind of country it was in which Fortune found these plants in China something over a hundred years ago, but I should guess at light, open woodland or parkland. At all events, they should be planted where they are not exposed to sun all day but are not in deep shade either. *M. japonica* and its variety flower in February and March.

For the seaside counties and the warm south-west there is a Chinese or Formosan mahonia which can be compared for nobility with *Rhododendron sinogrande*. The leaves of the magnificent species, *M. lomariifolia*, are as much as two feet long, the leaflets being up to four inches long, so that the whole leaf is enormous. The shrub attains about eight feet, sometimes more, and the inflorescence consists of a score of clustered erect racemes about six inches long, forming, therefore, a great bouquet of the yellow, fragrant flowers at the termination of each main shoot. Owing to the fact that it is not by any means universally hardy, although I know that it grows well in Gloucestershire where it can be cold, this species is not very easy to buy and it may be necessary to ask your nursery to order it for you; it will probably not be listed in their catalogue. Tender though it may be, I have seen it doing very well indeed in a courtyard well protected from cold winds in one of the colder counties. *M. lomariifolia* flowers later than the others named, in April or May, but perhaps earlier in the warmest parts of Cornwall. I forgot to say that the flowers are sweet scented like those of *M. japonica*. The shrub never reaches its full size in England, or rather perhaps one should say that it has not yet done so, for it was only introduced by Lawrence Johnston of Hidcote, in 1931. In Yunnan and Burma it makes a thirty- or forty-foot tree.

The mahonia which flowers right through the winter, beginning in November and becoming more and more floriferous until its zenith in March, is *M. napaulensis*. This comes from the Himalayas but perhaps not from very high up because it is not perfectly hardy and although it may be planted with confidence in the south and west, in the colder parts of the country it should be given a site chosen for shelter and warmth. It looks very like *M. japonica*—I for one would not undertake to tell one from the other at a glance—but in detail it differs. Its flowers are borne in racemes about a foot long and if they have any scent it is ephemeral, for I have never smelt it. The pretty berries look like clusters of miniature damsons, they have that same very beautiful blue bloom. The shrub is usually about six feet tall but in very favourable sites it may be much more, I believe. I have never seen a big one.

Many years ago I saw in Dublin what must, I think, have been the mahonia referred to by Bean as growing in Phoenix Park and being sixteen feet tall; I recall it because the short flower racemes, no longer than those of *M. aquifolium*, were not confined to the tips but occurred all up the stems, which made the whole shrub a great improvement on the commonest of the mahonias: this apparently, is *M. pinnata*. It is not easy to buy and is not usually listed. Most of the best nurseries, at least in the south, however, have *M. fremontii*; the flowers of this species are not better than those of *aquifolium* but it is valuable for its foliage which is very glaucous, that is 'blue'. This species comes from the south-western United States and must be given a very warm, dry, sunny spot if it is to do well. It is of a suitable size for growing against a south wall.

A mahonia which is dwarf in stature but gigantic in foliage, and which has very long flower racemes held strikingly erect, is *M. nervosa* which I have seen only in the United States, although it was introduced into this country well over a century ago. Like some other north American shrubs and trees it does not really 'do' in England, although nobody seems to know why it should not. I should be interested to hear from anyone who grows it.

There is a great deal wrong with that article. The fact is that when I wrote it I was relying on the labels under which my own mahonias had been delivered to me; and on several authorities, as well as nurserymen's catalogues, which did not agree about the distinguishing of species and varieties. It is *M. napaulensis* rather than *M. lomariifolia* which has gigantic leaves. *M. lomariifolia* flowers in mid-winter, not spring and its leaflets are the most beautifully shaped in the genus. *M. japonica* and *M. bealii* are separate species, only *japonica* being fragrant; it has, too, paler flowers and drooping rather than erect racemes of flower. I tried to correct some of my mistakes at a later date.

THE MAHONIA MUDDLE

December 7, 1963

Reviewing some books a week or two ago I had occasion to suggest that it is not a good idea, if you have to make a rigorous selection of your shrubs for want of room, to plant the commonest of the mahonias when there are much better ones no more difficult to grow. I wrote about these splendid plants not very long ago but make no apology for reverting to the subject, for now is their season; but this time I shall confine myself to those which are the best garden plants taken all round. I must, therefore, leave out my own favourite, *M. lomariifolia* because it is not perfectly hardy and its immensely tall and gaunt habit is not universally admired. For the garden where there is, in fact, room for only one or two mahonias, there is really not much point in looking beyond the two varieties described below: to do so would be, as the French say, to look for noon at two o'clock.

First there is the mahonia which is called by W. J. Bean, and by Hillier in his catalogue—these two authorities are quite good enough for me—*M. japonica bealei*. There has been much discussion about the name; maybe it should simply be *M. bealei*. Glancing over the catalogues of the principal nurserymen I find that Veitch of Exeter have this plant under the same name as Hillier; that Scott of Merriot lists two different species, *M. japonica* and *M. bealei*, the confusion being worse confounded by their explanation that what they now list as *japonica* they formerly sold as *bealei*. The plant I mean seems to be their present *bealei*. Jackman of Woking lists it thus '*japonica* (formerly called *bealei*)', and I am merely assuming it is the same plant though it could be the *japonica* of Scott's catalogue. Wallace of Tunbridge Wells list both *japonica* and *bealei*. Notcutt of Woodbridge list the plant I have in mind as *bealei*; at least, I think they mean what I mean. Treseder of Truro agrees with Hillier and with Veitch. Waterer of Bagshot also agrees with these three but adds the synonym *hiemalis* for the varietal name. To add to the fun, Bean's description does not sound much like the plant in commerce at all. However, if you ask for it under the name of *japonica bealei* you have a good chance of getting the right one. It grows to about six feet tall and spreads over more than that; it is immensely vigorous, the shoots of the season being great, stout things growing almost visibly. The flowers are bright golden yellow, in racemes about six inches to nine inches long, curved, carried at the top of the shoots in clusters of several or many very prettily arranged like a fountain. These flowers are at their prime in February, but I have seen this plant well in flower in January or even earlier. The flowers are scented. The foliage is magnificent, the pinnate leaves being up to about eighteen inches long, hard, stiff, shining and, to handle, damnable.

Now, as to the second good garden mahonia: I invite correction if I have got the following story wrong, but here it is as it was told to me. There was a box of seedling mahonias from *japonica bealei* seed at the great Slieve Donard nursery in Co. Down, Northern Ireland. The whole box was bought by a visiting customer, a famous gardener. The plants turned out to be a cross, which had come about naturally in the nursery, between *japonica bealei* and *lomariifolia*. The hybrid is now in commerce, although not plentiful and rarely listed, as 'Charity'. I have it here, a young plant but flowering; it was in flower in Mr F. L. Fortescue's garden at Buckland Monachorum on October 30. The flowers are equal to, but much earlier, more plentiful and longer lasting than, those of *japonica bealei*. The foliage is very fine indeed, for with the size and substance of *japonica bealei* the leaves have something of the exquisitely formal shape of *lomariifolia*. Finally, the vigour and bushy habit, to obtain which it may be necessary to stop the main leading shoot, are admirable.

But the story does not end so simply. Next to some plants of 'Charity' in Mr Fortescue's marvellous garden were some which I took to be simply superior specimens of that variety. Well, they were not . . . not exactly. Mr Fortescue had long been trying to make the same cross; after difficulties too technical to describe here, he succeeded, but by the time he had raised his seedlings to flowering size, 'Charity' had come into the world and had even received the R.H.S. Award of Merit. Mr Fortescue's seedlings are going into commerce now, but it will be a long time before they are plentiful and for the time being you cannot buy them. Whether they too will be called 'Charity' or receive another name, I have no idea. Meanwhile, Mr Leslie Slinger at the Slieve Donard nursery, probably kicking himself for having unwittingly deprived himself of a splendid new variety to add to the honours of that grand firm, also set about making the cross deliberately, and also succeeded. My specimen of his seedling has not yet flowered. By the foliage I cannot distinguish it from 'Charity'. So this hybrid exists in three forms, possibly indistinguishable, but up to now Mr Fortescue's is the best I have seen.

These two winter-flowering shrubs are among the best of all plants for shrub gardens. It occurs to me that one reason for not recommending *japonica bealei* for general planting is that it may be rather intolerant of lime; it is said to favour peaty soil and some shade; I have it growing like mad in raw clay and full sun.

EVERGREEN FOLIAGE (OR CHOOSING EVERGREENS FOR FOLIAGE)

Since that was written I have again had to correct myself; but it will be clear from the confusion of nursery catalogues that I was not the only one in trouble with the naming of mahonias. Other species have since been planted.

We did not confine ourselves to those evergreens, like myrtle and mahonia and the southern barberries, which make a display of flower, but became interested in those which depend, for their beauty, solely on their foliage.

At one time in the past, English gardeners and the owners of parks were more interested in evergreens than in any other kind of plant. Gilbert White, writing to Daines Barrington about the terrible frosts and snows of the years 1768, 1776 and 1784, in two of which the temperature at Selborne fell below zero Fahrenheit,* was much concerned for his Portugal laurels, his cherry laurels, his bays and hollies and ivy. It was, I suppose, the introduction of *flowering* evergreens which began just over a hundred years ago and has since continued, although the stream is drying up now, which changed the whole picture. Now there is some small movement to change it back again. I found myself in company recently with a distinguished garden designer, an artist who has worked not only in Britain but all over Europe and he dealt rather harshly with me for my perhaps rather indiscriminate planting of flowering shrubs.

The problem, of course, is to reconcile one's plantsmanship, one's love of plants, with some clear and integral design in the garden; for any such design, if it is to be artistically valid, entails restraint in planting, the rejection of more species than one accepts.

* Jan. 1768; Jan. 1776 and Dec. 1784.

I asked my new acquaintance, whose clear thinking on this subject, whose artistic integrity and whose great experience commanded respect, what rules one should try to work to: they are those of all the arts. Then what should one aim at in practical terms? The creation of a garden which should be a work of art rather than a collection of pretty plants; the careful regard for scale; simplicity; but, above all, he said, give your garden a firm skeleton so that even years of neglect will never leave it simply a shapeless mass of weeds with a few poor exotics hardly surviving, but will leave it obviously an artefact whose firm lines remain. Then, let all that part of the garden visible from the house be such that, although it is a picture changing monthly with the seasons, daily with the weather, hourly with the light, it is there for good; does not, therefore depend on such ephemeral plants as herbaceous perennials; nor upon, or rather nor solely upon, plants whose beauty is in their flowers. We should, even in a small garden, be planting more big trees. We should be making more use of evergreens; and not, by any means, only the green ones, for the silver and golden-leaved shrubs and trees often make far more effective use of light, especially in the dark months of winter, than the green ones.

All this is very sound, of course. It happens that in the course of this year I have become acquainted with evergreens I did not know before, and have been planting them, or have found them growing here. All of them are of value in forming permanent features in a garden, creating that skeleton which gives the garden its shape and which can, in season, be dressed with more ephemeral beauties, those of flowers and berries.

At Buckland Abbey garden are some very fine big plants of a bright-leaved evergreen I have planted here, *Eleagnus pungens* var. *aureo-variegata*. It is a dense bushy plant which may attain to fifteen feet and spread over a considerable surface, but can be kept smaller by pruning; the oval, wavy-edged leaves have dark, glossy green margins and bright golden-yellow centres varying in shape and area. The whole plant seems to radiate light of its own accord, but its colour is so strong that one would have to be careful what flowers were placed near to it.

I have written with enthusiasm of *Choisya ternata* as a flowering and fragrant shrub. But this, too, is most valuable as an evergreen. It is much hardier than is generally supposed. I have seen good use made of it for the forming of a massive feature in the garden by planting a number of specimens close together and, as they grow into one mass of foliage, so carefully pruning them—with the eye of a topiarist—as to form one great, sweeping integral body of foliage, repeating, perhaps, the sweep of a sloping lawn. This admirable plant is very easily propagated from cuttings, will stand considerable frosts, is indifferent to drought, but does not much like cold winds.

Osmanthus illicifolius is one of the pleasantest foliage plants I have ever come across. This is the name it commonly bears in nurseries, or gardens where labelling is attended to; its correct name is probably *O. fortunei*. It is a compact, dense, light-radiating bush clothed almost to the ground with its leaves and naturally shapely. The leaves are very like those of a holly, yet the whole bearing of the plant is different so that what one says on first seeing it is, 'Surely that isn't a holly?' rather than 'What a fine holly!' The leaves are silver, like the silver hollies, but with very dark green margins and the whole plant so bright that it would light any dim corner. It is a cultivar from Japan, being a hybrid between *O. aquifolius* and *O. fragrans*, and it is extremely hardy, surviving zero temperature without harm. Many of this genus can be planted as flowering shrubs; some of them flower very late in the autumn and the flowers, small white tubes, are sweetly scented; but the principal use of the genus, which by the way is closely related to privet and to olive, is as an evergreen.

Photinia serrulata is another evergreen which I have planted here. It is a Chinese relative of our thorns, but it has much larger leaves, oblong, leathery, about four by two inches, a pleasant dull green when mature. But the shoots and leaves of the young, new growth are not green, but a reddish brown, rather the colour of autumn beech leaves, which gives the whole plant a most striking appearance. Again, one could consider *P. serrulata* as a flowering shrub or small tree, since it does, at least in the warmer parts of Britain, produce large corymbose panicles of small white flowers which are succeeded by berries resembling our common haws. However, these are secondary considerations, and photinia should be used as an evergreen. It is hardy in all but the bitterest years. A really savage frost sustained for several days will cut the whole shrub to the ground, but provided it be well established before that happens, will not usually kill it, and it will spring into growth again just as some eucalypts do after being cut down by cold. The sort of frost I am thinking of occurs about once in eight or ten years, so that I still think photinia is worth planting in England.

A year in their company has completely converted me to two very common evergreens, golden privet and aucuba laurel. I still dislike golden privet clipped to form a hedge, although it does make an admirable hedge, of course. But a specimen of this shrub planted in a corner which needs lightening is most effective, glowing brightly against darker plants or a fence, and forming a shapely, almost spherical bush. As to the aucubas, in really deep shade and under the drip of big trees they flourish wonderfully, producing large and handsome leaves very variable in their markings and depths of colour, and brightening the darkness of a shaded walk. I do not much care for the variegated ones, which are those most commonly to be met with. The plain greens are handsomer, and also they produce much larger leaves, in some cases enormous ones. These notable evergreens require no kind of care at all and are so free from pests and diseases that I have never seen so much as one leaf damaged.

A foliage plant which, again, brings light into the garden by its power to pick up and reflect whatever light there be, is the 'Silver Queen' variety of *Pittosporum tenuifolium*; a single specimen would make an admirable chief feature in any small garden, a group in any large garden. Although not hardy in the north, this species is either hardier than it has been supposed or is becoming so by being grown from seed in England. It is certainly growing well and resisting quite hard winters in Hertfordshire. It seems indifferent to soil, growing equally well in peat or chalk.

I have, as a matter of fact, planted other and more interesting evergreens since then, and shall revert to the subject. The garden, or wreck of a garden as it was when we first took it over, suggested the use of evergreens and was, indeed, badly overrun with uninteresting ones; almost the only really good plant which we found in it, excepting for naturalised cyclamens and a fine cedar, was, in fact, a flowering evergreen.

SALVAGE FROM A WRECK
December 31, 1960

As far as I can see, very little has been planted in our new garden since the beginning of the century, and it is as strikingly poor in good shrubs as it is rich in trees. The shrubs are numerous enough, but they are a dull lot, and by comparing them with what, without doing anything extraordinary, we shall plant in their room, one gets a very good idea of the advances made in this kind of gardening during the last fifty years.

The qualities of one shrub which has, however, obviously been in the garden for a long time did make me wonder why we see it so rarely in modern gardens: this is a *Choisya*, a mono-specific genus, the species being *ternata*. It seems to have no close kin and no varieties. The specimen in our garden is about five feet tall and as much through; a bushy, well-filled evergreen whose foliage has such a bright, youthful look that the plant has a pleasing air of spring out-of-season. The leaves have three obovate leaflets and the whole bush is strongly aromatic. Some people find the scent of the crushed leaves offensive, but I thought it pleasant enough after the first shock, strong and spicy and rather like a concentrated essence of orange-peel. It is probably the general bearing of the shrub, its shiny evergreen leaves and starry-white flowers, rather than this scent, which gives it its vernacular name of Mexican Orange.

Choisya is a native of Mexico and therefore not perfectly hardy. In the eastern counties it would require an exceptionally warm and sheltered site, or a wall. It has an outstanding quality for town gardens: the oiliness of the foliage is protective and it can stand the filth and foul air of great cities better than many evergreens. Our specimen is slightly in flower now and it will continue so until April and May, when the principal flush of blossom is to be expected.

The garden is very well provided with conifers, some of them of no great interest, but all of them bar one in their prime. Three of these species will give us great pleasure, the chief of these being a fine cedar, *Cedrus atlantica*, a spreading head of dark green foliage surmounting a straight and massive trunk. At the moment it is covered with small golden cones, and it requires the attention of a forester, having suffered from ivy and from crowding. This species is not, of course, for the small garden; but I should like to see it as often planted in large ones as it used to be, and municipalities should make more use of it with the future in mind. More suitable for medium-sized gardens are the thuyas: *Thuya occidentalis fastigiata*, as we have it in several specimens, is a stately, columnar tree about thirty feet tall and skirted to the very ground, so that where it stands on what will be lawn, it can be mowed round instead of under, a great mercy. Its gracefully held foliage is beautifully whorled and a very bright, cheerful green.

We find that we have several specimens of *Cryptomeria japonica elegans*. This is a bushy, broad-based, roughly pyramidal tree about twenty feet tall, whose light and feathery foliage gives, from a little distance, the impression of tamarisk. When we first saw these trees they were green, but by the end of November they were in process of turning a tender, rosy red, a delightful colour which one sees usually only in sunsets: such is the admirable autumn habit of this species, yet I cannot recall seeing it recommended as a shrub or tree for autumn colour. It seems to have one fault, unless our specimens are exceptional: planted on its own, it is straight and fairly sturdy; but where it has been drawn up by the near neighbourhood of other trees, 'outgrowing its strength', as it were, its wood has revealed considerable weakness, so that several of these trees have taken an ugly bend and are seriously misshapen.

There is one tree which we shall value both for itself, for its venerable if rather frowning grandeur, and, above all, for its inhabitants. This is a very tall, very old, and I fear moribund *Pinus nigra*, an Austrian pine looking rather like an ancient Scots fir, whose highest branches sustain a populous rookery. I understand that many people would wince at the notion of living cheek by jowl with such garrulous creatures as rooks and would as soon think of setting up a home in the House of Commons. But the talkativeness of rooks has certain advantages: as I do not understand their language, I am free to think that they are talking sense; I happen to enjoy their cries, and rooks are among the most entertaining birds to watch at home.

This new garden could be dated, if by nothing else, by its 'laurels'. There is only one specimen of the true laurel, *Laurus nobilis*, the biblical Green Bay Tree; and far from flourishing as an encouragement to the wicked, it is nearly dead of its infirmities.* Perhaps it would be foolish, and even rather too cynical, to expect a bay tree to have done well in what was formerly a vicarage garden, and in the very shadow of a pretty little church, but we shall plant a new one, and, likewise, at least one specimen of the only other species of this genus, *L. canariensis*, a magnificent plant, though doubtfully hardy in any but south-western gardens. But the garden's 'laurels' are those of the late eighteenth century and early Victorian shrubberies and hedges. There are two genera involved here: *Prunus* and *Aucuba*. The common or cherry laurel is, surprisingly, a close relative of the plum and the peach: it is *Prunus laurocerasus*, and has dingy black branches and stiff, almost oblong, evergreen leaves. This dismal shrub has been planted on such a scale beneath the trees, to form, I suppose, a shrubbery undergrowth, that it is going to cost me a small fortune in labour to get rid of it. To the best of my knowledge there is only one use for it, and that is in the making of wreaths, so that the longer I can do without it, the better I shall be pleased. It has also been extensively used as a hedging plant in our garden, and in that form it is inoffensive. There are also some hedges of the smaller-leaved *P. lusitanica*, a rather more distinguished member of the family, although its very dark leaves are somewhat depressing. A single specimen grown tree-shaped is not a bad ornament, but, all the same, the fuss poor Gilbert White made when severe frost threatened to kill his Portugal laurels is remarkable evidence of the excessive taste for evergreens evinced by his generation.

So much for the prunus 'laurels'. The other laurel which isn't is *Aucuba*. This is that evergreen shrub of countless Victorian front gardens in interminable suburbs, with spear-head leaves of very dark green in the less commonly planted species, and lighter leaves speckled with yellow in *A. variegata*. They bear oval red berries and were, in the not distant past, the sole 'props' with which innumerable small urban boys were obliged to make do in imaginatively creating their simulacra of those teeming jungles they had read about in the admirable adventure stories of the late nineteenth and early twentieth centuries. The aucubas seem to me at least superior to the prunus laurels; and our garden, true to its

* After treatment this made a good recovery.

period, has a damp, dark, curved walk bordered by some really splendid specimens of *A. variegata*, which have seeded themselves quite freely. These we shall retain. I cannot pretend that they are among the best of shrubs, and although ours look clean and healthy, one cannot look at them without the eye of memory covering their leaves with soot and lending the ground beneath them that look of being quite dead, peculiar to the less floral, less arboreal of London's suburbs. But . . . well, they were the shrubs of my childhood environment; and there is something appealing about that sunless alley between the aucubas. Perhaps it is simply that I am falling a victim to the thriving vogue for Victoriana.

II.
Laurus cum flore.

Chapter 7

Plants from the Southern Hemisphere

Many of the plants of the southern hemisphere are tender in the average climate of Britain but flourish in the south and west; even there the most interesting of them are apt to be damaged or killed in a hard winter. Considering the superior riches of the north temperate zone in this field, why should any gardener be bothered with southern exotics? For one thing there is often an attractive strangeness about southern hemisphere plants: they accomplish their purpose by using curious and amusing variations on the means employed by the plants of our own hemisphere: no northern hemisphere plant, for example, has flowers like the South African proteas, the Australian banksias and callistemons. In most of the flowers of the northern hemisphere the petals, in some the sepals, are the most spectacular organs which make the beauty of the flower; in many flowers of the southern hemisphere, however, this office is done by highly coloured massed stamens. Then again, by bringing flowering plants from across the equator we can fill gaps in the flowering series: southern plants often stick to their own flowering time and consequently make their display in our autumn or early winter. Nerines, for example, do this, and schizzostylis and, among flowering shrubs and trees, the eucryphias. I am not sure, however, that even these arguments are not, rather, rationalisations, and that the real reason why some of us grow or try to grow these exotics is because they exist. I made my own beginning in this field with climbers.

EXOTIC CLIMBERS

October 6, 1962

We have three exotic climbers in the greenhouse. I have found on experiment that just as a number of the plants which receive the qualification 'greenhouse' in the R.H.S. *Dictionary of Gardening* can be grown in the open if you find a warm enough corner for them, so, too, a number of plants which are qualified 'stove', can be grown quite successfully in a greenhouse which is heated only during cold weather. The most outstanding case in this class is the superb grape 'Muscat of Alexandria', which I have grown for many years in an unheated greenhouse, getting very good ripe muscat grapes, but about six weeks later than one would expect to have them.

The greenhouse we have built here, to my own design, which is not a conventional one, has room for some ornamental plants as well as fruit plants. Before the house was finished, I planted beside one of its main supporting pillars of western red cedar, a *Mandevilla suaveolens*. This because I admire its enormous 'jasmine' flowers, and because I like, when I enter the greenhouse, to be at once assailed by a richly sweet exotic scent which I should find intolerable in a living-room. *Mandevilla*, although it is called Chilean jasmine, is more nearly related to periwinkle than to jasmine; however, it is a twining climber, with large elongated heart-shaped leaves and a great many slender stems. It is immensely vigorous, especially in a greenhouse, and needs a good deal of control, for new shoots are apt to get themselves all over the place. It has a strong inclination to go straight up, and as it is usually convenient to train it, after a certain height, along a horizontal wire, it needs to be given a twist round the wire fairly often. Its flowers are carried in axillary corymbs, six or eight together on stalks, and they are two inches in diameter and two and a half inches long, pure white trumpets of five segments with a graceful twist to them, like some periwinkles. The scent is the same as tuberose. This plant is fairly easy to propagate, growing from cuttings. I have seen a specimen of *Mandevilla* bearing its seeds, on the wall of The Moult, at Salcombe: they are extraordinary, a pair of pods as much as fifteen inches long to each flower, very decorative and curious.

Mandevilla can be grown out of doors: it is deciduous and not all that tender. It is well worth trying it on a really warm wall with shelter from the cold quarters, even in those counties which are not remarkable for their mildness of climate, though it would be a waste of money, I suppose, to plant it in a really cold part of the country. However, everyone can grow it in a glass porch or a cold greenhouse.

This is not the case of the most spectacular flowering plant I have ever seen. When my wife and I were in Grand Canary we saw, on the garden wall of a villa in the hills, about sixty or seventy yards of flaming red passion flowers growing on an immense old vine with thousands of ramifications climbing posts and trees, hanging down to the road and clambering everywhere. What was unusual in so gaudy a plant was that it had great distinction, and the individual flowers were of a pleasing perfection of symmetrical design, which is the case with all this genus. This plant was subsequently identified* as *Passiflora racemosa*, although whether the type or a remarkable variety I do not yet know. This species is down in the R.H.S. *Dictionary* as 'stove'. But the conditions in which it was growing where we saw it, not far from the town of Teror, were by no means those of a stove house; they were much nearer those of a cool house with frost protection. I have therefore planted a *P. racemosa* in the greenhouse and it is growing with the usual alarming vigour of the genus. I hope it will flower next year and will not disappoint us with a poorer colour; what I am chiefly afraid of is that it may grow too big and fast to be kept in hand. A much hardier member of the genus is, of course, *P. cœrulea*, which will grow on a wall in even quite cold places. I had a big on in Kent; and about three miles away, in a lane often filled with snow in winter, there was an enormous plant of the species which was never much harmed by cold so far as I could see, and which set great quantities of fruit, some of which ripened in hot summers. It was, however, completely shielded from the north-east winds. In the south-west this species can be allowed to clamber over trees. I wonder whether anyone still has the ivory-white variety 'Constance Elliott'? I have never even seen it.

Lapageria rosea is a monotypic liliaceous Chilean climber which looks nothing much when it is not in flower, and very beautiful when it is. I have seen several in flower this year. It is apparently best to plant it where, although exposed to the south for warmth and protection from the cold quarters, it is also shaded either by trees or by a high wall. My own specimen, not old enough to flower yet, is rambling among the twiggy growth on the bole of an old oak-tree, and I notice that when it is allowed to make its own way, it does shrink from the sun and keeps well behind the

* Incorrectly. See page 85.

leaves of the oak. An acquaintance of mine near Salcombe has it planted in a really dense shade of conifers, on a fence, where it flowers magnificently. But it should, in most parts of the country, be considered as a greenhouse plant. At Dartington Hall gardens I saw this plant in flower during the first week of September, trained to the span of a greenhouse in cool conditions. It was obviously very much at home. The stems and leaves are hard and wiry; the flowers are elongated waxy bells of perfect form and a rich crimson colour, each bell at least three inches long and about half as much across the mouth. There is a pure white variety which I have not yet seen or found in a catalogue. Here we are going to see whether the plant will flourish out of doors before we try it in the greenhouse, for we have a limited amount of room. It is propagated very easily by layers, and sets fruit with viable seed in a greenhouse.

Of the clematis we have here, the one which attracts the greatest admiration from visitors is a young but very vigorously growing plant of *C. florida* var. *bicolor* which seems also to be known as *C. sieboldii*. Moreover, everyone who has not seen this before says exactly what I said when I first saw it, which was in that magnificent Sussex garden, Great Dixter, where Mr Christopher Lloyd is particularly good with clematis, though, come to that, I don't know what part of gardening he is not good at. What I said was, 'It looks just like a passion-flower'. The flowers, about two inches in diameter, consist of a very regular ring of sepals which look like petals, within which is a boss of purple. I have found this clematis a little difficult to establish in ordinary soils or in clay, but very easy in really peaty, leafy soils such as suit ericas. This is rather odd and uncharacteristic of the genus, but there it is. A young specimen whose roots were planted only this spring very close to those of a *Rhododendron mucronulatum* which is growing with extraordinary vigour, has made ten feet of growth on two leaders, climbed right up into a rather sparse and sickly yew tree, and flowered freely for some months. Its growth, however, is alarmingly soft, and I can only hope it will harden off a little before the winter. However, the species apparently comes from Japan, so presumably it is perfectly hardy. Much less so, so that it must be grown in the greenhouse everywhere but in the extreme south and west, is the New Zealand *C. indivisa*, a most beautiful clematis with pendant white flowers. This is an evergreen, and I saw a fine specimen grown in a porch by Mr Fortescue at Buckland Monachorum, and flowering in May. Some comment on the above. The plant we saw in the Canary Islands was not *Passiflora racemosa* but, probably, the much more spectacular *P. incarnata*. As for *P. racemosa* it has, since I first wrote about it, grown enormously and is now rather a nuisance in the greenhouse. Its richly purple flowers are borne in very great number from April to November on racemose flowering shoots which are often nine feet long. It never sets any fruit. My question about the variety 'Constance Elliott' of *P. cœrulea* was answered by the gift of a small plant and this, planted out in the open, has grown well but not yet flowered, probably because it was cut back by one cold winter.

We soon got over the timidity of confining southern hemisphere exotics to the greenhouse and began to try them out of doors.

BOTTLE-BRUSH PLANTS

May 18, 1963

Having just paid a short visit to Kew Gardens, which I try to do from time to time, I want to write something about the shrub, or perhaps I should call it a small tree, which I thought quite dominated the Temperate House in mid-April, *Callistemon citrinus* var. *splendens* and its allies. The elegance of bearing, the subtle colours of the foliage, and the spectacular form and colour of the flowers of the several callistemons in the Temperate House are all bound to remind any visitor of how well worth trouble these plants are in any garden where it is at all possible to grow them.

First of all there is the question of hardiness: of the species I had planted out and fully exposed in this garden, one survived the ferocity of the late winter without any damage at all, *C. salignus*. All the others were more or less damaged, but *C. rigidus* was not quite killed. It should be said that these plants were all young ones and that they had no protection whatsoever, being planted right in the path of the east wind. I have little doubt that where a protected situation can be given, several callistemons can be considered hardy in regions where the temperature does not fall below fifteen degrees Fahrenheit, which is as much as to say that they would come through normal winters almost anywhere on the coast and in many places inland; in western gardens; and in Irish gardens.

The two species which are thought to be the best as ornamental plants are *C. citrinus* var. *splendens*, and *C. phoeniceus*. *C. citrinus*, both the type and the *splendens* variety, is a tree to about twenty feet in Australia; but as one sees it in England it is a shrub to about twelve feet. It flowers when quite small; at Overbecks last year there was a seedling raised by Mr Edward Pilkington, about three feet high, and flowering freely. In time it makes a trunk of softish wood and many long, drooping, and recurving branches of rather lax wood, carrying the lanceolate leaves which are about four or five inches long, half an inch or a little more wide, and, in all the young foliage, softly flushed with coppery red. For those who have never happened to see it before, the flowering habit is fascinating: the flowers have no petals, but a vast number of inch-long stamens which, in this variety, are a very rich crimson and in at least one other species, crimson-scarlet tipped with gold. These stamens are arranged in a regular cylinder, exactly like a bottle-brush, up to four inches long and two inches in diameter. They occur at the tips of growing shoots, the shoot constituting also the stem of the flower. As the shoot continues to grow, the flower is as it were left behind and as, moreover, the very hard woody seed capsules remain on the plant for many years, you can find three or four sets of these seed capsules at intervals along any well-grown branch of the shrub. In flower, in spring and again in autumn, the plant is very beautiful, and the flower colour is vibrant. For the benefit of those familiar with it, the colour is almost that of the rhododendron 'Elizabeth'.

I believe that the way to grow this lovely Australian shrub in English gardens is on a south wall; its long, slender growth makes it manageable as a wall shrub, and where it can be planted between buttresses it will receive so much protection from all cold quarters that it should survive the winter. In any case, on a wall it is not difficult to give extra protection during very cold spells.

C. speciosus var. *phoeniceus*—probably the correct form of the name—is described by Mr Ernest Lord in that admirable book *Shrubs and Trees for Australian Gardens* as 'probably the best and most brilliantly flowered of all Australia's bottle-brushes'. This variety, unlike the type which is a small tree, is a shrub about six feet tall, of lax and open habit, forming a fountain-shaped bush of many-branched stems. The leaves are about three inches by a quarter of an inch, and they are either a red-flushed green or, at least in quite a number of the seedlings I have raised here, a fine, coppery red. Among my seedlings I have at the moment one which is perhaps a new variety, for it has no green at all. The flowers are very much like the ones described for *citrinus* 'Splendens', but the colour is flame-red. The vernacular name of the shrub is 'Fiery Bottle-brush'. It is very easy to raise it from seed and it grows fast. The seed is minutely small and needs careful handling: I mix it with silver sand, spread the mixture over the surface of the compost, shade the box or bag it in polythene, and do no top watering. Germination of fresh seed is something like a hundred per cent. It is, I discovered, absolutely essential to keep potting on; the one thing which callistemon will not stand is being pot-bound.

C. rigidus is hardier than the above two. The shape and size of the bush are much the same as the last, and specimens rarely exceed six feet. The leaves are smaller as a rule, but not always, and certainly narrower. The flowers are very similar, perhaps rather smaller, and they are of a less vibrantly flaming red. To do well I think that this callistemon may need to be growing in the sunniest, seaside gardens in really warm soil; it survives worse conditions very well, but it does not flower freely where the soil is cold and the atmosphere damp.

C. salignus is native to several parts of Australia, including Tasmania. Tasmanian shrubs are, on the whole, a good deal hardier than mainland Australian shrubs, and this one has come through our shocking winter remarkably little the worse. It has very narrow, sharp pointed leaves which are bronze red on opening, later dark green and so closely set on the stems as to look almost imbricated. It is famous in Australia for standing up to drought. The bottle-brush flowers are not much longer than they are wide, pom-poms rather than bottle-brushes; they are pale creamy yellow. The leaf size is extremely variable: there is a huge old bush of this at Knightshayes with leaves so small that I exposed my ignorance by doubting that it was a callistemon at all. Some leaves were sent to a botanical authority in Australia who wrote back to say that the plant was certainly *C. salignus* although it was true that the leaves were very exceptional.

There are, in the books, other callistemons, but since they do not seem to be grown here even by specialists I suppose that they are even less hardy than those I have described. The one famous for gold-tipped stamens (i.e. gold anthers, but they are noticeable in other species) is *C. rugulosus* and there is a callistemon, *C. pinifolius*, with green flowers, but it comes from the warm N.S.W. coast and would obviously be impossible here.

A point I have never seen so much as mentioned about these plants is that they all seem to have aromatic foliage. The scent is something between rosemary and eucalyptus, and not unlike that of myrtle. It is impossible to handle even small seedlings without getting your hands covered with this pleasant scent and we found that the leaves and stems of those callistemons which were killed by cold in the winter were, when withered, very richly aromatic.

If you get callistemons established it is, I understand, a good idea to cut back the old wood quite hard every third year: this pruning is said to result in a much freer flowering, presumably because new wood is more floriferous. But with a genus so very marginal in our climate, it is a case of first manage to keep your callistemon long enough.

TIBOUCHINAS
November 9, 1963

Friends who called to see us during September and early October were much taken with two plants in the greenhouse, so much so that even the curious and beautiful *Passiflora racemosa* with its immensely long racemes hanging like a flowered curtain, was overlooked. The two plants were a very small lemon bush bearing ripening fruit; and a specimen of *Tibouchina semidecandra*. Of the lemon I shall write on another occasion, for it is not just any lemon but a natural dwarf which reaches maturity from seed very rapidly and bears its fruit continuously.

The tibouchina here in question is one of a genus containing well over one hundred species, all of them native to South America and most of them tropical. A few of them were, and perhaps still are, grown in hot-houses, but no hot-house is required for *T. semidecandra* var. *floribunda*. It is, in fact, so nearly hardy in the warmer parts of Britain, that some enterprising gardeners have managed to keep it for several years out of doors on a warm wall. In the end, of course, along comes a sharp winter like the last one—

I see that *The Times* gardening correspondent is gloomily forecasting yet another—and kills the plant. This is quite unimportant, for like all sub-tropical shrubs this tibouchina grows very fast indeed; and it is so easily propagated from cuttings at any time of year that nothing could be simpler than to have half a dozen young ones in pots in the greenhouse, or on a windowsill for that matter, at all times, so that outdoor stock can be replaced. As well as the specimen in the greenhouse, I have one on a wall in the open; it has been there since last April and it has flowered and grown just as generously as the plant under glass.

T. semidecandra var. *floribunda* is a shrub which can easily grow seven or eight feet tall in time, but which can be kept shorter and bushy in a large pot. Its habit is pleasantly symmetrical, with branches opposite and smaller branches also opposite on the big ones. It has hairy green stems, large, bright green, hairy, ovate leaves, so that even for its foliage it is one of the handsomest plants in the garden. At the growing tips of all the shoots appear, in summer and right through to late autumn, and perhaps all the year round if you never 'rest' the plant by withholding water, clusters of bright crimson buds. These open in succession to display large—say two and a half-inch—flowers of a very rich blue-purple which is at once velvety and, somehow, translucent. The leaves, I forgot to say, have prominent veins which mark them with a very attractive pattern. In each flower cluster there are from one to six flowers open at the same time, and on a plant which is well-branched and so has plenty of flowering shoots, the result is spectacular. For beauty, and for its immensely long flowering period, this shrub is to be strongly recommended.

As I have said, *T. semidecandra* var. *Floribunda* is tender and though some gardeners manage to keep it alive and flourishing out of doors for a few years, on a sheltered wall, this is not practicable in most gardens. But there is another way in which it can be enjoyed in the open, among other shrubs, rousing bitter envy in the breasts of visiting gardening friends, and that is to grow the plants in large pots, say eight-inch ones, and, in summer, say in mid-May, move these out of the greenhouse and bury the pots to below the rim in a border or shrubbery. These pots can then be lifted in October and returned to the greenhouse, where, over winter, they can be kept rather short of water to check the growth and rest the plants.

In spring the main growths can be pruned back while the tibouchinas are still in the greenhouse, the object being to retain the bushy character of a plant which is apt to grow rather leggy and gaunt if not pruned.

It is not necessary to expose the plants to full southern sun; I find it does well on a north wall. Some protection from wind is desirable, because the lovely flowers are very delicate and easily blown to pieces by strong winds, though for that matter they are almost immediately replaced by new ones. The compost recommended for these shrubs is turfy loam; but I find that they will grow very well in J.I. No. 3 compost if in pots; and, in the open, in ordinary garden soil which has had some peat worked into it.

I have recently become a member of the Society for Growing Australian Plants, by the simple process of paying the small subscription. The Society has branches in all the Australian states and its work can be of interest to English gardeners in the following way: a great many Australian plants have not yet been brought into cultivation; members of the Society are constantly doing this work; from time to time it is possible that plants which might be fairly hardy in Britain will be thus brought into horticulture; the Society publishes a journal, *Australian Plants*, with good down-to-earth descriptions of plants and the methods of cultivating them, and in this journal progress can be followed and good new plants watched for.

The current number of the journal has, for example, an article on Grevilleas. Now as everyone knows, most grevilleas are tender but some are hardy: *G. sulphurea* and *G. rosmarinifolia* both came through last winter in many English gardens where, for example, rosemary plants were killed by cold. Well, there may be other and even better hardy ones. The only thing is, one has to realise that familiar terms when used by antipodean gardeners do not mean the same thing. Here is a quotation from the June number of *Australian Plants*:

> *Grevillea pteridifolia.*
> A tree 15 to 20 feet, leaves pinnate with very narrow segments of from four to eight inches, glabrous above and silky beneath. The flower is of a rich golden yellow and carried on a terminal raceme of often over six inches in length. This is an extremely beautiful grevillea . . . most adaptable to cultivation and very hardy.

It is from an article by L. H. Cockburn and the grevillea in question is a Queensland plant. Now when I say of a plant in English gardens that it is 'very hardy' everyone understands me to mean that it will not be killed by an English winter; it will, therefore, tolerate temperatures even down to zero F, although it will rarely have to do so. Does Mr Cockburn mean the same thing? Of course not; it is, in fact, difficult to know exactly what he does mean, because he is not writing for us but for Australians who know what is to be expected of their climate. I think we can say that he means the plant will stand any amount of either cold or drought which it may have to encounter in Australia. Yet this is the sort of thing I look for in *Australian Plants* because I know that a plant of whatever kind so described will stand some degrees of frost at least, and may be worth trying here. Of course, it would be ruinously dear to buy such exotics from Australian nurserymen, even if one could, and import them by air. What one does is to get seed of the chosen plant and try it that way.

Again, we get, in the same article but under another head: 'Quite easy of cultivation but will be cut back by heavy frost.' It would be interesting to know what a Queenslander means by 'heavy frost'. Probably something less damaging than we mean.

It is by the cultivation of new exotics that, in the long run, the plant material of our gardens is enriched; and it is in the carrying out of trials of such plants that the amateur can make a useful contribution.

GREVILLEAS
April 18, 1964

Late in March we were planting out two, and thinking about planting out a third, species of a genus which we have propagated from cuttings ever since we first saw it in West Country gardens. If you look for grevilleas in the books you will find that most of them are, in Britain, greenhouse or hothouse plants, but two of them are much hardier than they have a name for being, one indeed ruggedly hardy; and there is a third worth trying outside in a warm corner. The point about the two I call hardy is that they are ideal plants for filling a low gap in the sunshine, being sprawling but densely-furnished shrubs of the kind which, unless staked and pruned, tend never to show a leg.

Grevillea sulphurea grows well in any neutral and gritty soil, in loam, even in clay, and certainly in peat. It is a native of New South Wales, but I think it must be a mountain plant, for it has withstood twenty degrees of frost in our garden, and it is notable that, having been planted with some common rosemaries by way of a horticultural joke, it survived undamaged eight weeks of frost wind which killed the rosemary stone dead. For this reason, and despite the expert opinion one reads on it, I consider this grevillea to be absolutely hardy. The bush, usually about four or five feet tall and much bigger in the other dimensions, looks like a rosemary, although not on close inspection, for its leaves are much narrower and finer, and they are not glaucous on the lower surface. It flowers very freely, usually in spring but often at other seasons; its flowers are in groups or terminal racemes, a group of single flowers forming an inflorescence which looks like an individual bloom, or almost. They are hard to describe, being something like a slender and uncurved honeysuckle flower; botanically, this flower is a split calyx whose two segments are elongated and curled back, pale yellow in colour, and a style, sticking out between them, also yellow. There are no petals. The general effect of the flowers is spidery; and of the plant, that of a biggish rosemary which has enlarged its flowers and turned them yellow.

Not quite as hardy as this is one very like it in general appearance, and even more like a rosemary bush, a fact expressed in its name, *G. rosmarinifolia*. It has rather broader and stouter leaves, they are darker in colour, and the flowers, again of the same kind, typical proteaceous flowers in fact, are a dull crimson. They are very effective when the bush is flowering well, which it does in full sunshine and warm summers. I have known this to flower, however, at some very odd times; it is apt to remember it is Australian and come into full flower in late autumn. It is not a bad plan to plant these two species together, with *sulphurea* placed north and east of *rosmarinifolia*, thus providing it with a measure of protection.

The third grevillea is much tenderer and has to be specially managed, usually by planting out in May and bringing back inside again in November. This is the very pretty dwarf *G. alpina*, not more than twenty-four inches tall, full and well-rounded, so that it is very suitable for growing in a large pot which can be taken out and plunged in a border during the summer, but brought under glass during the winter. The leaves are narrow, elongated ovals, usually between half an inch and an inch long, and their downiness makes them a kind of sage-green. The flowers are white or pale yellow and red, both colours being in the expanded and curled sections of the calyx. The style, sticking out prominently as in the other species, is similarly bicoloured. A good sunny position, both within the greenhouse and outside when you bring it out, will ensure free flowering, and when well covered with flowers this is a prettier grevillea than either of the others, although in view of its tenderness, not so good a garden plant. I have looked it up in Bean who says that it is about as hardy as *sulphurea*; well, it isn't, nothing like. The garden in which I judge the hardiness of these marginal shrubs is that of a friend of mine at East Portlemouth, where the climate is as mild as anywhere in England and where the most improbable shrubs and trees flourish in near frost-free conditions; even in that garden, this grevillea is not reliable.

But there is something very odd about this all the same; because *G. alpina* is, as its name implies, an alpine plant from the mountains of New South Wales, and in theory it ought to be the hardiest of the three. What I think we need is fresh stock of it, from seed collected at the greatest possible altitude. It has lately been noted, for example, that there is a marked difference between the hardiness of specimens and strains of *Eucalyptus gunnii*, and that when we grow Australian plants in our gardens, we need always to get the highest mountain strains, in which case they have a very good chance of proving perfectly hardy.

They are not, of course, by any means the only southern hemisphere plants which I grow. There are the myrtles already referred to and we also have a number of leptospermums, the New Zealand Ti-trees, which seem quite hardy here and which, with their tiny leaves and masses of small flowers, are very pleasing, light and airy plants. Our white flowered ones (*L. scoparium*) were brought here originally as small self-grown seedlings which I was allowed to take from the woods round the great Abbey gardens on Tresco, where this species is well naturalised. The red-flowered variety (*L. scoparium* 'Nicholsii') is less hardy but survives with us.

Long before planting such shrubby or tree genera, however, I had some acquaintance with southern hemisphere bulb and herbaceous genera. The following account probably marks the beginning of that acquaintance.

NERINES AND AGAPANTHUS

December 19, 1959

In the matter of nerines I am very much a beginner, but an enthusiastic one. I can hardly be said to have been properly aware of their existence until a few years ago, when I happened to be the sympathetic observer of a struggle, over nerines, between the head gardener of a great house and his employer, one of the most distinguished living gardeners. This head gardener fell victim to a consuming passion for nerines—possibly he had been smiled on by a water nymph, for that is what the name signifies, though the genus has no liking for water—and as the usual want of labour had driven his employer to restrict greenhouse accommodation to the minimum, there really was not room for his nerines *and* for his employer's favourite plants. The latter were apt to be huddled into corners or even stood outside in the cold, to make room for more nerines. And beautiful though the genus is, the proprietor of the garden and greenhouses felt a good deal aggrieved by this consequence of the gardener's passion.

One of the large numbers of things I did not then know about nerines is that a species of this genus is fairly hardy and can readily be grown out-of-doors; had I known this no doubt I should have started growing them sooner. But since a great many gardeners seem as ignorant as myself about these flowers, I had better say something about the genus in general.

Nerines belong to Amaryllidaceæ, that is, they are related to amaryllis and hippeastrums, but not to the lovely agapanthus, which is liliaceous. They are natives of South Africa, from which we have so many magnificent species; they are, of course, bulbous, and so increase by offsets, doing this, at least in the case of *N. bowdenii*, so generously, that a few bulbs soon increase to a great quantity. The flowers, numerous in good varieties, are carried in a gracefully open head on a slender scape, and the colours include a wide range of pinks and reds, to a vivid scarlet; also white. Most nerines set seed here, the seeds being fleshy and substantial, and germinating quite readily if left, hardly covered at all, on the surface of the compost. It is, of course, from seeds that good new forms are obtained, so that it is well worth while propagating from seed as well as offset bulbs.

For most gardeners the only interesting species of the genus will be *N. bowdenii*, since that is the one which can be grown out-of-doors, at least in the milder counties, although one friend of mine who grows them in large quantities for market says that 'mildness' does not seem to matter, and that the species is hardier than it is generally supposed to be. It is from him that I have a good deal of my information. He bought a whole bed of *N. bowdenii* at a sale of nursery stock necessitated by a liquidation, and has been very successful with these plants, being especially struck by the great rate of increase.

However, since there is some question about the absolute hardiness of these nerines, it is best to choose for them a warm site in the garden. I have a dwarf wall recently planted to the grape-vine 'Pinot Meunier', the 'Dusty Miller' of old English gardens. At the foot of this wall I have set the bulbs of nerines, where they are very hot in summer, which is fine, provided they are given *some* water. But as the soil under this wall is rather 'clouty' as we say in east Kent, I dug the holes for the bulbs much deeper than necessary and much larger, and put in a bottom of potsherds and gravel to make sure of clean drainage. Moreover, since we seem to have a particularly ravenous and omnivorous race of soil fauna, the holes were refilled, when planting (as for lily bulbs), with a compost made from the soil taken out mixed with a great deal of very sharp grit, as at least some protection against mice and the larger slugs. I do not know that either of these creatures eats nerine bulbs; but my experience is that they will eat pretty well anything excepting the poisonous baits especially prepared for them.

For some reason the time to break up a clump of nerine bulbs which has increased to the point where replanting is desirable is neither in the winter, after flowering is over, nor in spring before growth starts, but in July or even August, although, out of doors, they flower in late September and October.

N. bowdenii have pale pink flowers with a line of darker pink on each segment. And since they flower at a time when there is not a great deal of flower in the garden, they are very valuable for cutting.

For the richer colours it is necessary to have recourse to the tender species; but they are not particularly difficult to grow. You buy the bulbs in August, and although various composts are recommended, they seem to be happy enough in John Innes potting compost. However, like agapanthus, the richer you feed them the less they flower, so use only quite small pots, plant with the neck of the bulb just showing, and stand them on the cool-house staging—never in a hot-house—in the sun. Do not water them until the flower spike appears, which is before there are any leaves. Then water well and keep the soil thoroughly moist throughout the season of flowering and until the leaves begin to look dashed and turn yellow. Then reduce and finally stop watering altogether, put the pots out of the way on the greenhouse floor and leave them dry until growth begins again in the following August. Restrain the generous inclination to repot; it will, of course, have to be done eventually, but the later the better, and these plants will do better crammed into an apparently over-crowded pot, than if given ample room and nourishment.

In this respect they resemble agapanthus, which, however, are not bulbous but have a mass of thick, fleshy roots. If those roots are given ample room and the plants often repotted in fresh compost, they fail, in my experience, to flower; whereas, crowded into a too small pot, and by ordinary standards thoroughly pot-bound, they flower quite readily.

This, of course, refers only to agapanthus in pots, that is the tender varieties with rather broader straplike leaves. There are several species and probably some hybrids; all are beautiful, the great blue umbels of flowers held on tall, graceful stems rising out of the clumps of leaves like giant bluebell leaves.

Like some nerines, some agapanthus are hardy. Moreover, one very beautiful species, *A. orientalis*, is said to be so fond of water that it does not mind bad drainage and will do well on the margins of lakes or ponds, or beside streams. I have not so grown it, but it must be admirable in such situations. Colours available within this species are from pure white through china-blue, light blue, dark blue to a sort of rich hyacinthine blue.

A difficulty with this genus is that its taxonomy is in a muddle:

until not very long ago only one species seems to have been recognised, *A. africanus*; now about ten are distinguished. Nurserymen have not, on the whole, caught up with the South African botanists, and it is difficult to be sure that the plants you are buying are hardy enough to be grown out of doors. But almost certainly the practice of planting agapanthus in tubs and bringing them under cover in winter is not necessary; some are tender and they can be treated very much like nerines as to climate and water, although they need larger pots, of course. Others are hardy and having been planted out of doors, can be left there.

Incidentally, not only are most, and perhaps all, species of agapanthus evergreen, but in several one of the attractions is the variegated leaves: *A. orientalis* var. *variegatus* (still in some lists as *A. umbellatus variegatus*) has white leaves striped green; *aureovittatus*, which I saw for the first time this autumn, has striped yellow leaves. And a lot of varieties seem still to be simply unobtainable here, notably *monstrosus*, whose colossal umbels have several hundred flowers each.

Since that time, and the move to Devon, nerines and agapanthus have become familiars of my own garden. The nerines one plants and forgets until they have so increased that they must be dug up and spread out. As for agapanthus, I raise these now from seed received from the South African Botanical Society, which means that ours are a variable lot but all of them 'natural' plants, superior in delicacy and charm to the heavy, burly and over-large garden hybrids.

Here is an account, published in June 1961, of a first encounter with a Chilean shrub which has, since then, also become a familiar, growing in my own garden but to be seen at its magnificent best only in Cornwall and in Ireland.

THE LANTERN TREE AND THE FIRE TREE

June 17, 1961

Plant lovers should not really drive cars; years ago I became expert in keeping my eyes moving in a scanning motion so that even at fifty miles an hour or more I can spot any outstanding wild flower beside the road while still keeping the road under observation as it were; I have not had an accident yet, though a fortnight ago I confess that only the brakes and skill of the man behind me avoided one when I spotted a fine specimen of *Gladiolus byzantinus* growing on a bank above a ditch. But I came nearest to disaster when, years ago in Ireland—near Cork—I was drawn across the road in a sudden swerve, as by a powerful magnet, by the flaming spectacle of a shrub looking over a garden wall, which I had never seen before and which captivated me entirely. A man driving a donkey cart who almost lost his life as a consequence, being Irish, first offered to sell me the donkey as a safer means of getting about, which of course it is; and when I declined, nevertheless, called upon God to bless me with a fervour which showed that he thought I had much need of divine help to get through the day, the way I was going.

The shrub was *Tricuspidaria hookerianum*, but currently called *Crinodendron lanceolatum*, and I have been lately delighted to realise that I can now grow it, for I have found one fine specimen in a garden not so sheltered as ours and less than five miles away; and two more within twenty miles. *C. lanceolatum*—sometimes listed by the few nurseries which have it has *C. hookeri*—is not, as one thinks on first examining it, an erica closely related to rhododendron, but one of the three species belonging to the family Elaeocarpaceae, and all natives of South America. And this, as they say, is the worst of them, for they are not perfectly hardy. The two species of garden quality are Chilean and they can be grown in Cornwall and parts of Devon, in South Wales, Southern Ireland and South-west Scotland, wherever, in short, the climate is mild, moist, and normally free from frosts of more than two or three degrees. Crinodendrons, like so many American plants, are intolerant of lime in the soil: they require a peaty loam on the acid side of neutral. Where there is room in a large green-house, *C. lanceolatum* makes a splendid cool-house shrub, although capable in time of attaining twenty or thirty feet. As a rule it is smaller, about ten or twelve feet. Its vernacular name is Lantern Tree, it is upright and rather stiff in habit, making good, hard wood, and the very numerous narrowly elliptic leaves are from four to six inches long. Flower buds form in autumn and remain dormant all winter as small, tight balls. It is when these open in late May or early June that the patient and fortunate gardener is rewarded by a generous flowering, hundreds, on a big tree thousands, of rich crimson, urn-shaped flowers hanging on long stalks, each nearly an inch long and three-quarters of an inch in diameter. Each single lantern is a delight; the whole constellation on a well-flowered shrub, breath-taking.

Apparently crinodendrons are not hard to propagate from half-ripened cuttings taken in August and kept close; and they are not dear; the only catalogue in which I can find the species offers plants at half a guinea.

While on the subject of shrubs or small trees which are half tender and can only be grown in the mild west and in peaty loams, there is another which, in Southern Ireland and in Cornwall, can be spectacular, and this is the Fire Tree, *Embothrium coccineum*. Another South American, the type is rather tender but it attains fifty feet in the south-west. The flowers are racemes of tubes with recurving petal-like lobes and a long style; they are very numerous and they are flame-red, so that an embothrium in flower looks like a conflagration bursting out of the ground. The variety *longifolium* comes not from Chile but from Tierra del Fuego—appropriately enough—and is hardy all along the South Coast as far as one can tell from the limited experience of this shrub or tree in England.

A southern hemisphere genus much more familiar to all English gardeners is *Fuchsia*. But not until we lived in the West Country did I have much success with it in the open border. A single species—*F. magellanica*—is hardy enough in Kent; and it is more or less naturalised in Cornwall, parts of Wales and Ireland, and parts of Devonshire. In the West Country several can be grown as free-standing shrubs, although apt to be cut to the ground by frost in winter, to grow again, however, in the following spring.

FUCHSIAS

August 19, 1961

We have in flower here at the time of writing five varieties of fuchsia, and if we have only five it is because we have not yet had time to plant any more. For I have every intention of growing as many varieties of this admirable genus as can be persuaded to survive our ordinarily quite mild winters; and even in much colder districts it is not necessary, if varieties be carefully chosen, to go through the old elaborate routine of winter storing the plants dry for replanting the following May or June. It is true that Bean, having said in *Trees and Shrubs Hardy in the British Isles*, that 'in the milder parts of the British Isles, like Cornwall, South-West Ireland, Isle of Wight, Isle of Man, etc.' fuchsias grow 'into trees 10 ft or more high with trunks 6 ins or more through', goes on to say that they can hardly be called hardy shrubs, 'seeing that they are killed to the ground almost invariably' in colder, more northerly and inland localities. But the operative words for those whose gardens are not in mild counties are 'to the ground'. Excepting in the very coldest parts, where the earth itself may be frozen a foot deep in harsh winters, fuchsias are not killed *below* the ground if some care is taken to avoid this catastrophe, as described below. And since, being very fast-growing plants, they will make four or five-foot flowering stems in a single spring and summer and look at their best in late summer and early autumn, it is very well worth planting them even where the above-ground parts cannot be preserved through the winter.

In my experience of this genus, the best time to buy and plant specimens is in June, from the nursery, when the fuchsias will already be in flower in their pots. A good plant will be about one foot to fifteen inches tall, well branched, with half a dozen stems from the crown. It will cost between 5*s* and 10*s*. Fetch the plants yourself, so that you can keep them in the pots until you are ready to plant. They can be planted in a bed of mixed shrubs and herbaceous perennials; or in a special planting, say, with paeonies. The paeonies give the bed colour early in the year, the fuchsias late, and their respective foliage and habits are in pleasant contrast. This, of course, is where the fuchsias cannot be expected to survive the winter above ground; where they can, then a different plan must be adopted, for they may grow far too large to be mixed with anything but other large shrubs. The soil should be a fairly rich loam and the hole you dig for each plant should be deeper than seems necessary so that the top of the pot soil can be about two inches below the surface of the garden soil. As for manure, fuchsias respond quickly to a light dressing of dried blood, and to water in dry spells. On the other hand they are almost incredibly drought-resistant when well established. I once had an old and rather large, woody fuchsia plant in a tub in a summerhouse. It was neglected, for some reason, throughout almost a whole year. The soil in the tub was by then bone-dry, but after a single copious watering the plant revived and began to grow; two of its offspring are now flourishing here.

The hardiest fuchsias are varieties of *F. magellanica*, a species very variable in its habit which comes from southern Peru or Chile, down to Tierra del Fuego. Its variety *riccartonii* is the hardiest of all, and this is the one which you see forming hedges in western Ireland and in Wales, in Cornwall and south-west Scotland; and which, in warm corners of Devonshire gardens, grows into tall, bushy tree-like shrubs of great beauty. The flowers are not borne in terminal racemes as in some of the large-flowered and more spectacular kinds, but in the leaf axils all up the stems as they grow, so that the variety, and in fact all varieties of this species, are very floriferous.

Fuchsia-growing *par excellence*, the cultivation of tender and hot-house hybrids, the use of standards, the training of climbing and procumbent varieties, is a very specialised art and I do not propose to write about it. The only varieties which the amateur who wants to leave his fuchsias out all year round should plant, are those which are called, by slightly stretching the meaning of the word, hardy and can be treated as if they were herbaceous perennials. And it is desirable to get them, if possible, from a nursery which specialises in them and understands their behaviour. Here are a few names of such varieties:

'Howlet's Hardy'. This has red sepals and a deep purple, bell-shaped corolla with overlapping petals, which gives the flower a very good form. When mature the plant must be allowed a square yard to itself and its shoots, all flowering, will reach about four feet tall by August, when it flowers, continuing to flower until the cold weather.

'Mme Cornellison.' The sepals are red and the corolla white. I have found this very free-flowering.

'Lena.' This has flesh-pink sepals and a mauve corolla or 'skirt'. I find that the sepals are often more or less reflexed, a pleasant feature. My own plant of this is still young and not two feet tall, but covered with flowers. In maturity the variety has gracefully arching stems attaining four or five feet in a season after being cut to the ground in winter. It needs about two feet by two feet of surface.

'Tom Thumb.' For nearer the front of the plantation as it does not surpass two feet in height even when old. Flowering from early August to late October, its flowers are exquisite, the sepals carmine and the skirt a clear blue-purple.

'Caledonia.' The flowers are in two shades of pink and the plant spreads to occupy a large area. It is not one of the best but it seems to put up with colder winters better than most.

'Margaret.' This is a magnificent fuchsia, covering a six-foot frontage (as estate agents call it). I have seen it taller than myself in August although cut down in the previous winter. The flowers are very large, with reflexed crimson sepals and the skirt of pale violet.

There are many others and they are all good. Propagation is very easy. Here is my own method, but others are quite as good: take cuttings of small side-shoots pulled off in August; they should be free from flowers or flower buds. Plant each one separately in John Innes No. 3 compost in a small (2 inch) pot. Plant the pots, touching each other so that their rims are at soil level, in a rectangle of soil such that it can be covered by a single cloche. Water very thoroughly; mulch with peat or compost; put the cloches in place and close the ends with glasses. Whitewash the south-facing glass of the cloche. If you do this you leave the cuttings alone until next year, apart from weeding the covering soil. The whitewash will be removed by autumn rains, the little plants will grow away early in the year, under their cloche. A top glass of the cloche can be removed in May and the plants hardened. Later, remove the cloche entirely. In mid-June plant straight from the pots into the stations chosen for the plants.

With young plants, whether of your own propagating or from the nursery, it is possible to avoid winter cutting and so build up a bigger plant more quickly, by covering with a closed cloche (glass, not plastic; plastic cloches are fine in summer and useless in winter). When the plants are larger this is not really practicable: in districts where the winters are hard, don't wait for frost to cut the plants down, do it, to the ground, yourself, and then cover the place with a straw or bracken litter several inches deep, to be removed in the following late spring or early summer. In mild districts, do nothing whatever and hope that the superterranean parts of the plant will survive as well as the root: in that case, you may get almost a tree-fuchsia.

To my short list of hardy fuchsias I would now add one more, the best of all; its name is 'Mrs Popple'.

Early in 1962 I had my interest in Australian plants stimulated by a small book; I don't think I was then familiar with Ernest Lord's magnificent, *Trees and Shrubs for Australian Gardens.*

PLANTS FROM AUSTRALIA
March 17, 1962

When he first encounters Australian plants in one of the gardens which can grow them, the gardener is very apt to be completely captivated by their charm; I know two who have been led to try specialising in these plants whose forms of leaf, flower, seed and general bearing are so different from those of either the old world or the Americas, that they have the special attraction of the exotic. I have received from a kind correspondent in Australia a beautifully printed booklet reproducing, mostly natural size, some colour photographs of native Australian flowers by Mr Frank Hurley, a very good photographer indeed, with fascinating subjects to record. It has occurred to me to wonder how many of these plants are, or can be, or could perhaps be, grown in our gardens.

The subject on the cover of Mr Hurley's booklet is *Callistemon lanceolatus*, the Crimson Bottle-brush. It is unfortunate that callistemons, like so many Australian plants, are not hardy in the average climate of Britain. Yet I am surprised that Bean did not even include any reference to them in his great book, for there is no doubt at all that some of this genus are hardy in Cornwall, in Devon, in the south-west of Scotland and in parts of Wales; and I have not much doubt that some of them could be grown on warm walls in several other parts of the country. My own very young and tender plants showed no reaction whatever when the thermometer fell to 24°F for three days in succession. Callistemons make shrubs or small trees of erect habit, they will stand any amount of wind, their leaves are for the most part long, narrow and pointed, and they are evergreens. The flowers are extraordinary, their beauty being formed solely by the mass of long and innumerable stamens arranged in the form of a bottle-brush all round the flowering stem, below the terminal tuft of leaves. From observations made this summer I think that callistemons must be tolerant of salt in wind, and can be grown close to the sea. I have noticed, on the Devon coast, that they remain undamaged where broader-leaved plants show the characteristic salt scorch. The possible species are *lanceolatus*, synonym *citrinus*, with four-inch bottle-brushes in some shade of red; the variety *splendens* has magnificent crimson flowers. And *pinifolius* has needle-like leaves. I do not know of any nurseryman growing these plants, and those of my friends who have the genus in their gardens have grown them from seed; they seem to grow very fast.*

The most spectacular of Mr Hurley's subjects is *Telopea speciosissima*, called the Waratah, the emblem flower of New South Wales. The genus belongs to the Proteaceae and this species looks very like a South African protea. The flowers, as large as a good big tea-rose, are crimson, a mass of handsome stamens surrounded by bracts of the same colour—at least I think they are bracts and not petals. Telopeas are evergreen shrubs or small trees and one of them scrapes into Bean, *T. truncata*, for it comes from the mountains of Tasmania, has been very successfully grown in Sussex, and is, therefore, moderately hardy, perhaps quite hardy. I have never seen this one but Bean says the flowers are rich crimson and 'much the same shape as those of *Embothrium coccineum*' (same family). Again it would be necessary to get seeds from some friend in Tasmania, or perhaps an English seedsman.†

Mr Hurley has some lovely photographs of eucalyptus in flower. There are, of course, many eucalyptus enthusiasts in Britain but I think I am right in saying that the hardiest species are not those with the prettiest flowers. When I was in Tresco at Christmas-time one of the *E. ficifolia* trees still had one tuft of belated flower; it was a gorgeous translucent orange colour. But Bean does not include this one among the eucalypts hardy in our island, although I know quite a number of healthy trees of it growing in Devon coastal gardens.

* Callistemons are available from some nurseries, including Treseders of Truro and Hilliers of Winchester.

† Plants are offered by the Slieve Donard Nursery, Newcastle, Co. Down, Northern Ireland.

In Australia Blandfordias are called Christmas Bells. These are beautiful cool-greenhouse plants in our country, although they could perhaps be put outside in the summer. *Blandfordia grandiflora* is a beauty, a tall, narrow-leaved, liliaceous herb whose flower stems are topped by red and yellow bells with the waxy texture which distinguishes a few of the more exotic rhododendrons and one or two other valued exotics of our gardens.

The acacias, which florists call mimosa and the Australians call wattles, naturally figure among Mr Hurley's subject. Several species can be grown in England either in the warmer counties or on specially protected sites elsewhere. I know of a flourishing group in Hertfordshire. The hardiest and luckily one of the best is *A. dealbata*. Both young and mature plants of this in my garden came through the cold spell, with eight degrees of frost for several days, without harm. *A. melanoxilon* was damaged but not killed. My favourite of this genus is *A. verticellata*, which looks rather like a tree heather until the thousands of minute bottle-brush flowers come out. Acacias grow so very fast from seed that it might be worth growing them even where they are apt to be killed in winter; a couple of mild winters, and we often get them, would enable them to reach a fair size and perhaps to flower.

We have, as natives in this country, a number of umbelliferous herbs, some of them gigantic, others small, all of them coarse, and having either white, cream or dirty pink flowers. The Australians are more fortunate in their *Didiscus coeruleus*, the Rottnest Daisy, for this has a sky-blue umbel of flowers. It is either an annual or biennial and if you can get seeds of it, you just plant them where the plant is to flower; as it rarely exceeds eighteen inches in height it should be towards the front of the border.

This is but a small sample of a magnificent flora; how one would like, for example, to have some of the boronias growing in one's garden, those delightfully flowering relatives of our common rue. They can be grown in pots and stood outside in the summer, but they will not stand an English winter, alas. Among the trees, too, the banksias, which flourish on Tresco, would make a remarkable addition to our flowering trees, and I do know at least one garden in Devon where they are doing very well at the moment, and, of course, they can be grown in Cornwall. However, it is wiser for most of us to try only the genera, and the species, which are known to stand a good chance of survival.

The principal comments I would add to this are that *Acacia dealbata* in our garden subsequently survived much lower temperatures than those mentioned in this article, for two specimens of it came through the atrocious winter of 1962/3. And that *Telopea truncata* can be seen at its best in Irish gardens: there is a magnificent specimen of it at Mount Congreve in Co. Waterford.

In September 1962, just before the worst and coldest winter in living memory, I again reverted to the subject of southern hemisphere exotics for English gardens.

LATE-FLOWERING SHRUBS
September 29, 1962

No experience in gardening is pleasanter than a success after failure has been admitted and accepted. When, before the cold weather of last winter, I planted corms of *Zantedeschia rehmanii*, from South Africa, I did so in three different sites, knowing nothing about their tastes. We thought the cold had finished them off. Then, suddenly, in late August, they began to reappear in all three sites and one of them bore a flower within a few days of popping through the soil. The stalk is fifteen inches long and the flower has the same form as the yellow 'arum' that is, it is a narrower, less open spathe than most white ones; the colour is a good clean pink on the inside, a pinkish-green on the outside. Most of the corms were raised from seed. In a year or two we should have quite a nice clump of this little arum. But that is by the way.

I have been noting, chiefly in the very lovely gardens of Dartington Hall, whose superintendent, Mr Johnson, has done remarkable things with a soil by no means easy for many of the plants he grows so well, what shrubs, sub-shrubs and small trees are best planted for late flowering. Of those we saw there, we have planted some here already, but others we must take steps to get.

A small tree which greatly took my fancy at Dartington was hoheria; there are several kinds there, one having a weeping habit, but they are all equally graceful. I cannot myself distinguish the species, but there are apparently three in cultivation here, *Hoheria vulgaris*, *H. lanceolata* and *H. angustifolia*, or else all these are simply varieties of one species, *H. populnea*. At all events, the plant is a tree not less than ten feet and not more than thirty feet tall; it is evergreen, comes from New Zealand, and is hardy at Kew; it should have quite a wide range in Britain. In late August it becomes covered with pure white starry flowers in the leaf axils, so that the whole plant is snowy. The habit is tall and narrow, but not stiff, on the contrary very graceful. Even small gardens could find room for it. At Dartington these trees are surrounded by seedlings rising from the seed they have dropped. But they are commonly increased by cuttings.

The glory of the shrub gardens at Dartington at this late season, and despite the quality of the many kinds of hydrangeas in flower, are the eucryphias. Two kinds are grown there: there is one magnificent specimen of *Eucryphia* × 'Nymansensis' and all the other specimens appear to be *Eucryphia glutinosa* or *E. Intermedia*. The noble bearing, graceful ramification, clear green of the pinnate foliage and the delicacy of the cup-shaped, pure white flowers, with their boss of faintly red anthers, all make eucryphias some of the loveliest small trees in creation. What conditions are necessary to grow them? Well, it depends on the species, even on the variety.

First, *Eucryphia cordifolia* from the island of Chiloë, illustrious as the source of all our large-fruited strawberry varieties, is tender. It dies at Kew, but survives in the south-west and in parts of Sussex. It has simple leaves, two-inch cup-shaped flowers in the leaf axils, brick-red anthers, and will attain a height of fifty feet. It seems to be tolerant of lime for it is a success at Highdown. *Eucryphia glutinosa* is not; this one is much hardier although it also comes from Chile: it is enormously floriferous in August and into September. We have both of these here. I have also planted *Eucryphia lucida*, a Tasmanian species with very fine foliage and capable of growing to a hundred feet, though I shall not be here to see it do so, if it ever does. It is not to be compared with the first two for garden quality, or so I understand. I have never seen it really in flower, although ours bore about a dozen flowers the size of half-a-crown this year.

Eucryphia × 'Intermedia', of which I have two forms, both very young plants, is a cross between the Tasmanian *lucida* and the

Chilean *glutinosa*, which appeared as a chance seedling at Rostrevor, Co. Down. A very attractive eucryphia, and very vigorous in growth, increasing at twice the pace of the others. Another natural hybrid, this time originating at Nymans, between *glutinosa* and *cordifolia*, is *Eucryphia* 'Nymansensis'. It has advantages over both: although *glutinosa* is, at least in my garden, deciduous, 'Nymansensis', which is as hardy, is an evergreen, like most eucryphias. The flowers are large, two and a half inches, and have yellow anthers which stand out beautifully against the pure white of the petals. *Eucryphia glutinosa* and *Eucryphia* × 'Nymansensis', with their upright yet graceful habit, their relative hardiness, the evergreen habit of the latter, their size at maturity, and their great beauty in the very height of the holiday season, should be tried by some enterprising south-west town council as street trees, I don't believe this has ever been done, and I feel sure that it is very well worth trying.

I.
Cerasus flore pleno.

Chapter 8

Small Flowering Trees

Despite the originality of the two major English garden styles, our gardens trace their descent back through Renaissance Italian to the Hellenistic gardens of early Roman imperial times whose first patron and pioneer was Lucullus. The most important element of the plant material of these gardens was, perhaps, the small tree—cypress, laurel and box. But the ancients seem to have had only two flowering trees, myrtle and oleander, and myrtle rarely attains tree size or, rather, tree shape. The great wealth of small flowering trees in English gardens now is a product of nineteenth-century activity in plant introduction from Asia, South America and Australasia. English gardens are probably richer in such trees than those of continental Europe, for the relative mildness of our climate favours those which come from the southern hemisphere. The first of these small flowering trees which I ever fell in love with and wrote about was, I think, *Arbutus unedo*.

THE STRAWBERRY TREE
November 21, 1950

Finally, for the greatest of all winter-flowering and fruiting beauties, there is the one tree in my garden which I visit every day from now until January, for the sheer lust of the eye: *Arbutus unedo*. Planted ten years ago as a very small plant from a pot, our specimen is now about nine feet tall and rather more through the widest part. Year after year, in October, November and December, it is covered with panicles of waxy, translucent flowers and, at the same time, last year's ripe fruit, which is a vivid scarlet and has a curious granular surface texture. This shrub is something of an historical curiosity, for there is no obvious reason why it should have been so assiduously cultivated for thousands of years that it has spread and naturalised itself all over Europe, wherever it will survive the winters—it is quite hardy—from its original habitat in the eastern Mediterranean littoral. True, it is very beautiful, and evergreens flowering and bearing fruit in mid-winter are not common. True, also, that the berries of this strawberry-tree are edible, although some ancient peoples believed them to be poisonous. Neither of these reasons is sufficient to account for its wide and very early diffusion, especially as Dioscorides was of opinion that the fruit was, indeed, poisonous, though Galen notes that it was commonly eaten by rustics in Italy, as was the case in Ireland many centuries later.

The most plausible explanation of the great numbers and wide distribution of this little tree is that it was one of the plants used for the ancient Greek and Italian *leaf forage* plantations. The Mediterranean climate is not kind to grass; by July there is virtually nothing for the cattle to eat; nor does autumn produce the fresh green 'bite' for sheep and even cattle, which we, in the north, expect. The foliage of certain shrubs therefore took the place of grass, such shrubs being planted along the borders of fields, ditches and paths. The cattle were not always brought to the growing fodder; the leaves were often stripped from the arbutus by hand, mixed with those of olive and vine prunings, and fed to stalled beasts. Whether the larger kinds of cattle relished this diet, it is difficult to say; cows are extraordinarily adaptable in this respect. In some parts of the world they are commonly fed on seaweed; I once met a cow which was fond of fresh herring. Goats, of course, prefer foliage to grass, being browsers. And sheep certainly enjoy a change of diet, for some of my neighbour's broke into the vineyard last year and stripped a row of vines of their leaves in a matter of half an hour.

It seems, then, that we probably owe the winter beauty of the *A. unedo* to the Mediterranean peasant's shortage of fodder. The deciduous trees were useful until leaf-fall—Cato advises farmers to feed their oxen on the leaves of 'elm, poplar, oak and fig'; but in winter, the strawberry-tree must have been available. In addition to the beauty of flowers and fruit, the little tree offers that of its always fresh-looking foliage, always richly green and never tired or disfigured: the reason for this is its habit of renewing its foliage constantly, but not steadily. It seems to wait until it has grown a new set of young leaves on one branch or several, and then, all at once, will suddenly drop the old ones, which will be found thick on the ground one morning without the tree showing any signs of nakedness.

Not all, by any means, of the little, flowering trees which are such a source of delight to the eye, are exotics introduced from outside Europe.

BLACKTHORN, LABURNUM AND MAY

May 27, 1961

But the most valuable, because earliest of spring-flowering trees, is our native blackthorn and I have sometimes wondered why it is never treated as a garden plant. True, the hedgerows are full of it so that there might seem to be no point in giving it valuable garden space; but whereas in the hedges it has no particular shape, in the garden it can be grown as a specimen and with some protection from wind and some judicious pruning, preferably in the spring, a blackthorn makes a small tree of great beauty twice a year: in March or early April when its almost jet black wood and long, handsome thorns are so beautifully decorated with clouds of tiny, pure white rose-shaped flowers; and in autumn when the tightly clustered fruit ripens to the extraordinary matt blue-grey which it owes to the dense, 'bloom'. It seems, however, that this autumn embellishment is confined to the south of England: a north country friend was telling me recently that although he had admired blackthorn in flower since boyhood, he had never seen sloes on a tree until he came south. I suppose that it is very rarely warm enough, in the north, at the flowering season of this beautiful small tree, for the fruit to be 'set'. Blackthorn is remarkably adaptable in other respects, though: on exposed and windy sites, instead of refusing to grow it will form a prostrate ground-hugging shrub beautiful in both flower and fruit. Such naturally wind-trained shrubs can be seen on Dungeness, or could until the Atomic Energy Commission invaded that fascinating habitat of so many interesting plants and birds.

Facing me as I write is a laburnum, *Laburnum anagyroides*; it has been in flower for a fortnight and will be in flower for another. It is about twenty feet tall and it is probably the most graceful tree in the whole garden, so charmingly hung are its long racemes of golden flowers. This plant is neglected by writers simply because it is so common, a suburban tree. But set it in a mixed plantation, as it is with us, backed by dark conifers and in the near neighbourhood of a copper (not the red, the true copper) beech, and its great beauty becomes apparent. There are, by the way, better varieties than the common laburnum. *L. alpinum*, often planted in the suburbs, is almost too free with its flowers; but *L. alschingeri*, which may attain well over thirty feet but can also be grown as a bushy shrub, not only has longer racemes of flowers than common laburnum, but better foliage. There is also, in this genus, or half in it to be precise, a plant which, although of no great beauty, indeed it is rather ugly, is one of the curiosities of horticulture: *Laburnocytisus* × *adamii*. It is of the rather rare class of chimaeras or graft-hybrids: the original plant grew from the mixed tissues at the point of graft junction between a common laburnum and a *Cytisus purpureus*. It is a crazy, mixed up tree which bears some laburnum, yellow flowers, some purple cytisus flowers, and some intermediate between the two and a depressing brown colour.

A native small tree also neglected by writers and which certainly would not be if it were an exotic and difficult to grow, is the red may. To see this tree at its best, you have to visit some of the pleasantly leafy older suburbs to the south-west of London. These suburbs are almost arboreta with houses concealed among the fine trees and shrubs, and there you will find very old red may trees which have reached a great size for their species, and which, in May and June, are magnificently in flower. A specimen tree of this variety, set against evergreens and so that it can be seen all round, is as beautiful as many of the finest exotics and would cause great excitement in the horticultural world had it only had the good fortune to have been introduced from Yunnan.

The may trees belong to the genus crataegus which includes over a thousand species from the common hawthorn of our hedges to difficult exotics. The red mays can be either *C. monogyna* var. *sesteriana*, in which case the flowers are double and the plant may be a tree as tall as thirty-five feet or more; or *C. oxycantha*. In the latter case the tree will not pass twenty feet at maturity: the variety *coccinea* bears single scarlet flowers; the variety *coccinea plena*, double scarlet flowers; *rosea* is a single rose-pink, and *maskei* the same colour but with double flowers. The species *monogyna* includes two very interesting white-flowered varieties; one is the famous winter-flowering Glastonbury Thorn; the other a dwarf, *semperflorens*, which makes a perfect miniature tree rarely exceeding five feet, even after half-a-century of growth, and producing its flowers continuously or in bursts from June to August.

Among the best of the small flowering trees are the cornels although many of them are, commonly, shrubs rather than trees. Although some of the best of them flower better in the east than in the west of England, for with the exception of the tender evergreen species they require sunshine in summer to flower well and are not affected by winter cold, I did not become interested in them until I had a West Country garden.

THE CORNELS
December 2, 1961

Perhaps the handsomest large shrub or small tree in this parish at the time of writing this piece, that is in mid-November, is a fine specimen of a cornel about a mile from my house; I believe that it was planted only about seven years ago, but it cannot be less than fifteen feet tall and twenty feet through; I think that as many people stop to look at it now, when it is covered with its large raspberry-like fruits as big as medlars and a dull crimson in colour, as did so in May and into June, when the plant was well covered with the great flower-like bracts. All the cornels are growing in popularity but it is a wonder to me that they have not been much more widely planted in the past; the one in question, for example, *Cornus kousa*, was introduced over eighty years ago and it is not difficult or demanding about soil although it does best in deep loams, it likes sun but will tolerate some shade, and it is hardy. Despite these advantages it is not really common. The true flower of this species is inconspicuous but about each inflorescence are arranged four large, cream-coloured bracts which look like petals, the whole 'flower' having something of the look of a clematis. I have already mentioned the fruits which add to the beauty of the tree in autumn. Although *C. kousa* is deciduous, it seems reluctant to let go of its leaves which remain fresh after those of other trees have been shed; after a hot summer the leaves, before they fall, turn a deep bronze red, so that this species is valuable for its autumn leaf colour. So is its variety *chinensis*, whose leaves turn crimson and whose bracts are larger than in the type.

A more beautiful plant than either is *C. capitata*, an evergreen species, but one which cannot be so widely planted since it is not perfectly hardy, although the best specimen known to me, a plant about twelve feet tall, wide-spreading in its habit, well furnished with branches and most graceful in its bearing, puts up with a certain amount of frost and some cold east wind every year. However, it is apparently unwise to plant *C. capitata* anywhere but in the south-west. The big fruits, very like those of *C. kousa*, look most attractive in November among the fresh green of the leaves. But the great beauty of this, Bentham's Cornel, is in May when the big flower-like groups of bracts, four or six to each inflorescence, appear. They are a rich sulphur yellow. Bean says that the fruit is often spoilt by birds; I have just been examining the nearest specimen of *C. capitata*, which is loaded with ripe fruits, some of them one and a half inches in diameter; very few seem to have been pecked.

The cornel so beloved of Americans as Flowering Dogwood is *C. florida*. This, too, is a very beautiful shrub, or rather small tree; the bracts are white or greenish white in the type, rosy red in the much lovelier variety *rubra*. It is quite usual to hear experienced gardeners advise against planting this cornel on the grounds that it is not hardy; this, of course, is absurd, for the species flourishes in New England, New Englanders make a festival of driving out of the cities to see the wild dogwood in flower, and in its native habitat it has to suffer every winter temperatures which occur in England not two or three times in a century. The fact remains that dogwoods in Britain rarely look happy and I have a theory about this; they have, for their supposed tenderness, been most commonly planted in quite the wrong parts of England. The cool, damp summers of the south-west do not suit them at all. Where do peaches do best in England out of doors? Suffolk and the east coast. Why? Hot dry summers and autumn heatwaves ripen the new wood as it is rarely ripened in the west. I believe that the same would be true of *C. florida* on one condition, that, like peaches, the trees be planted *high* and on a site with really good *katabatics*—an outlandish word meaning air drainage. For the flowers with their protecting bracts are formed in autumn and open in spring; they are ruined if caught by a May frost. You see the difficulty? In those parts of Britain where May frost is not to be feared, the wood will not ripen; and where the wood ripens, there are apt to be May frosts.*

However, there is an American cornel which does not suffer from this incompatibility with our climate since it comes from the western part of North America, including that region whose climate is most like our own. This is *C. nuttallii* which Bean describes as the noblest of the genus. I have planted it here, but the finest specimen of it I have seen was in Sussex. As a rule it remains a shrub in gardens but where it is well suited it may grow into a tree; in the wild it may attain seventy or eighty feet, apparently, but it is not likely to grow so large in England. It is deciduous and fairly hardy. The bracts, six to each group surrounding the bunched inflorescence, are very large, cream fading to white and finally to green. As they may be three inches long, the whole 'flower' can be six inches in diameter. The species is apparently not likely to be at its best or to live very long in the colder parts of Britain, but in the maritime counties and the south-west it can attain a great size and a considerable age.

A very hardy cornel is *C. alba* which has no bracts and whose cymes of small flowers are of no great merit: it is planted for its winter beauty, for in autumn the young stems turn brilliant red and they, after leaf fall, are most decorative; the variety *sibirica* is supposed to be better than the type. The species is one which forms a dense thicket of suckers and must, therefore, be planted where it will not intrude upon other, less vigorous shrubs. The variety I planted was *C. a.* 'Sibirica variegata', for this, with creamy yellow leaf margins, is handsome in summer as well as winter. I did not find it very easy to establish; it suffered from some kind of die-back of the growing tips. But this seems to be an unusual misfortune.

C. mas is a European native and the garden name for it is Cornelian cherry; the name is derived from the large, bright red fruit which is borne rather too sparsely as a rule but which, where the shrub is really well suited, makes it a very handsome object in autumn. However, the species is not planted with that in mind but for its very early flowers: these appear in February and often in

* Probably more important is the fact that this cornel does not form flower-bud in the cool, moist western climate, but does so in the hot summers of eastern Britain.

great abundance. Each inflorescence is enclosed in four small, hairy bracts; when these open they expose the umbels of flower. The individual flower is very small, but the umbels are striking because of their form and bright yellow colour. They are borne each on a short stalk growing from the last season's wood, so that in a good flowering specimen the whole outside of the plant may be covered with them. The flowers appear before the leaves so that *C. mas* looks best when planted among evergreens, and since it attains twenty feet or more in time, Portugal laurel makes a good companion for it. There are a number of varieties, all of them good: some of them are not easy to buy. The variety *aurea elegantissima* with its golden cream and pink-flushed leaf margins, is the prettiest. For a small garden the ideal variety is *nana*, a compact shrub with the merits of the type. In *xanthocarpa* the fruits are yellow instead of being red. All varieties of *C. mas* are indifferent to cold in winter, but if fruit, as well as flower, is to be borne they really need rather hotter summers than they get here and it is wise to plant them with full exposure to the sun.

This piece about cornels did not even mention one with which I became acquainted later, and which is perhaps the most beautiful small tree we can grow. The most perfect specimen of this, *Cornus alternifolia* 'Argentea', which I have seen is in Mr Richard Grove Annesley's garden, Anne's Grove, County Cork. Its branches are 'tabulated', its pointed, twisted leaves bright silver. Another magnificent species of this genus is the Chinese *C. controversa*, remarkable for the tiered symmetry of its bearing.

One cannot plant everything in a garden of only three acres, but I sometimes have the chance to ensure that good flowering trees are planted in other people's gardens:

THE JUDAS TREE AND OTHERS

September 2, 1961

An acquaintance of mine recently inherited some landed property and a fine house but very little money to go with it. It is a beautiful place and he and his wife decided to live in it although it would be a great strain on their resources. The formal garden is small and manageable without paid help, but it is extended by about ten acres of trees, mostly oak, too densely planted to constitute a park, and too thinly planted to be forest. It is a curious fact of our economy that if you want to buy timber it is fabulously dear, but when you come to sell it, it is worthless: the few trees cut from my friend's plantation to give the rest a better chance to make good timber thirty or forty years hence, did, however, make a small fund with which my friend proposed to 'garden' the plantation and he asked me to go and see the place and advise him on what flowering shrubs and trees he could plant in small clearings and beside the main path through the wood.

The trees for such a purpose must not grow too big; and they must be such as will 'do' when surrounded by other trees. It is, of course, useless to plant any kind of flowering tree without any outlet to the light of the sky at all. But in all but conifer woods planted for industrial purposes to make a great deal of tall timber as quickly as possible, there are breaks in the canopy of leaves formed by the established hardwood species, a sort of skylight in the leaves; and several kinds of flowering trees, set under these openings, will grow very well. Part of my friend's problem was solved with varieties of *Camellia japonica* but I do not want to discuss them here. What did occur to me when we were dealing with this job was that several of the flowering trees we discussed fulfilled not only the conditions set by his case, but also those of the man with a small or medium sized garden who wants to have flowers over his head as well as under his feet.

A tree of curious beauty which should be much more widely planted in England and might well be used as a street tree in southern towns, is *Cercis siliquastrum*, the Judas Tree. It is a leguminous plant and the genus includes six other species which need not detain us as they are either inferior in beauty or not hardy. The name is misleading: the tree was introduced to the north side of the Mediterranean in the sixteenth century or earlier from Palestine, where it is native among other places, and was named *Arbre de Judée*, Tree of Judaea; this somehow got itself corrupted to Judas Tree, perhaps by way of Jewish Tree.* In time a Judas Tree will attain forty feet and I have seen fine stands of it even

* I think this derivation more probable than the commonly received one that it was supposed to be the tree from which Judas hanged himself. *C. siliquastrum* cannot be recommended to would-be suicides.

taller among deciduous hardwoods in south-western France. But as a rule and in any case for many years it is smaller, and has a shrubby rather than an arboreal habit. The wood is grey speckled with lighter colour, and the young foliage bronzed. The mature foliage is glaucous so that the blueish tinge is in pleasant contrast with other foliage as the shape of the leaves is also, for these are heart-shaped, rather like apricot leaves. In fact, at a quick glance, it is possible to mistake a shrubby Judas Tree for an apricot bush.

It is in May that the great beauty of the tree appears. Once the tree has begun to flower, which it does not do until it has reached seven or eight years of age, it soon becomes almost covered, in May, with clusters of purplish rose-pink pea-flowers on stalks so short that they are not noticed. And when I say covered I mean *covered*: branches young and old, and even the trunk of the tree, seem suddenly to sprout flowers in the most singular way until the whole tree is closely dressed in colour. Judas Trees are lime-tolerant, like a good fat loam, and must be planted in full sun. Never buy a tree more than a foot or eighteen inches tall: older plants die if moved. You can propagate more trees from seed, which germinates easily; and, very occasionally, from suckers produced while the tree is still young. There is a white-flowered variety, *C. siliquastrum* var. *album*, but I cannot find it listed in any nursery catalogue and I have hitherto failed to buy a specimen.

EUCRYPHIAS

For general purposes the most interesting of the lovely eucryphia family is the one known to those who believe it to be a variety of *Eucryphia glutinosa* as *E. glutinosa* var. 'Nymansay', and to those who accept that it is a natural cross between *E. glutinosa* and *E. cordifolia*, as *E.* × 'Nymansensis'. It is an evergreen tree and although it may well be capable of growing to fifty or sixty feet if one parent really is *E. cordifolia*, it does not in practice grow to anything like that height. It is an evergreen, it is fairly hardy and whereas *E. glutinosa* is a lime-hater, *E.* × 'Nymansensis' tolerates chalk and in fact was first flowered by Sir Frederick Stern in his famous chalk garden of Highdown. The stiff, handsome pinnate leaves always look bright and fresh. In flower, a good specimen of this tree is breath-taking, for the pure white flowers with their great boss of yellow-anthered stamens are well over two inches in diameter and of a thick, waxy substance; moreover, on a good specimen they are very numerous. Propagation is by cuttings or layers, but seeds are sometimes produced and in favourable conditions self-sown seedlings may be found. In fact this is the origin of the Nymans species.

MYRTLES

No myrtle is, alas, perfectly hardy in England; they are none the less worth planting, for even if cut down by a severe frost, they shoot up again and I have known one very fine *Myrtus communis* tree, a glorious sight in flower, which has been cut down and has regrown no less than three times. *M. luma*, which comes from Chile, is no hardier and it may even be less hardy, but it is well worth planting in the mild south-west and elsewhere against a wall, although even on a wall the species has been killed by frost at Kew. I possess a photograph of an *M. luma* growing in Cork which was about twice as tall as the books say it can grow; however, it does not as a rule exceed twenty-five feet, making a spreading dark evergreen which flowers in late summer when it turns almost white with the great number of flowers. In suitable climates the seeds germinate freely and seedlings appear all over the place. If you can keep the tree alive into old age the trunk and older branches become one of its beauties, for the bark then turns a rich cinnamon brown. In my view the best way to plant this species is in a small glade open to the south but surrounded on all other sides by trees larger than itself. Or, in town, in a courtyard protected by buildings from the coldest quarters.

MAGNOLIAS

All the magnolias are beautiful, but for me the most beautiful are those with pendent flowers. It is all very well to rave over the beauty of *Magnolia campbellii* and wait thirty years for the flowers, but you cannot see them unless you have a tall tower handy so as to climb up and look down on the tree. Of those with more or less pendulous flowers, *M. wilsonii* makes a small, tidy tree about twenty feet tall, deciduous, flowering at ten or twelve years old, the flowers are four-inch hanging cups of white petals with crimson stamens. There is a very lovely specimen of this tree at Stourhead and though it is not very easy to establish it is worth repeated efforts and every care. I have found that young plants of *M.*

wilsonii which look sickly will quickly recover if screened against wind until they are established; in any case this species greatly dislikes a windy site.

I had, of course, much more than that to say about magnolias—much of it, written over a period of years, is collected in the next chapter. I do not want to digress into that special subject now, but to deal with two other small trees with which I was very taken in Devon gardens and have since planted in my own.

HOHERIA AND OLEASTER
October 31, 1964

Flowering trees have always had their place in the large garden; for the garden of medium size and for the modern small garden, most of these plants are too large. It is therefore of importance to have some knowledge of those which are of manageable size and there are two with which, seeing them first in other people's gardens, and then planting them in our own, I have of late years fallen in love. When I describe them as 'small' it is best to bear in mind that I do so in the context 'trees' which, as a category, are the largest of living creatures.

The genus *Hoheria* looks like poplar to the eye of the inexpert, but in fact belongs to the mallows, with hibiscus and hollyhock. The particular species I want to concentrate on was formerly 'referred to' *Plagianthus* (how I love botanical jargon), and is treated under that head by Bean* even in the 1951 edition; but by 1956, when the *Dictionary of Gardening* (R.H.S.) was published, *Plagianthus lyalli* had becone *Hoheria lyalli*. When, however, you find hoherias in a garden, especially where there are several or many and these old, and where seedlings, often copious, have been cultivated, it is very difficult indeed to put a name to these trees. And it is really not very important. However, I am taking as my 'standard' plant one at Dartington Hall which is strikingly beautiful, and which is labelled *H. lyalli* var. *glabrata*. I have seen this same variety in the garden of Anne's Grove, County Cork, where the genus is abundantly and variously represented, and from which came the seedlings I am cultivating.

* *Trees and Shrubs Hardy in the British Isles.*

H. lyalli var. *glabrata*, then, is a small shrub-like tree, up to about twenty feet in height, but in shape often more or less fastigiate; it is deciduous in cold climates, at least partially evergreen in milder ones; it comes from New Zealand and is, therefore, not ruggedly hardy. Very cold winters may kill it to the ground, but it springs up again. This did not happen in the south during the winter of 1962–63, and I therefore think that it is safe to recommend this plant for all but the coldest parts of our country. There are, in this and in other species of hoheria, and as far as I can be sure in all hybrids, two kinds of leaves, though Bean does not give this as a character of the species we are discussing, which is surprising for it is very striking. Some leaves are from two to four inches long, half as wide, heart-shaped at the base, tapering to a point, and with more or less serrated edges; but with them in young plants grow about as many leaves similar in shape but less than half as large. The foliage is downy or glabrous, according to variety, but perfectly smooth and even gleaming in the one in question, if it be a good form. It is more or less silvery, light green, and it has the poplar-like quality of shimmering in movement. This tree flowers in July or very early August, and it then becomes absolutely covered with clusters of flowers in every leaf axil or new growth. Each flower is on its own stalk, drooping; each is well over an inch across, saucer-shaped, translucent or pink towards the centre. The flowers are somewhat reminiscent, though smaller, of those of *Abutilon vitifolium* to which, indeed, the hoherias are related.

Those living in milder countries may like to try another little tree of this genus, *H. populnea*. This is evergreen. In both species (at least I think so but I have noted it only in specimens I would not dare to identify specifically), there is a notable change in the foliage as the trees come to flowering size: the number of the small kind of leaves diminishes; while the larger kind becomes dominant.

As to the proper use of hoherias in the garden, I suggest planting them in place of other, unflowering, background trees; of using them, for example, to mark and beautify corners and turns of paths; and, finally, as specimens on or beside small, sheltered lawns. Certainly no gardener in the south or along the seaboards should deny himself one or more specimens of this most attractive small tree.

My second subject is an *Eleagnus*. There are, as you probably know, both evergreen and deciduous kinds, but all have one thing in common, the scaliness of young shoots and foliage, a scaliness which produces effects of singular charm, for the young growth of, for example, that fine variegated evergreen *E. pungens aureo-variegata*, look exactly as if they have been dipped in that kind of gold paint which is made by suspending real gold-dust in a varnish or other liquid medium. In the species I want to write of here, the effect is the same but the colour is silver instead of gold.

E. umbellata is a small shrubby tree about fifteen or twenty feet tall at maturity and, unless it has been pruned which it can be, wider than it is tall. It comes from China, from the Himalaya and from Japan and, deciduous, is perfectly hardy. I call it deciduous, but it often retains quite a lot of its leaves especially in mild winters. These leaves are oval, pointed, about three inches long and half as wide. The young ones are shimmering silver; in the mature foliage the upper surface is a bright, matt green, and the underside a shining silver, so that, when moved by a breeze, the gleam and shimmer of the whole tree is a sight of very great charm. But it is not for its foliage merely, though it could well be, that I like this tree so much. In June it bears an enormous crop of flowers: these grow in small clusters all over the plant; they are like little bells or funnels, each about the size of a harebell flower, creamy on the inside, but on the outside silvery with the characteristic scales of the genus. I do not say that these flowers are spectacular; they are not; they are enchanting, which is not the same thing at all. But, and here is a small mystery, why does not the great Bean, why does not the R.H.S. *Dictionary*, refer even in a single word to the most important attribute of these flowers: that they are intensely and very sweetly fragrant? This really is odd, for in suitably warm and moist conditions of the atmosphere I know of no flowering tree which so deliciously scents the ambient air; and though the scent has not the carrying power of, say, lilies, still it is very strong and pervasive all about a mature tree in flower. Can it be that the Dartington form of this tree is a special one? If so I am in luck, for I bought my plants from the small plant-shop in that great garden, knowing them to be from the fine tree familiar to me; and I have since struck cuttings of these, so that we now have several young specimens.

Both the hoheria and the eleagnus described here are fast-growing trees, but especially the hoherias which, like so many Australasian plants, do, for some reason which nobody has ever explained to me, grow very much faster than northern hemisphere plants. For example, when I was at Anne's Grove in September of last year, Mr Annesley very kindly gave me a handful of chance seedlings of hoherias; they were small, fragile things perhaps four or five inches tall. Planted in a nursery bed when we reached home in October, they now average, just about a year later, thirty inches in height, and are firm, woody, and much branched. Some have been planted out into their final stations and it would not surprise me to see them six feet tall by this time next year. This great speed of growth makes it worth while to grow one's hoherias from seed, if you can get it. A word of warning, not from personal experience: the seeds of this genus are set in such quantity and germinate so readily in southern moist, peaty gardens, that hoherias can become 'weeds' in some British gardens. As to the eleagnus it is easily grown from cuttings; I use, as material, soft tip-growth and root it in the closed case over bottom heat; but for all I know harder wood can be rooted, although Bean says that deciduous 'oleaster', the vernacular name, should be increased by seed. As to situation, I find that both these trees will stand some shade, but it must not be deep shade and at least one side of the tree should be exposed to sunshine.

It may be of interest that one year after this was written the hoherias in question were from five to seven feet tall and bushily ramified. No doubt about it, if you want a garden in a hurry, plant Australasians.

Frittillaria.

Chapter 9

Magnolias

November 26, 1960

In the past, most fortunately, many gardeners planted magnolias. It is my impression—I can only hope a false one—that these trees are more rarely planted now. If this is true,it is a great pity, for magnolias are among the most beautiful of the flowering trees, are not particularly difficult to grow, are for the most part hardy, or at least hardy enough, and live to a great age. I suppose that the smallness of so many modern gardens would be advanced as the reason for the decline of magnolia planting. If so, it is a bad reason; there are small species and varieties as well as large ones, and one of the finest has always been chiefly used in the vertical, not the horizontal, plane, that is treated as a house-wall plant so that it occupies hardly any garden space at all.

Of the genus, which has eighty species, my own favourite is *Magnolia wilsonii*, of which I am planting two in my new Devon garden. I first saw this tree at Stourhead, and was greatly taken with the way in which it carries its flowers: most magnolias hold their flowers erect or nearly so, but in *wilsonii* they hang down, nodding and trembling to the slightest stirring of the air. They are bowl-shaped and very regular, about three or four inches in diameter, and produced in sufficient number to give the tree its full beauty in May or early June, without being so numerous that one does not have a chance to appreciate the form and texture, and incidentally, fragrance, of each individual flower. The tree at Stourhead is, I suppose, about twenty feet tall, and I have seen one other like it at Wisley, if I remember rightly. Apparently *M. wilsonii* very rarely exceeds twenty-five feet and is usually smaller, although it is a true tree rather than a shrub. It is, therefore, not only one of the best magnolias, but one of those which can be planted in a small garden. One odd thing I have noticed about this species: The R.H.S. *Dictionary of Gardening* advises planting it with some peat; one of the principal nurserymen stocking it lists it specifically as lime-tolerant. I have seen it in both acid and neutral soils.

Another small shrubby magnolia, which I do not much like myself but which is certainly useful in small gardens, is *M. stellata*. From personal experience, I do not believe that this one *does* tolerate lime, although it may not insist on a really acid soil. It never did well here* and a poor specimen which, having refused to grow, was given away to a friend with a peaty soil in Sussex, there began to flourish. An experiment with a single specimen is not conclusive, of course; half a dozen other factors may account for this curious behaviour. But I do not advise planting *M. stellata* in the chalk counties. For neutral and acid soil gardens it has, however, many good qualities; it forms a spreading, well-shaped shrub about eight or nine feet tall when fully grown, and as much or more in diameter. It is the earliest of all magnolias, flowering before the leaves appear, in March or early April, and far more lavishly than other magnolias, producing a great mass of narrow-petalled, starry, white, fragrant flowers which become shot with pink as they age; there is a variety, *rosea* ,whose flowers are pink from bud, but it is a poor colour. My objections to the species are two: the first is perhaps rather perverse: it bears too much flower, so that the form is lost. And the second is that, blooming so early, the flowers are frequently seared by frost, whereupon they turn brown and flabby and look horrible. The second objection need deter nobody with a sheltered garden in a warm county; and the first is personal and idiosyncratic.

The wall magnolia takes up no space in the garden, and we owe a debt of gratitude to those thousands of house-owners who, in the past, planted this magnificent species, *M. grandiflora*, for the pleasure of future generations; it is a debt we can only pay by doing as much for our posterity. *M. grandiflora* is an evergreen—I should have mentioned that both *wilsonii* and *stellata* are deciduous —and in its native land, the south-east of the United States, it sometimes attains eighty feet or more. Planted in the open in England, it does not exceed about forty feet, but on walls of tall houses often grows to the eaves. It should be given a warm site. One of its beauties are the leaves: they are as much as a foot long, spear-shaped, dark, shiny green on the face in all seasons, and rust-red beneath. The flowers, rarely numerous, are individually magnificent, great cream-coloured 'tulips' nine inches across,

* i.e. in Kent.

produced over a period of three months, beginning in July. The flowers are fragrant, and the rich scent will drift in through the windows of the wall clothed by this glorious tree. The type is often distinguished by the extra name *lanceolata*, for the variety *M. g.* var. *furruginea*, with rounder leaves, flowers a little earlier. A good pot-grown plant will cost you from a guinea to 25*s*: the capital increment on this investment should be expressed by the sign for infinity, since you cannot put a figure on the pleasure the tree will be giving fifteen, twenty-five or a hundred years hence.

Wilsonii and *stellata* present no difficulty in transplanting, but *grandiflora*, being an evergreen, may give, and should receive, a little more trouble. What kills evergreens after transplantation is drought, especially when they are planted near a wall. The soil to receive the young plant should be prepared in advance, and it should be rich in water-holding compost, or peat or leaf-mould, and thoroughly soaked. After planting, do not keep on watering, for it is perfectly possible to drown a young tree. Given that the soil is thoroughly moist, and having watered-in the tree, mulch it with old hay, or dead leaves or bracken. It is usual to plant evergreens in spring, and in parts of England and, for that matter, of Scotland, though not Wales, March and April droughts are common: in Kent and Essex, for example. Inspect below the mulch from time to time and moisten the soil if it tends to dry out; top syringing with perfectly clean rain-water can help the plant in that period before the sap begins to rise and maintain its foliage. Best of all, if you can screen the plant from the dehydrating east and south-east winds, do so.

There seems to be some confusion as to the species *M. liliflora*. The only one known to me is a bush not more than ten feet tall, rather untidy, with flowers which are purple outside and white within. It flowers in May. But I have seen it described in catalogues as a low-branching tree attaining forty feet or more. Is this perhaps a *liliflora* × *obovata* cross? But *obovata* has pure white flowers.

M. wilsonii is not the only magnolia with pendent flowers, although I think it is the best. *M. sieboldii*, in some catalogues as *M. parviflora*, is a small deciduous tree which attains about 15 feet at maturity, more or less, according to the local climate and soil. Its flowers hang like little cup-shaped lanterns from late April or

May, and throughout June, displaying as they spread their white petals a richly-purple centre of massed stamens.

Finally, the *M.* × *soulangeana* varieties, which are numerous, have the most colourful flowers: *rubra*, with mauve to purple flowers, blooms in May, and sometimes exceeds twenty feet, × *soulangeana* itself is the one whose flowers are stained cyclamen at the base, while *alba* has the same graceful, shapely habit, but dead-white flowers.

Since that was written I have learned a little more about magnolias. One comment on what I wrote about *M. grandiflora*: the Italians favour and cultivate a very handsome fastigiate form of this species; I saw rows and rows of them in the great tree and shrub nurseries of Pistoia, in Tuscany, tall narrow, symmetrical trees of great beauty. There is, too a form which is pyramidal, also much favoured by Italian gardeners.

VARIATIONS ON A THEME
June 2, 1962

A surprising number of gardeners are, in the matter of magnolias, in much the same case as Squire Weston of 'Tom Jones' in the matter of music: it will be remembered that the squire knew two tunes: one was 'God Save the King'; the other was not. To a very large number of people in Britain there is *Magnolia grandiflora* and, perhaps, vaguely, another kind of magnolia. But there are at least thirty species growing in English gardens. All of them have come from either the southern half of the United States, or from the Far East. There are probably quite a lot of other species waiting to be 'collected'. Some no doubt, will never be English garden plants, for they are native to Malaya and would probably not be hardy enough for our climate. Of those in cultivation here, three are evergreen and the rest deciduous. I am particularly interested in this genus at the time of writing, for in March and April I deliberately set out to see as many of the spring-flowering species and varieties as possible, since I wish to plant a number of them myself. As well as seeing magnolias in gardens, I was able to see a fine range of sprays and branches in flower at the Spring Show of the Cornish Garden Society.

The genus is very accommodating in almost every way; apart from being beautiful in both flower and foliage, most magnolias are hardy, although some of the evergreens are less so in the north; although their taste in soil never seem to have been very clearly established, most and perhaps all of them with a little help from the gardener, will grow in a wide range of soils including chalk, although Sir Frederick Stern found three species, including the lovely *wilsonii*, which were not happy in his famous chalk garden at Highdown. Finally, there are magnolias for all garden sizes, from medium-sized shrubs to giant forest trees. In short, one can write about them with the hope of interesting gardeners of all kinds and all over the country.

Of the evergreens, *M. grandiflora*, with its shiny bronze-shot leaves and succession of big, tulip-shaped creamy flowers, is the hardiest. It is usually planted against a house wall; this is not, in warm places, necessary. This magnolia should stand free as a specimen, preferably in deep loam. But all magnolias make a lot of surface root, feeding in the leaf-mould of the top layers of soil; therefore they should not be hoed, but either hand-weeded or, better, mulched with peat, compost, or rotten straw and bracken. I think they respond to mulching with farmyard manure. Of *M. delavayii* I have written quite recently and will only remind you that it has magnificent foliage much larger than that of *M. grandiflora* and that the scent of its big creamy flowers is best at night; the species is not hardy north of Kew, or even at Kew. The third evergreen is *M. nitida*, a plant very rare in cultivation. It was discovered in South-East Tibet by Forrest in 1917, growing at about 10,000 feet, but it is hardy only in the west and south of our islands. It makes a small spreading tree of leaves resembling those of *M. grandiflora* but smaller; its flowers are also smaller, cream, fragrant.

For small gardens the most useful magnolia is *M. stellata*. I have already described it. It rarely exceeds ten feet in height at maturity, and about the same measured through the head of the plant. This species succeeds well at Highdown in chalk; yet nurserymen of experience will tell you that it is intolerant of lime and I failed with it completely in Kent. I have it growing apparently happily in Devon, but it is too soon to tell whether it is going to settle down. My advice is to plant it with a great deal of peat and leaf mould in the soil. And to mulch it with peat or bracken. Also for small gardens are two of the most beautiful of the genus, *M. wilsonii* and *M. sinensis*; the latter makes, if left to its own devices, a big shrub rather than a tree; the former, too, but it can easily be limited to a single trunk and persuaded to form a small tree. Both have saucer-shaped flowers five or six inches in diameter, and a bunch of crimson or purple stamens. In *wilsonii* these flowers are pendent, an unusual habit for the genus and a very attractive one. In *sinensis* the stalks of the flowers seem to be stiffer and to hold the flowers out, but as the fruit forms its weight makes it pendent.

The majority of the magnolias have either white or cream flowers, but there are some very lovely exceptions. The commonest coloured-flowered magnolia is one which I do not recommend, *M.* × *soulangeana*. I know that it is much admired and easy to grow; but I have yet to see a shrub of this variety which is really shapely, and I find the purple of the outside petals, which is the colour of some large onions, ugly. However, *de gustibus* . . . and all that, and it is true that there are several varieties of better colour. The lemon yellow flowers of *M. cordata* are very beautiful, borne on the naked stems before the leaves appear; the colour is much deeper in some specimens, the scent is disagreeable. This species is very suitable for the small garden, as it grows slowly and does not exceed about ten feet in Britain, and it flowers freely when it is very much smaller than that. There is another yellow-flowered magnolia, a big tree this time, *M. acuminata*, but its flowers are a poor colour and of no merit.

There are several pink-flowered magnolias: *M. campbellii* makes an enormous tree in time. I would urge *young* gardeners who do not propose to keep moving to a new house but have settled down for life, to plant this glorious magnolia. Nobody over, say, forty can be sure of seeing a *campbellii* he has planted in flower, but somebody should be planting them for posterity. This year the flowers, all opening in early March, were spoiled by frost even in Cornwall and Devon. This too often happens further east and north.

The magnolia which made the greatest impression of all on me this year was the *M. sprengeri* at Caerhays. This species was introduced by Wilson in 1901 but there are two forms; one has small white flowers; in the form called 'Diva' the flowers are very large and rosy carmine. *M. sprengeri* makes a very large, spreading tree and 'Diva' is rare, I believe even very rare, in cultivation. I should say at this point that some of the magnolias I am discussing are hard to get; *delavayii* is not easy at the moment because the hard winter damaged a great many young plants in nurseries; *nitida* is very scarce; so is *sprengeri* 'Diva'.

The easiest of the pink-flowered magnolias to buy and to grow is *M. veitchii*, so named by Bean. This is a hybrid between *M. campbellii* and *M. conspicua* (syn. *denudata*) produced by Veitch of Exeter, the nursery from which it may still be had. It makes a thirty-foot spreading tree and bears blush-pink flowers six inches long in April on the leafless branches. Even from seed it comes into flower within ten years, so that it has not inherited the slow habit of the staminate parent. This is one of the best magnolias for any part of Britain. Its pistillate parent, still in some lists as *conspicua* and so labelled in my garden, although I understand that *denudata* is correct, is likewise an exceptionally beautiful species. In this the very pure form of the flowers, tulip-shaped in youth but opening to cups, the thick substance of the petals, and their absolutely pure white, give the whole plant great distinction. I have a plant of this species not more than three feet tall, yet it has already flowered. It makes in the end, where it is well suited, a spreading tree of about thirty feet, and it should be planted against a background of evergreens where possible.

Although nearly all magnolias have splendid foliage, the outstanding species in this respect is *M. macrophylla*. It does not much exceed thirty feet in height, but its leaves are not infrequently thirty inches long and up to a foot wide. The flowers, borne after the leaves have come out, are also enormous, perhaps a foot in diameter, and fragrant. At the opposite end of the scale for leaf size is *M. salicifolia*, a tree up to forty feet but usually smaller, with narrow leaves three inches long and medium-sized pure white flowers.

Magnolias are best planted among deciduous hardwoods so that they receive some sunshine, but also some shade and some protection from wind. But they are also capable of standing quite alone, though I do not think that the very large-leaved species are really happy when so exposed. But, as I said, the genus provides something for almost all conditions, and as Bean wrote, 'Perhaps no group of exotic trees gives more distinction to a garden than a comprehensive collection of magnolias'.

Rosa Damascena flore pleno.

Chapter 10

Camellias

It is only in the West Country that ordinary gardeners are interested in camellias; for, despite their hardiness, only west of Exeter, excepting for some great garden enclaves in Sussex, are they taken seriously as flowering evergreens for the shrubberies and borders. You can tell at once if a gardener is a serious grower of this genus: he pronounces it camĕllia; the rest call it caméllia. Although the genus has nothing approaching the number of species, varieties and hybrids of the rhododendron or the rose, it is one of those which arouse special feelings of almost passionate admiration; which has its own international learned society meeting in annual conference; and which rouses, in its specialists, the devil of fierce controversy.

In my Kentish garden I had one camellia bush. Only after moving to Devon and seeing the grand camellia walk at Dartington Hall, did I start to plant camellias for myself. Meanwhile, I had seen them where they flourish like the wicked.

CAMELLIAS IN PORTUGAL
February 20, 1960

My title this week is slightly fraudulent, for although I do indeed want to say something about camellias, it is really an excuse to write about the Portuguese gardens I have been looking at during the past few days: all public gardens, and all with camellias in flower, as indeed, the camellias in the West Country, not much less than a thousand miles farther north, are, as to the earlies, in flower. Which is one more item of evidence that we have the best gardening climate in the world.

Because their delicate flowers can be kept at perfection for much longer by giving these shrubs the protection of glass, the myth that camellias are not hardy has been widely propagated. The fact is they are quite as hardy as the hardy rhododendrons and, incidentally, require the same kind of soil, although I doubt whether they are quite so implacably 'calcifuge'. I have three specimens, two very small and one medium-sized and growing fast: all are on the north wall of the house, which delays their flowering, so that the flowers when they appear are not exposed to damage by morning sun after night frost. I noticed that even in Portugal persistent rain, although it was warm rain, browns the edges of the petals, especially of the white and pale rose varieties.

One of the best displays of camellias I have ever seen—as of rhododendrons—was at Heligan, in Cornwall, where plants of both these genera have attained tree size. But there is an avenue of tree-sized camellias as far east as Battle Abbey, in Sussex. Not for years, however, have I seen anything like the camellia garden of the Penha Palace, near Sintra, in Portugal: I do not know its extent, but one can walk for a long time by winding, cobbled paths among coppices of camellias some of which are certainly twenty feet tall, and all of which are large, healthy and free-flowering. The flowers are of every shade of rose-pink to deep crimson, and one or two of the shrubs flowered almost orange, while many were white. I saw no singles, which is a pity, for I think them even more beautiful than the doubles. In fact, I fancy that a real camellia specialist would criticise this lovely garden on the grounds that, although well kept like all the Portuguese gardens I saw, there have been few recent plantings of new and improved varieties, such as those produced from the Chinese species *Camellia saluensis*, and *C.* × *williamsi*. But this is carping: a garden must be considered as an integral work of art, not a botanical collection, and on those terms the Penha Palace camellia garden, with the sound of running water for ever in one's ears, the hilly site, the interplantings of great New Zealand tree-ferns, rhododendrons, exotic conifers, araucarias, the splashes of golden yellow from the mimosa and others acacias —many of them large trees, growing beyond the camellia zone— and the way in which resting-places have been contrived at points which give one a view over the garden so that one can see the whole beauty of the camellias in flower, is one of the finest in the world.

In a sense, the Penha Palace garden is an English garden, in so far as it is laid out with consummate art to suggest nature. This is equally true of another remarkable garden, also very rich in camellias, not very far away—I think it was about a fifteen-minute drive, certainly not more—the garden of Monserrat. But as it was, apparently, made by an Englishman (I had some difficulty in understanding the name as pronounced by my Portuguese driver, but I think it was Sir Herbert Cook), the Bodnant-like layout is not surprising. I use that comparison advisedly, for I was reminded of Bodnant by the extreme hilliness of the site, the maze-like wanderings of innumerable, well-kept paths, the ubiquity of water, and the art with which species from the four corners of the earth had been combined to produce a natural landscape of tranquillising beauty which yet could never have happened in nature; that is, without the aid of a skilled artist-gardener.

Since I have compared Bodnant with Monserrat it should be said that Bodnant brings together more, and horticulturally more interesting, species. Monserrat is now Government property, and it is very well kept, but the hand of a master-gardener, breeding new hybrid shrubs and constantly planting the best new varieties, the hand, in short, of a Charles Puddle at Bodnant, is missing. But that having been said, this enormous Portuguese garden—where for an hour and a half after I was due out I still wandered, completely lost—is one of the most beautiful I have ever seen. Of the shrubs and trees, camellias, a very early cream and mauve rhododendron, acacias, including the florists' mimosa, mahonias in several species, and various prunus and pyrus ornamentals were in flower (January 20). The scent of the mimosa and the sound of water from streams and waterfalls filled the garden as a background to birdsong. Oh, yes, and magnolias, their vast heads of bloom standing out very handsomely against such strange garden-fellows as tree-ferns nine or ten feet tall and colossal agaves, and overtopped only by tall palms and eucalyptus trees.

Camellias, again, are a feature of the municipal gardening in Lisbon itself. Lisbon is a city of outstanding charm in two kinds: on the one hand, the old, very steep, winding and richly coloured streets of the ancient city—not so ancient, really, since most of it was destroyed in the great earthquake which features in Voltaire's *Candide*—and on the other, magnificent, broad, double avenues, with two or four carriageways separated by gardens. In those gardens, those in the Avenida de la Libertad, for example, I saw not only camellias in flower, but numerous annuals and perennials as different in kind as stocks and marigolds, and arum lily and *Strelitzia regina*, the latter with its strange orange and blue flowers like the head of a crane or heron. To the most remarkable of the gardens of Lisbon, however, I propose to devote a whole page—the covered, tropical garden called the 'Estufa Fria', at one end of the lovely Edward VII Park, is worth all that. Meanwhile, to return to camellias, in a more brass-tacks spirit for the benefit of those gardeners who have never tried planting them, but might like to try now that the myth of their tenderness has been disposed of.

I am far from being a camellia specialist, but to the best of my belief the older ones in cultivation, and still the most important numerically in the nurseryman's stock, are varieties of *C. japonica*. But this species has been reinforced by the introduction of Chinese camellias, and the finest new hybrids remarkable for being free-flowering and for remaining in flower over a long period of time, derive from these species. Chinese or Japanese, the plants are perfectly hardy, all evergreens, and the damage due to frost or rain will be confined to the spoiling of some flowers. Their soil should be free of lime, but they are not as insistent on a very low pH value as rhododendrons. They will tolerate full sun if deeply and consistently mulched, since they will not stand drought. They will also tolerate dense shade, and do well in partial shade. The best mulch for camellias is probably a mixture of leaf-mould and neutral peat: I have heard though I don't know how true it is, that they are as fond of tea as we are, and should be mulched with tea-leaves. As a matter of fact, this is true of most shrubs, since tea-leaves are relatively rich in nitrogen.

A few starting varieties for beginners ought, I think, to include 'Donckelaarii', which seems quite easy to grow, and whose white-striped red, semi-double flowers are charming; the large, pale pink single called 'Apple Blossom', but only where the site is a warm and sheltered one, for the flowers spoil easily; and what I think is the most beautiful of the whites, *alba simplex*, which is also a single. Noted in my camellia garden wanderings here and abroad, I have starred *althaeflora*, a late-flowering variety with large, fully-doubled red flowers; the very graceful *saluensis* × *cuspidata* hybrid 'Cornish Snow', which has carmine buds opening to single white flowers; and the relatively fast-growing, free-flowering *williamsi* hybrid 'Donation', whose numerous flowers are rose-pink with carmine veins.

WINTER-FLOWERING CAMELLIAS
November 4, 1961

I was given my first camellias by the head gardener of a very great house simply because I came from that parish in Kent whence his work had exiled him to the dukeries. He was rather like that formidable Scots head gardener in Mr Michael Innes's *Hamlet Revenge*, who won't let the duke have flowers from the hothouses. For when I hesitated to accept the camellias because it occurred to me that they really belonged to the head gardener's employer, the man gave me a look which both cowed and reassured me; it was clear that the gardens were *his*, not his employer's. Perhaps it was that overbearing frown which started me growing camellias.

They have been grown in England for at least two centuries; but although most of the species are more or less hardy, and some of them very hardy indeed, for though camellias come from India, China and Japan, they live at great altitudes, they were, until quite recently and in all but relatively few south-western gardens, treated as tender and grown under glass. I dare say that this was because they look and 'sound' exotic shrubs; because they are, in fact, good greenhouse subjects, growing faster under glass than in the open; and because the flowers are easily damaged by weather.

There are four species with their varieties and hybrids which are of the greatest garden value. There are others you can grow if you wish, including *Camellia thea*, if you want to grow your own tea; this can be grown in the milder counties but it has no ornamental value when compared with its congeners.

All camellias need a good deal of peat or leaf-mould in the soil which should be free from lime. I grew them in a chalk district by raising beds of peat, loam and leafmould above the general level so that chalky water could not drain into them; but this was easy for I grew only one or two camellias. They are not as intolerant of a high pH as rhododendrons. All camellias also like a great deal of water; as everyone knows, the rainfall in their native lands is very much higher than ours. We have a damaged gutter on our house and I won't have it repaired because it happens to spout water down on to one of our camellias; that plant has grown twice as much as any other in the place; I am taking the hint, and I shall try to see that all our camellias receive the equivalent of eighty inches of rain every year. But this also means that drainage must be perfect. Before coming to the winter-flowering species I will run through some others.

C. japonica varieties will stand zero Fahrenheit temperature—that is, over thirty degrees of frost. They make, in time, very tall shrubs, even small trees. They grow rather slowly, however. They flower in April to June. They do not like full sun and are often planted with a north house wall behind them but will do even better if the partial shade they enjoy is provided by oaks or by conifers. Varieties of this species, and of the other species I have knowledge of, flower very young; it is normal to see a camellia bush eighteen inches high covered with blossom, and I have a notion that this habit inhibits growth. As they can be moved without harm during their early years, it is possible to plant them close and at the front of a shaded shrub border at first, moving them as they get too big for that position. As an example of their precocious flowering, my own *C.* × *alba-simplex*, a single-flower beauty of great purity, bore three flowers when it was one foot tall, following a winter when the temperature had been down to seven degrees Fahrenheit.

The most spectacular camellia is the old garden variety of the species *C. reticulata*, a variety selected in China centuries ago and grown here for 150 years. This spring-flowering species is not very hardy and should only be planted where frosts are slight and of brief duration. Its flowers are blush-pink and the size of tea plates. Varieties and hybrids of *C. saluensis* are as hardy as *C. japonica*; the numerous flowers are soft pink and borne over a season of many weeks; they set fruit regularly and the seed, ripe in September, germinates fairly easily in gentle heat with lots of water. Its best hybrids are a *saluensis* × *cuspidata*, 'Cornish Snow', and the *williamsi* garden camellias, the best being 'Donation' which has shell-pink to peach-pink flowers and is superb.

I am writing this in the second half of October. There are about thirty camellia plants in the garden, none planted more than ten months ago and none more than four years old. The flower-buds on my small specimen of 'Narumi-Gata' are now showing colour, for 'Narumi-Gata' flowers in November and December. This is because it is a variety of *C. sasanqua*, the winter-flowering camellia of Japan. If this species has not been as widely planted as it could and should have been, it is not because it is not hardy: it will stand thirty or more degrees of frost without showing the slightest resentment. But its flowers, of course, are apt to be browned by frost, although in some varieties they seem to remain undamaged even covered with icicles. In any case, of late our winters have been postponed until January, November and December are often very mild even in the east, and you can always pick the flowers before a severe frost if you listen to the forecasts. 'Narumi-Gata' has large, white flowers and they are fragrant.

I also have here a small specimen of the variety 'Crimson King', which has an earlier season. 'Narumi-Gata' starts in November and flowers until February; 'Crimson King' starts in October and flowers until January. The flowers are large and crimson but not fragrant. I am not sure, but I believe that fragrance in winter-flowering camellias derives not from *sasanqua* but from another species which often appears in nurserymen's lists as a variety of *sasanqua*, and that is *C. oleifera*. Perhaps this is a garden species, though Bean treats it as a natural one.

C. s. var. *rosea plena* has about the same season and much the same strong, bushy growth as 'Narumi-Gata', but its fully double flowers are pink. I am much less bigoted in my preference for single over double flowers in the case of camellias, because the form of the flower, in good varieties, is so perfect, so almost stylised. *C. japonica* doubles are apt to bear curiously piebald or striped pink and white flowers, slightly reminiscent of the rose commonly and, I believe, mistakenly, called 'York and Lancaster'. I do not care for this and I have not seen it in *sasanqua* varieties, but it may occur in them, too.

Although *C. japonica* varieties seem best planted in semi-shade or even in quite deep shade, though they should have clear sky, not tree-tops, right above them, it is possible and perhaps desirable to plant winter-flowering camellias with some exposure to direct sunshine. It is true that the same winter sun which warms the buds into flower may, by thawing them out too quickly after frost, damage them as well. This can be avoided if the shrubs can be given such a position that the sun does not reach them until an hour or so before noon—that is, if they can be given a place with exposure to the south and south-west, but protection from the south-east and east, which is, in any case, desirable, for no evergreen enjoys days of drying and freezing east wind.

I do not think it wise to use manufactured fertilisers to hasten the growth of camellias, and in any case it is by no means sure that they respond; if you want to hurry them up a bit, mix dried blood with Irish moss-peat, which as a pH of 4, and use that as a mulch; and keep them well watered all the time.

Geranium III. Tuberosum.

Chapter 11

And other Winter Flowers

When we moved to Devonshire I flattered myself that at last it would be worth my while to plant for winter flower. Our first winter—the one of our move—was encouragingly mild and wet. Then, *âte* following close upon *hubris*, came the severe winter of 1961–62; and the atrocious winter of 1962–63. It begins to look as if the period of mild winters is over. But we still persist in our belief that Devon winters are mild, or, at least act, in the garden, as if we still believed it.

Fortunately, there are some genera, and those among the most pleasing in their forms and colours, which seem more or less indifferent to weather.

THE HELLEBORES

January 30, 1960

For years I had no success in trying to establish Christmas and Lenten roses, the hellebores, in our garden. There was no apparent reason for this failure. The genus (*Helleborus*) has a score of species, and all of them, as well as their hybrids, like some shade, rather heavy, moist soil, and good drainage. These conditions we could give them. There is a good deal of chalk in our soil, but these plants do not object to that.* Moreover, a wood not very far away was, and is, completely carpeted with the sub-shrubby *H. foetidus* which is with *H. viridis*, one of the two species of this genus native to England. This species, often as much as two feet tall in the wood in question, has dark, shiny, rather rubbery-looking foliage, and green, cup-shaped flowers. It flatly refused to grow in our garden.

In due course I discovered that the hellebores are among those plants which must be moved as soon as they have finished flowering, or even while the last flowers of the season are still in being. Also that they ought to be moved very quickly, spending as little

* This was in Kent.

time as possible out of the ground. Once we had realised that, there was no further difficulty. Even so, the one species which refuses to live with us is our own *H. foetidus*. Fortunately, it is not one of the best, and as it does not flower until April, it cannot be regarded as valuable, since what we look for in the genus is the winter-flowering habit.

The two species I prefer among the dozen or so I have seen in flower, and certainly the best in our garden, are *H. niger*, and its successor in point of time. *H. macranthus*. *H. niger* is the Christmas rose, but it never flowers by Christmas in our garden. It is, however, usually in flower in the first week of January: the name Christmas rose is quite an old one, so that, if we nowadays find it in flower on, say, January 5, it would, under the Old Calendar, have been in flower by Christmas. It is an evergreen rarely a foot tall, with pure white flowers about two inches in diameter. In some plants the flowers are tinged with pink, in ours with pale yellow. It is perhaps the harsh time of year at which it flowers that gives the blooms an unearthly, transparent luminescence which makes this species so beautiful. If one has enough to make picking flowers for the house worth while, it is a good idea to place a cloche over one or two clumps, not to force the flowers, but to protect them from damage. They last very well in water.

At the moment of writing, while *H. niger* is in full flower, the base of the leaf-stalks of *H. macranthus* is a tight mass of flower-buds, and some of the buds are beginning to rise on their stems. Our single, large clump of this species grows at the base of a cypress where it is perfectly happy and can be seen from the sitting-room window. The first flowers will appear towards the end of this month, and if past experience is anything to go by, the plant will still be carrying numerous fine flowers at the end of April. It always gives us this three or four months' continuous display and provides flowers for the house through times of snow and frost. Like *H. niger*, it is an evergreen, but it is an altogether bigger, more substantial plant, with longer flower-stems and rather larger flowers, of the same ethereal white shot with greenish-yellow. Flowering with it, or a little later, is *H. abschasicus*, with much the same habit but pink flowers. We have yet to establish it here.

It is a good plan with this genus to devote a bed to it, as near the house as possible, and to plant for succession, even though this is rendered unnecessary by the long flowering season of some species and their hybrids. Succeeding *H. macranthus* comes *H. odorus*, a species which comes from the Balkans and bears its yellow-green cup-shaped flowers on eighteen-inch stalks in February. The flowers are sweetly fragrant. And, finally, to wind up the winter by flowering in March is a species which I have not yet established in our garden but have seen flourishing elsewhere in the parish, *H. corsicus*, which is almost a shrub, its tall flower-stalks carrying upwards of a dozen yellowish-green, two-inch flowers.

Those are the species with which I have experience, but I propose to extend it by at least one more, the beautiful Caucasian *H. guttatus*, first because it has larger and more spectacular flowers than the others, and, secondly, because it is another of the species which really flowers in winter, beginning with January. The flower-stems are very tall, up to four-feet, the flowers as big as a coffee saucer, white, rose, and cream, spotted purple. It is, however, rather difficult to buy plants; in fact, I have not yet succeeded in doing so. In addition to these and quite a lot more species, there are numerous hybrids. But named varieties of the hellebores seem all to be of the later-flowering *H. orientalis*. These, the Lenten roses, I hope to deal with later; they are not really winter-flowering kinds.

The hellebores are, of course, Ranunculaceae, and so are the next most valuable of the winter-flowering herbaceous perennials, the Winter Aconites. With these I had exactly the same difficulty as with the hellebores: however often and carefully I planted the tuberous roots one buys in shops, nothing whatever came up. But in the garden of a friend who lives near Canterbury the aconites have become quite a serious weed, spreading like wildfire. They are, moreover, so large and fine, with such luminous golden-yellow flowers, that I think they must be the hybrid called *tubergeniana* (*Eranthis cilicica* × *E. hyemalis*). At all events I was given a good big box full of these aconites, lifted without much disturbance and swiftly replanted in our own garden. Since then we have not looked back, and the first flower opened this year on January 3. It looks very much as if *Eranthis* is another of the genera best moved at the height of, or just after, the plant's most active season. Books, and nurserymen, generally advise moving aconites in early autumn. In my view the time to move them is just after flowering, and while the very short-lived leaves are still green and fresh. Now that we have established aconites, we are gradually increasing the number of their sites in the garden, planting them under shrubs and in the wild garden, where we hope that they will seed themselves and increase, for the warm yellow of these charmingly formal little flowers is a great comfort in mid-winter.

Ideally, aconites and snowdrops go together, and where they are so established nothing looks pleasanter under trees. But here, yet again, we have had precisely the same difficulty. Dry snowdrop bulbs bought in shops never—with us—grow. We must have planted hundreds, but it has all been wasted money and effort. I am not suggesting that this is the general, or even a common, experience; but it is certainly mine. I find nothing to account for it in the books. But after some years of such setbacks, we tried getting bulbs from a neighbour as soon as the flowers were dead, but before any withering of the leaves had started, and in clumps with the earth still on them. This was better: we at least got *some* snowdrops, although they are still relatively unsatisfactory in our garden.*

Galanthus, the genus to which snowdrops belong, has about fifteen species. The so-called common snowdrop, the one most usually grown, is *G. nivalis*, but when you have said that, you have not said very much, for it is very variable in form and markings depending on whether your stock originally came from Mount Athos, or the Caucasus, or south-east Europe, or one of a dozen other places where distinct varieties are found. The species which gardeners usually refer to as giant snowdrop, a very fine kind, is *G. elwesii*. It comes from Asia Minor and it should be given a particularly favourable site fully exposed to the sun. But some large snowdrops are hybrids: those, for example, between *G. nivalis* and *G. plicatus*, a Crimean species not very easy to distinguish from the common snowdrop, have much larger flowers than either parent species. And *plicatus* has its own large flowered variety, *maximus*. But whatever the species, size or form, I wish someone could tell me whether it is the soil or the gardener who is at fault in the matter of my failure to persuade these enchanting little winter flowers to increase and flourish with us.

* This was in Kent.

SOME WINTER-FLOWERING SHRUBS
October 29, 1960

Perhaps the greatest change in our gardens which has taken place in the last half-century has been in their winter beauty. The Victorians made great use of evergreens, many of which had been introduced by their predecessors of the eighteenth century. These evergreens were greatly valued: they were foremost in Gilbert White's mind when he wrote to Daines Barrington about the bitter winter weather of 1768: '. . . the snow on the author's evergreens was melted every day, and frozen intensely every night; so that laurestines, bays, laurels and arbutuses looked, in three or four days, as if they had been burnt in the fire.' For those gardeners who have valued evergreens, what follows is worth noting. White says: '. . . a neighbour's plantation of the same kind, in a high, cold situation, where the snow was never melted at all, remained uninjured.' And he goes on: 'Therefore it highly behoves every planter who wishes to escape the cruel mortification of losing in a few days the labour and hopes of years, to bestir himself on such emergencies . . . and to see that his people go about with prongs and forks, and carefully dislodge the snow from the boughs: since the naked foliage will shift much better for itself, than where the snow is partly melted and frozen again.'

It was for the most part after White's day that the exotic conifers were added to Victorian gardens. But there seem to have been very few winter-flowering shrubs available to gardeners until this century.

Viburnum fragrans was introduced from China in 1909. It is a deciduous shrub and my own specimen, at nine years of age, is eight feet tall and about five feet through, and increasing in substance every year. It is not a very elegant shape, but it is improving with age. Propagating it is no problem because it has a habit of self-layering its lower branches; if none happen to be near enough to the soil, it is easy to peg one down. It is usually said to begin flowering in November, but there are several strains or forms, and ours usually produces a few flowers in September, more in October and November, and flushes throughout the winter and into the early spring. Its flowers are modest little pinky white clusters, with a delicious spicy scent, very striking in a warm room when a few sprays are cut and brought indoors.

Good though it be, I would not plant the species, but one of the better forms of *V. fragrans* × *V. grandiflorum* called *V.* × *bodnantense*. The latest and perhaps best of these is Messrs R. C. Notcutt's 'Deben', but this is a recent introduction, and better known is 'Dawn': the best specimen I have seen is about ten feet tall and eight feet through, and from October until March it is covered with flower clusters, twice the size of those produced by *V. fragrans*, and which, in bud, are a vivid pink, though the flowers are white when they open. 'Dawn' is as fragrant as the parent species.

It is at this time of year that *Arbutus unedo* is in its great glory, with last year's fruit beginning to turn vivid scarlet, while this year's flowers, each individual like a floret of lily-of-the-valley but waxy and almost translucent, hang in graceful racemes. There is surely no lovelier ornament of the winter garden. But I have written of this splendid shrub before and will add here only the reminder that, though an ericaceous plant, it does very well on chalk.

A surprising number of gardeners say 'witch hazel' when they mean *Hamamelis mollis*. Witch hazel is *H. virginiana*, flowers in October, and is not nearly so fine a plant. The type *H. mollis* was introduced in the late nineteenth century but does not seem to have made much of an appearance in gardens until well into the twentieth. It is, at its best, a stout, handsome shrub whose young branches are covered with a soft grey or buff down and whose substantial, hairy leaves of a beautiful hazel green have much the same colour on the reverse side. The curiously starry, golden-yellow flowers with mahogany-red calyces first appear in January and are at their best in February, when our native hazels are in flower. A variety called *pallida*, with soft yellow instead of hard gold petals, was introduced about twenty-five years ago. Both should be planted.

I have heard the name Winter Sweet applied to more than one plant, but I believe that it properly belongs to *Chimonanthus praecox*. This is probably one of the oldest winter-flowering shrubs in our gardens, having been brought here from China at least two centuries ago. Yet it is not as common as it might be. In the open it reaches about eight feet, but it will go higher against a tall wall. Being deciduous, the flowers, which begin in November and continue to burgeon until March, appear on the naked, much branched stems. They are about an inch in diameter, with narrow waxy yellow petals and purple centres, so that they look starry. And they are very sweetly scented.

Being a horticultural optimist—probably to make up for pessimism in other fields—I always regard February as the beginning of spring: technically, however, it is still winter, so that *Daphne mezereum*, which flowers in that month, can be considered as an ornament of the winter garden. In the type, the fragrant flowers are purple and I like neither their colour nor their clotted look: I would, therefore, plant var. *alba* instead, or, best of all, a group of daphnes, for they are small shrubs, with one purple among the whites.

Progress notwithstanding, the best winter climber is still *Jasminum nudiflorum*, with its bright green naked stems and brilliant yellow flowers all through the winter. Only, of course it is not really a climber at all, but a sprawler. True, you can tie it up and keep tying it up, so that it is forced to clothe a wall—a north one will do quite as well as a south—but what this admirable plant really wants to do is not to climb up but to fall down. If your garden is on several levels, it can be set on a high place and allowed to cascade downwards. But I did recently see an ingenious way of making it really cover a wall, and yet allow its flowering shoots to droop. The roots had been planted very close to the wall—this matters less, in that the species seems to be able to flourish in either bone-dry soils, sodden soils, or no soil at all—and then a screen of wire netting fixed to battens at an inch or two from the face of the wall. The main stems of the jasmine had been kept inside the netting, but all the sideshoots, at levels from a foot or two from the soil to the top of the wall, had been allowed to come through the netting, which in the end they more or less concealed.

Another good and this time uncommon winter-flowering climber for the sheltered garden in one of the milder counties, is *Clematis calycina*. This species is an evergreen introduced from south Europe in the late eighteenth century, but rarely seen in gardens today. The ferny foliage turns a rich deep bronze in winter and the flowers, which appear quite freely from November to February, are curiously like certain winter-flowering hellebores: they are about two inches in diameter, greenish-white and spotted reddish-purple. It is useless to plant this clematis or its near relative *C. balearica*, where keen frost is to be expected.

Among the flowering cherries, *Prunus subhirtella* var. *autumnalis* is a small, twiggy tree which bears a mass of delicate single-white flowers in late October or early November, and again in flushes during December and January, and often into March. *Prunus davidiana* is not a cherry, but either an almond or a peach: it has an ungraceful erect habit, but the large rose-pink flowers appear in February, and there are white-flowered and red-flowered varieties.

FLOWERS IN DECEMBER
December 24, 1960

The garden plants which are in bloom at the beginning of December are of two kinds: the belated flowers of autumn which look rather dashed and *fin de saison*; and those whose proper flowering time it is. Chrysanthemums can be given an extended season, at least until a sharp frost kills them, by erecting an all-round screen of hop-netting. This year we have had no real frost yet, with the result that nasturtiums, one or two 'Bowles hybrid' veronicas, and, surprisingly, fuchsia, are still in flower, as well as a few penstemons, roses of course, and some antirrhinums which were not intended to flower at all this year.

To me there is a definite distinction in the appearance of the flowers which are simply lingering on, and those which are really in season now, though I would perhaps be hard put to it if required to define that distinction. These autumn and early winter-flowering plants, again, are of two kinds: those which are by nature winter-flowering; and those which flower in the summer of the southern hemisphere, or rather in its spring, and, having been brought north of the equator, have still not changed their habit and seem to be governed by some sort of time mechanism rather than by the seasonal weather. I daresay that some scientific work has been done on this but I confess that I have not come across any explanation of the fact that, for example, *Schizostyllis coccinea*, the Crimson Flay or Kaffir Lily of South Africa, about which I was so enthusiastic when I first discovered it in a Devon garden and transplanted it to Kent, persists in flowering in October, November, and well into December, instead of changing its habit to bloom in our spring. I can only suppose that day length and temperature of an English autumn are insufficiently different from those of a South African spring to upset the plant's habit. At all events I can report that during the first week of December we were still picking, in Kent, from their plantation at the foot of a dwarf wall facing south, very fine spikes of both the crimson-flowering type and the pink 'Viscountess Byng'.

Of all the autumn and winter-flowering herbaceous or tuberous-rooted plants, however, there are two which seem to me to surpass the rest, their frail beauty of form and colour is in such sharp and moving contrast with the rough grimness or tranquil gloom of the season: these two are *Iris unguicularis* and *Helleborus niger*.

We had a good deal of difficulty in establishing *I. unguicularis*, which used to be more euphoniously called *I. stylosa*, in Kent. And having succeeded at last, are now obliged to leave it. And despite the ugly, untidy mass of foliage which it produces, and which is its worst fault as a garden plant, we shall try to grow it in all its varieties in our new Devon garden. The only one which is perfectly easy to buy is the type and this, with its silky, fragrant, lilac flowers, is the one most commonly met with in gardens. For years we could not get it to flower; it produced nothing but a great mass of leaves. The trouble was, and apparently usually is, too rich a soil and too much water; and possibly also summer shade. Once we had set the tuberous rootstocks on top of a bit of stony, barren soil in full sun against the wooden wall of a shed, not planting them but simply wedging them in position with bits of flint and broken brick, they began to make plenty of flowers. They receive almost no water and I cannot imagine what they find to live on. In 1960 they produced their first flower in October and have since flowered every few days. The species has a pleasant habit of so hiding its flower bud that you never see it: one day there is only leaf, the next, one or two flowers in full bloom.

Half a dozen varieties of *I. unguicularis* are listed, but I know only three. *I. u.* var. *alba* is simply the white version of the type. It seems to be rather rare, for one hardly ever sees it in gardens. Both my other varieties are deep purple *I. u.* var. *lazica* and var. *grandiflora*, and inferior to the type, yet worth growing to mix with it and bring out the delicacy of its own subtler colouring. There is a variety, which I have seen only once and that was in south Spain, *marginata*, whose violet flowers are edged with white. I have not been able to buy it.

In the case of the genus *Helleborus* our luck in exchanging gardens seems to be in. It is true that *H. viridis* completely carpets a wood not far from our house in Kent; that we have successfully grown several species and varieties; and that one, at least, a Lenten Rose, has done exceptionally well. But when I did my first hour's work in the new garden, planting rooted potentilla cuttings against the low stone wall of a small courtyard, I discovered a number of hellebores, not all of which were easy to identify; and, what really is a great stroke of luck, equal to that great bank of naturalised *Cyclamen neapolitanum* which I shall always maintain was what, with the cedar, made us buy the house, there are numerous fine plants of what appears to be the *altifolius* variety of *H. niger*. I say, 'appears to be', because I must say that I find the varieties of hellebore very hard to identify; authorities differ in their botanical description from book to book; furthermore, there are probably many garden hybrids which have not been described at all, especially in old gardens. Thus the plants in our new garden, while they answer more or less to the description of *H. n.* var. *altifolius* are not yet in flower, which that variety should have been since late October. On the other hand, its flower buds are much too advanced for the type, for although that is called Christmas Rose I for one have never seen it in flower before mid-January, unless protected by a cloche throughout the autumn. In any case, the plants do not look like the type, nor do they look like the magnificent 'Bath Variety'.

Whatever our hellebores may be, they have seeded themselves quite freely, and there are some dozens of seedlings to transplant to other parts of the garden.

I have already written about the impression made on me by the acacias, including the florist's mimosa, whole forests of them in flower on a mountain road between the Portuguese-Spanish frontier and Lisbon. I have always intended to grow this tree in one or more of its numerous varieties, if I had a garden which was warm enough. Given a protected site, mimosa will grow farther east than is generally realised. I remember a house near Havant, during the war, where an enormous mimosa tree had grown clean through the shattered roof of a courtyard conservatory and had filled the whole angle between two of the house walls, where just after Christmas of a coldish winter, it was magnificently in flower. We associate this lovely flowering tree with the south of France and, of course, with Australia where most species come from, but, in fact, it does particularly well in Brittany, whose climate does not differ from that of our own south-western counties. Mimosa cannot be grown in the open in Kent, but I had a young specimen doing well in the greenhouse.

On the very day that I drove this, with some other plants which we are moving, down to Devon, I paid a short visit to the beautiful gardens of an estate very near to our new house.* And there, just in time to enable me to copy the notion, I saw what I have never seen before: a mimosa grown and trained to cover a vast area of the wall of a house. The work has been very skilfully done so that the whole wall is covered from a foot or two above soil level, to the eaves, with a close texture of the bright green ferny foliage. Another smaller area of wall has been similarly treated. Both looked like vertical lawns, and I noticed that the flowers were just beginning to show colour. The spectacle of this wall mimosa in full bloom will be something to look forward to. Meanwhile I have, of course, planted my own small mimosa against the wall of our house, with the same idea in mind. The genus is a very fast growing one, so that clothing a wall should not take too many years. I noticed that even in the warm climate of South Devon, the gardeners had 'lagged' the main trunk of the tree with sacking, presumably against the danger of a severe winter, which even Devon suffers from time to time; and which in East Kent killed a similarly trained tree on the wall of Withersdane Hall, Wye College, after three years' magnificent display.

PRELUDE
February 24, 1962

The first three days of February were mild and soft in south Devonshire, with that alternation of sunshine and cloud, with an occasional shower which makes the climate here so interesting and good for plants. The birds sang as if spring had come, the grass was growing and a good deal of bud movement was apparent to

* Dartington Hall. The species is *Acacia dealbata*.

anyone who looked as closely as we do. If the voice of the turtle was not yet heard in the land, the less harmonious one of the rooks certainly was; I fear they will again build in our tall remaining *Pinus insignis*, which is a nuisance. That is, of course, an 'early' part of the country but what we have in flower in early February is certain to flower all over the south within a few days, and all over the north within a couple of weeks. Some of these precocious plants are worth noting for future planting.

There is no need to say anything more than I have already done about snowdrops; they were a white groundsheet wherever we looked. Certain places which had, we thought, been carefully cleared of them last summer, and the bulbs replanted elsewhere in order to make lawn-mowing easier, seemed as crowded with the little white and green hoods as ever. Among them, and again there is no need to say much, were, of course, the gold and the blue crocuses and many of the earliest daffodils were in tall bud. Although none of our very early white sweet-scented violets were out yet, there were a few blue ones and also the 'Princess of Wales' cultivated variety was already carrying a few of its enormous flowers; I even found a couple of premature flowers on the Parma violets planted last summer. Of the daphnes at least four should be in flower at this season: the *odora*, its variety *odora variegata*, and the two mezereums, the type and the white. I have been able to confirm, this season, how much finer a plant is the white, by the way. It is true that, where it will flourish, *D. mezereum* with its curiously rosy-purple flowers, is a pretty sight, although I don't really like the colour, but the white variety has a purity and a quality of radiance the other lacks; moreover, although I am not experienced with it, I am assured that it is much more robust than the type which, you will remember, has a way of dying suddenly because of some virus disease; apparently the white variety is more resistant.

We had three kinds of hellebore in flower or nearly in flower, four if you count the not really very decorative *H. viridis* which in my perhaps perverse opinion, is a very handsome plant for its splendid foliage when it is *not* in flower and which, in any case, holds its pale closed buds in suspense for many weeks before it actually opens them much later in the year. The attractive ones were the Christmas Rose, as usual a month late, though some people have strains which really do flower at Christmas; a very lovely rose-pink species or perhaps variety, with enormous leaves, which I have not yet identified to my own satisfaction, and the reddish-purple *abschasicus*. We could, of course, have others, and I should like one day to make a collection of the really early ones. There used to be and doubtless still is a fine bed of many sorts at Sissinghurst, against one of the walls which enclose the herb garden there. But, as I recall them, they were later kinds, Lenten Roses; and for my taste many of the species are too tall for their form.

That remarkable shrub *Coronilla glauca* was in flower; it always is. It is a curious fact that hardly anyone looks twice at this shrub and yet it is well worth attention, with its always bright clean blue-green foliage and its little clusters of golden pea-flowers. It's an odd plant, for it rarely becomes untidy. What happens to the dead flowers? It always looks as if someone went over it every day and tidied it up, whereas, in fact, one never does anything to it at all. In the south-west and along the south coast, and I daresay in the west also, this shrub flowers all through the winter, spring and summer; in the less favoured parts of the country it flowers in spring and early summer. I like to let it straggle but with pruning it can become a very neat and compact plant. Also still in flower, and that since November, were bushes of *Viburnum fragrans*. The best of the varieties of this species is the one called × *bodnantense*, and apart from that one I am not at all sure that I would grow this shrub at all but for one thing, the delicious scent which it imparts to a room if you cut some sprays and bring them into the house. Ours are still too young for that. In winter this viburnum is gawky, and in summer its flowerless foliage is rather dull; I have literally never seen a specimen of the species, in any variety which was not unshapely.

In the last week of January I paid a flying visit to old friends at Wye College. We were taken round that most exquisitely well kept of all medium-sized gardens, Withersdane, the principal residential house of the College. This garden is interesting and beautiful at all times of year and if a plant *can* be grown well, then it is grown well there. It was, therefore, with relief that I saw the unsightliness of the Wye *Iris unguicularis*. With this iris one is in exactly the same difficulty, only much more so, as with the viburnum: it is an untidy mass of tatty-looking foliage among which the very lovely flowers are more or less concealed. On the other hand one certainly wants these flowers for the house. The only thing to do is to plant the iris in some sunny, well-exposed corner of the kitchen garden. I was much taken at Withersdane with a specimen of *Chimonanthus praecox* (*fragrans*) very prettily trained against a wall and richly in flower. This is a shrub which everyone should have; its curious, fleshy, yellowish-green flowers have a strong, spicy scent and are singularly beautiful in detail, with the centre of tiny petals purplish-red in contrast with the yellow outer ones and the sepals. It can be grown, of course, as a bushy plant standing free, but it seems to flower more richly and to grow taller when trained against a wall. I once saw this plant very cleverly used in a north Italian garden. It had been planted on the south side of an ancient and gaunt conifer, I don't know which one, and as it grew the branches were trained round the trunk so as to embrace it. The chimonanthus was an old and very big plant, and the lower eight or nine feet of the tree trunk had become closely netted in chimonanthus branches which flowered freely, the flowers standing out brilliantly against the black bark of the tree. I recall the flowers as quite bright yellow, not the pale, translucent colour of the chimonanthus one sees as a rule in England: I assume that it was the variety *grandiflorus*.

The flowers of our young *Hamamelis mollis* were over before the end of January. This Chinese witch hazel is usually at its best in early January, but its relation, the Japanese witch hazel, *H. japonica*, which is almost as beautiful a shrub, is often still in flower in February, so both should be planted. Meanwhile, the earliest of our rhododendrons was showing colour on February 2, and this is a very young plant which has not been here for a year yet. *R. mucronulatum* is a deciduous rhododendron which comes from China and Korea. It has a wiry, leggy growth of thin, tough stalks which, in summer, are covered with bright, insubstantial, pointed leaves. But at flowering time these stems are naked, and at the tip of each one is carried a cluster of five or six flowers which may open several at a time or singly and in succession. They are quite large, about one and a half inches in diameter when fully open, and the same colour, or almost as *Daphne mezereum* flowers. The flowering time varies with the weather; it can be as early as Christmas Day—it often is at Kew—or as late as April Fool's Day.

If it flowers early and is then caught by a frost—Bean says that five degrees will scorch the flowers—then it often produces a second crop of flowers later as if determined to produce a crop of seed despite the weather. It is such a good flowering shrub that I should be inclined to make special arrangements to grow it even in a chalk garden, by isolating it in a tub of peat safely above the general level of the garden.

NOVEMBER FLOWERS

December 1, 1962

In mid-November I made a few notes of plants which were still good to look at in our garden, not counting those which have been planted for autumn colour, and which almost all failed to show any colour this year; and not counting foliage plants like, for example, the 'Silver Queen' variety of *Pittosporum tenuifolium* which is beautiful all the year round. I noted that the schizostyllis were still quite effective, with plenty of flower; that many of the violets which seed themselves all over this garden were in flower several months too soon; that primroses and polyanthus had a few flowers; that the dead heads of hydrangeas were still attractive; that most of the simpler pansies were flowering—some of them will keep this up throughout the winter if past records are anything to go by. We even had a few wallflowers producing either a second crop of flowers or next spring's crop in advance. My wife treats a certain number of wallflowers as short-lived perennials by scrupulously cutting off the old flowers as soon as they are over and before the seeds form. They will then, unless the winter be very harsh, live to flower a second and, rarely, a third season. Best of all the groundlings were our fine collection of *Cyclamen neapolitanum*. Incidentally I wonder if other gardeners have the difficulty which I have in finding ripe seeds of this cyclamen. We have hundreds of plants yet I am lucky if I find half a dozen ripe pods of seed. I have no idea what happens to them. Mice? But we have two very industrious and predatory cats who kill any mice within the place, and incidentally have taken to fishing the golden orfe out of the little lily pond. And when I do find seeds of the cyclamen they take a whole year to germinate however fresh they may be when sown.

In my notes I discounted certain plants which were flowering quite out of season: three rhododendrons were doing this, including 'Elizabeth'. The other two, 'Blue Diamond' and *R.* × 'Yellow Hammer' very frequently flower in the autumn, so does *R. forestii* var. *repens*. By far the most beautiful flowers in November were the fuchsias and the hebes. I really do not know why more gardeners do not treat fuchsias as border and shrubbery plants. All that is necessary is to find out from a good nursery which of the very many varieties are called 'hardy'. None, of course, are hardy in the ordinary sense of the word. But those which are least tender can be treated not exactly as shrubs, but at least as perennials. They will go on flowering magnificently until the first sharp frost. Then, after that happens, cut them down to good hard wood (not to the ground, it is not necessary) and put a cloche over them, closing the ends with pieces of glass held in position by cane pushed into the ground. If you do this and unless the winter is very hard indeed, next year's new growth will spring from the wood you have left, and you will have a very big plant indeed, probably at least four feet tall by August. If the winter is so hard that the cloche affords too little protection, then your fuchsia will spring from below ground to make a perfectly good and floriferous plant by late summer. It is not true that this can be done only in the south-west. One friend of mine does it in a very cold part of Kent, and most successfully. My own triumph this year has been with the tender *Fuchsia splendens*: this stood out last winter, was killed to the ground, and sprang up again to make a good plant flowering beautifully in October and November. The flowers are long tubes with reflexed petals and are salmon pink with prettily protruding anthers.

I shall say nothing of the beauty of our wall-grown abutilons at this season, because they are confined by tenderness to the mildest gardens. But not only was the little hebe which is probably 'Everleigh Seedling' (but which may be one of half a dozen other kinds judging by the heavy mail I have had from readers about it), again in flower but a lot of the others were flowering, not the older plants, but those which are about a year from the 'cutting' stage. We had, in November, red-flowered and blue-flowered hebes blooming away merrily, in surprising variety.

Of our ceanothuses there is one which seems hardly ever to

stop flowering. This is the hybrid called 'Gloire de Versailles'. It has very large panicles of soft lavender-blue flowers and there were half a dozen good sprays of blossom in mid-November. In my opinion, and we have grown this hybrid for many years, in Kent and again in Devon, 'Gloire de Versailles' never lives very long. And the reason may well be that it flowers itself to death. In most parts of Britain it needs the shelter of a wall, for it is not very hardy.

It goes without saying that in November we had many roses in flower. Most of the 'species' and 'old-fashioned' roses, indeed, were over, even to shedding their leaves in some cases, although *Rosa moyesii* was, as usual, a glory of huge scarlet hips and the *spinosissimas* were still handsome, their hips being black. But not only did we have hybrid teas in flower, which is normal for November in many parts of Britain, we also found that the hybrid musks were flowering well, with a great many buds promising blossom later in the year. And, considered as very late-flowering shrubs, they are far preferable to the HTs. The latter, it is true, had plenty of bud and some flower; but the flowers were very much dashed by rain and wind, and the plants themselves, except in the case of the beautiful single-flowered. 'Ellen Wilmott', looked rather wintry. Not so the musks; their foliage was as fresh, their growth as vigorous, their flowers, though not so numerous, as intact and their fragrance as strong in November as in July. I have not before had much experience of these roses, and I must say that they were superb; I shall be interested to see how they behave later; at the time I made my November notes they had all the air of plants which intend to be evergreen.

I believe that I have hardly ever said anything in these pages about berrying plants for autumn colour. The fact is that we lose so many berries to birds here that growing shrubs and trees especially for their fruit is rather a discouraging occupation. Moreover, although we have planted, for example, several species of berberis, they are all too young as yet to be worth writing about. But I happen, by virtue of being locally known as a plant lover, to have come across a berrying shrub of quite outstanding loveliness this autumn. Across the garden from our house is the village school and the schoolmistress has become a friend. One of her pupils brought from her grandmother's garden a spray of a shrub, in fruit, wanting to know its name. It was brought to me. It was clearly an evergreen, with very handsome oblong-lanceolate leaves and clusters of small fruit growing from the tips of short twigs or fruiting-spurs. These 'berries' were a clear butter yellow with a noticeable brown 'eye'. I found the spray altogether more attractive than any red-berried shrub. After a good deal of difficulty and doubt I came to the conclusion that the shrub, which stands about fifteen feet high and is a grand sight, is *Cotoneaster salicifolia* 'Fructu-luteo' and I have every intention of planting a group of it somewhere. The berries are very like those of *Pyracantha rogersii* var. *lutea* another good yellow-berried shrub.

Coronilla glauca began to flower in October, having left off its last season of flowering in August. By mid-November it was quite covered with its graceful little corymbs, if that is the right word, of bright yellow pea-flowers and we know from experience that it will now be continuously in flower until next July. In the east, however, it will not as a rule begin to flower until April. Laurustinus, needless to say, was in full flower by the first week of November and it will be in flower for almost as long as the coronilla. For perpetual flowering these two shrubs are unequalled; among the herbaceous plants, I think it is the hardy geraniums or cranesbills which give us the longest season in flower.

Three weeks after that article appeared began the twelve weeks of the most bitter winter weather in living memory. Frost was unbroken throughout January, February and March and the snow so deep that for three weeks we were unable to use the car at all and for some days were confined entirely to the house, for even on foot it was dangerous to go out. Friends living on Dartmoor were supplied with food by helicopter. Many of our young tender plants, were killed. But a year later I was back to the subject of early winter flowers.

THOMAS HOOD REFUTED

December 14, 1963

It was, I believe, the poet Hood who wrote that work which begins

No sun, no moon;

No morn, no noon;
No dawn, no dusk, no proper time of day . . .

and which ends

No fruits, no flowers, no leaves, no birds—
NOVEMBER!

Of course, the unhappy man was obliged to live in London; but, moving away from that Great Wen, the poem, of which there is a great deal more in the same strain, becomes a libel. I have been looking over my weather record for the November just past; I find that we had a good many days of sunshine and that there was some sunshine on at least half the days in the month. It is true that we also had an enormous amount of rain, something like twice the average, I think; but it is also true that, for the gardener, this was a good thing: the water table was too low by the end of October; and it has been noticed by professional horticulturalists, chiefly in North America, that plants, especially evergreen shrubs, which have to endure spells of severe cold in late winter, resist better if there is plenty of water in the soil. We had many nights of clear and brilliant moonlight. The times of day were as proper as could be, marked by beautiful changes in the sky. As to leaves, not until the very end of the month were most of them off the trees, and for the greater part of the month there was a lovely display of golds and reds. Even at the very end of the month some garden shrubs and trees were still displaying handsomely, notably cotoneasters and *Eucryphia glutinosa*. The edible fruits were all gathered in; but there were still plenty of berries to be seen. Nor was it true that there were no flowers. I casually made a list as I walked round the garden before coming indoors on the last day of the month: still in flower were Kaffir lilies in both colours, one belated white agapanthus, chrysanthemums, a few *sino-ornata* gentians, and one *acaulis* gentian which seemed under the impression that it was spring and was coming splendidly into blossom. Rhododendron 'Yellow Hammer' was in flower; so were scores of primroses, two kinds of violets and *Omphalodes cappadocica*. We had good flowers on at least a dozen assorted hebes, some of which had been in flower for many weeks, perhaps eleven or twelve in one or two cases. A few of the periwinkles were in flower. Among the roses still blooming were 'Zephirine Drouhin', 'Penelope' and *sinensis mutabilis*. A large number of ericas were in flower, of course, this being the beginning of the season for *carneas. Tibouchina semi-decandra* was still flaunting its gorgeous purple against its wall. *Meconopsis cambrica* was in flower as usual, in odd corners all over the garden, although it is worth noting that in late autumn and early winter only those plants fully exposed to the sun continue to flower, while those in shade take a rest. Even a few hydrangeas were still showing fresh flower, although in most cases the heads had turned those extraordinary greens and buffs and browns with which this genus offers a second and very different display; *Helleborus foetidus* was coming into flower; both 'Hidcote' and 'Rowallane' hypericums still bore flowers.

There is no need to insist. And the November of 1963, although the day and night temperatures were perhaps unusually high, was not all that exceptional; I have notes of others as pleasant. In 1961 there were many days of sunshine in November, less rain, and much lower temperatures; I have no record of flower for that month, but we were really only beginning on our plantings at the time. November 1962 began mild and wet, but there were some cold days with sharp frost in the middle of the month which, however, ended mild again. I have records of flower for that year, including some camellias. But the leaves, in both 1961 and 1962, were not nearly so persistent on the trees, although there were not so many gales as we had this November.

I do not claim for this month of November that the display of flower is spectacular; it is, of course, sparse and scattered. But in a way it is all the more agreeable; in June one is overwhelmed; one cannot, as it were, see the trees for the wood (*sic*); but in November one can pause before each plant or group of plants which have been kind enough to go on flowering, and take in the exquisite forms and colours. And the colours themselves are not quite the same—they have less brilliance, an autumnal or even wintry fade-away look which contributes to the pleasing melancholy of the season.

In November there are certain plants which appear to be about to flower but are not; a visitor here drew attention to the way in which our *Pieris forrestii* 'Wakehurst' was covered with racemes (or should it be panicles?) of flower bud, and suggested that the plant was about to flower out of season and that this was a pity because obviously the flowers would be ruined by frost. The fact is, however, that this and other pieris, and they are representative of a small class of shrubs which have the same habit, make and display their flower buds in the autumn, hold them through the winter, and do not actually open the buds and show their flowers until the spring. This is the reason why one does not see these shrubs in the colder parts of the country as a rule: they are hardy enough for much more general planting; but only in the milder gardens do they have a chance to preserve their buds through the winter. Even in Cornwall and south Devon last winter the over-wintering flower buds of most pieris were withered by cold and as a consequence there was no flower. As it happens, even if all winters were going to be as bad, or if we had a much colder garden than is the case, *P. forrestii* 'Wakehurst' would not be left out of any planting of mine: for it is worth growing even where the flower buds are destroyed every winter. The young growth of this evergreen is a vivid, translucent crimson, far more striking than the flowers of many a good shrub. And this, again, is a score for November; for although the principal display of this very beautiful young foliage is in spring, after or during the flowering, when the plants make their main spurt of growth, yet as a rule there is a second and lesser movement in early November when the weather is mild, and this pieris may, during the first week of November, be looking very handsome indeed. Some photinias, too, although the colour of the young growth is not so fine, being a coppery red like that of the not-so-good pieris species, make a fine show in November.

A shrub which makes a very remarkable show in this same much abused month, which is very rare in gardens, and perhaps not very hardy, although the only big specimen I know was not damaged last winter, is *Euonymus fimbriatus*. According to the R.H.S. *Dictionary* it was introduced from the Himalaya in 1920; but the description in that great work says nothing of its qualities, and W. J. Bean knows it not. It makes a very large, bushy, evergreen shrub with four-inch long elliptical leaves, finely toothed. It has three colour phases: in spring the young growth turns the whole plant a fine coppery red. With the advance of the season this colour, as in other evergreens with the same habit, turns to green; but late in October and November the entire plant turns a gorgeous golden-yellow; one or two specimens of this fine euonymus would make great splashes of light in any garden big enough to hold them. The species does not seem to be in commerce, and since I have almost no experience of it in my own garden, our plants being rooted cuttings in their second year, it may, for all I know, be difficult in some way. I have never seen either the flowers or winged fruits of the species. However, they do not matter: this, like other evergreens, makes a specially fine display in the month of November, Thomas Hood notwithstanding.

WINTER FRAGRANCE

January 16, 1965

It is surprising how many of the winter-flowering plants are fragrant. We have been considering here whether it would not be possible to create a small scented winter garden, that is a corner, preferably with some shelter, in which a number of these plants would be grouped to mingle and concentrate their scent and to give importance to flowers which, with one exception, are rather insignificant when scattered all over the garden but would be effective if concentrated.

Such a garden would include, to begin with, a number of viburnums; the best of these were in full flower this winter on December 12, but they had then been flowering for some time and continued to do so thereafter. I should not, I think, put the species *fragrans* into the winter garden because × *bodnantense*, one of its hybrids, has more and larger and pinker flowers and they are just as sweet scented; there is a form of this called 'Dawn' which is the best and which carries the R.H.S. Award of Merit. One might, given enough room, plant *fragrans* 'Candidissimum' with it, for the sake of its pure white flowers.

There seems to be a good deal of loose talk in gardening circles about the sweet scent of winter-flowering mahonias. To the best of my knowledge and experience there is only one, and that is *Mahonia japonica*, all too frequently confused with *M. bealii*. For the quality of flower a number of these fine evergreens are to be preferred: *M. bealii* itself, flowering in January or February; *M. lomariifolia*, flowering in December and with really magnificent clusters of erect, butter-yellow racemes; *M. acanthifolia* with again, very handsome flowers, open in early winter, and really magnificent foliage; *M.* × 'Charity' flowering with great splendour in early winter. But, at least in my garden, none of these has a trace of fragrance nor has the enormous-leaved *M. napaulensis*. The flowers of *M. japonica*, open in mid-winter, or later, are *not* bright yellow; they are pale sulphur or deep cream; they are not in erect but in pendulous racemes; in foliage the species closely resembles *bealii* but is distinguished by the very large terminal leaflet. And this mahonia is very sweet-scented of lily-of-the-valley. Therefore one or more specimens of this would go into my scented winter garden.

If the winter garden were walled or hedged, it might be possible to plant, along the southern foot of the enclosure, not quite as understorey to the shrubs but as a kind of low background, the winter-flowering *Iris unguicularis* which many people still prefer to call *I. stylosa*. The type, and those of the varieties which I have met with, are all fragrant, and the colours vary from lilac to deep purple; there is a very beautiful white one, too. It is said that this iris will only flower if it is planted in very poor, stony soil, hardly soil at all, in fact, but gravel; and if it is so exposed that it is thoroughly baked by the summer sun. I think that the baking may, indeed, be important but despite what I wrote earlier, I have lately become doubtful about the matter of soil for I know clumps of this iris which annually produce hundreds of flowers and which are growing in quite good loam. Patience is the thing; old clumps seem usually to flower well, young ones do not. The foliage of this iris is very unsightly in the summer, but it seems to take no harm if, when the flowers begin to show in winter, the leaves are cut back with shears to half their length, to expose the flowers. On the other hand this exposure is not wise in frosty sites.

Chimonanthus praecox, formerly *fragrans*, can be planted free-standing but is best against a wall and in full sun. When it is old enough it will flower with regularity, but some gardeners I know have had this shrub for years and never yet seen a flower. The flowers, pale, waxy, cream or yellow with a purple or red stain at the heart, are among the most fragrant of all winter flowers and the winter garden should, of course, not be without this. The Award of Merit form is called 'Grandiflorus'; its flowers are yellow and the heart-stain a true red; in the variety 'Luteus' there is no red or purple stain. If the winter garden has a south-facing wall, then these Winter Sweets should be given space on it.

Our solitary young specimen of *Lonicera purpusii* began to open its flowers this winter early in December. Their fragrance is very sweet and pure, quite without spice but for that reason a favourite with many people. This is a very hardy, bushy, non-climbing honeysuckle. The flowers are rather small, cream in colour, by no means spectacular, but a well-grown bush of it can distil an astonishing volume of scent into the air. It will grow in any soil. Our specimen seems to be evergreen, taking after its *fragrantissima* parent and not after the other, the winter-flowering, fragrant, *standishii*. One might plant all three of these in a group.

Of the daphnes the best of the winter-flowering scented ones is *D. odora* of which I wrote recently that its variety *D. o.* var. *aureo-marginata* may perhaps be no variety but rather *D. japonica*. In the south and west and along the coast this daphne may be planted out in the open; but it is not perfectly hardy and should be given the shelter of a wall or of hardy evergreens in most gardens. It makes a small bush about four feet tall and as much wide, is very long-lived, is usually free flowering, the flowers being white and purple trumpets in small clusters. The scent is strong and delicious. Fortunately this is not one of the miffish daphnes, it is very willing to grow in any good loam, does not seem to mind whether the soil is limey or not, is very tolerant of shade but will grow in the sun and is, in short, one of the very best fragrant-flowered winter garden plants.

A mature and well-grown *Hamamelis mollis* is so spectacular, and is such a pleasure to the eye, that we tend to forget entirely that it also flatters the nose; the fragrance is usually faint, but very fresh and sweet and quite free from spiciness, which is a merit to some people, although personally I prefer something rather musky. The others of this genus in my garden have no scent; and the scent has been lost also in the *japonica* × *mollis* known as × *intermedia*. But in any case *mollis*, once established, and it can be difficult to start, is the best of its genus.

Scent in the flowers of Chilean plants seems to be the exception rather than the rule; I have heard this explained in the same way as the predominance of red in the flower colours: the flowers have to attract humming-birds, not insects. I have no idea whether this is true. At all events the azaras are exceptional, for they all have yellow flowers, mostly very small. *Azara microphylla*, a small and very pretty evergreen tree, is perhaps too late in flowering to belong to the winter season: it seems usually to flower in March; the scent is that of vanilla. But more remarkable for its fragrance is *A. petiolaris*, regarded as far from hardy and therefore rare in gardens and perhaps confined to the south-west, although Hillier's catalogue states that it has withstood twenty-seven degrees of frost in their nursery without suffering injury. This tall and rather narrow shrub bears its flowers in February and holds them into March; their fragrance is very remarkable, with extraordinary carrying power and if I were planting a garden for winter scent I should certainly include this azara.

Finally there is the magnificent tree-heath, *Erica arborea*. It is generally spoken of as flowering in early spring but it is still winter in this garden when it opens its myriad sweet-scented off-white flowers.

Here, finally, is a note taken from my mid-winter garden journal for 1964–65, of interest to gardeners who have greenhouses, and to which I can now add something more:

'In 1963 we had our first "crop" of lemons from the greenhouse, five or six fruits from the miniature lemon bush which came from Mauritius but is, we have been told, of Chinese origin. This year we have fruit, in greater quantity, on a young but very vigorous plant of Meyer's Lemon. This variety is said to be nearly hardy and it will stand a little frost. We have it in a greenhouse border, between one of the peach trees and a plant of *Tibouchina semidecandra* grown for its very beautiful purple flowers. The lemon tree is less trouble than any fruit tree I have ever grown; it does not need any kind of spraying, the Red Spider which has attacked one of the peaches does not invade it, it flowers almost all the time, filling the greenhouse with a delicious scent; and in January it was carrying a score of ripe fruits and a great many fruitlets of another generation. The lemons are small, whether because of the youth of the bush or naturally so we don't yet know. But they are perfectly usable and with lemons the price they are nowadays, a bush of Meyer's Lemon is well worth its space in any cool greenhouse.'

By the winter of 1965–66 this bush had proved itself one of the most valuable fruit plants we had ever grown. It had grown very fast, its fruit became larger, and it was borne in such quantity, ripening one crop in November and a small successive one in early spring, that it not only kept us in lemons of excellent quality but enabled us to give lemons away.

I. Lilium cruentum bulbiferum.

Chapter 12

Lilies

Although I did not really come to know much about the genus lilium until I made the acquaintance, which became friendship, with the greatest practical lily grower, breeder and specialist in the world, Mr Jan de Graaff of Oregon, I had, by 1960, some experience both of raising certain species from seed and of cultivating purchased bulbs of European lilies.

August 6, 1960

I confessed some time ago to being a novice with lilies; but I am beginning to find out a little about them. The policy of growing them from seed means that it will be a considerable time before we have a real show of such species and hybrids as can be grown here; but the success we have had in germinating and in growing on the seedlings of quite a number of varieties has encouraged us to make special preparation of a whole border, hitherto devoted to strawberries but now to be taken into the flower garden, so that as the young bulbs attain flowering size, we have somewhere suitable to put them. It is obvious that we are going to have far too many for the woodland part of the garden, especially as I now propose to plant more seeds of other species and hybrids.

By way of encouragement we have had a few flowers from our earlier 'pilot' attempt to grow from seed, and from the few bulbs purchased to keep us going in lilies. And this first season's experience has already taught us a good deal. The most interesting piece of information to come out of our observations touches the reaction of various kinds of lilies to high winds. Having read, for example, that *Lilium pardalinum* will not stand wind, we thought that all three groups of this beautiful orange-spotted-black turk's cap species had, in fact, been given adequate protection. However, whereas the one in the border was well out of the worst wind, the two in the woodland part of the garden turned out to be exposed to a severe south-west wind and will be so until such time as some berberis shrubs reach maturity and can screen them. The *pardalinums* in the border look happy and have flowered; the ones exposed to wind have produced flower-bud, much later, but their foliage looks for all the world as if it had been scorched by frost. But, and this is the point, *L. auratum*, planted within two yards of the woodland *pardalinums* and exposed to the same conditions exactly, have taken no harm at all, look fine, are well in bud, and their leaves, which for three days I watched streaming out like bunting in a howling sou'wester, show no damage whatsoever.

If, in that respect, the auratums, the lovely golden ray lilies of Japan which have given rise to some spectacular hybrids, have been a success, in another way they have given us our worst failure. Whereas seeds of all other kinds with one expected exception have germinated well, I have entirely failed to germinate auratum seed. The method I tried was the recommended one incorrectly called 'vernalisation' by analogue with certain treatments of wheat seed. You place the seeds, with some damp, clean sand or grit, in a glass jar, seal the jar, and put it for some weeks in a warm place, say the airing-cupboard or an electrically-heated propagator. You then take it out and place it for about a month or six weeks in the refrigerator, thereafter giving it another warm spell. I believe that the idea is to reproduce, for the seeds, the conditions as to temperature and humidity, which they would experience in nature if they fell from the seed-pod in autumn: a spell of early autumn warmth in soil still hot from the summer; a spell of severe winter cold; a spell of spring warmth. What should happen is transformation of the flat, flake-like seeds into tiny white bulbs which, when planted, at once start to grow. Whereas if you plant the seeds directly into the ground, they have to undergo the series of temperature changes described above before they can 'germinate' into bulblets and grow; planted in spring, they would not get their cold spell, and would remain ungerminated in the soil until, having experienced a winter cold spell, they would germinate a year later.

Unfortunately, nothing whatever happened to the seeds in my glass jars, although learned instructions were followed to the letter. At the end of the operation they looked precisely as they did at the beginning; assuming them to be lifeless, I threw them away. If I can get fresh seed this autumn, I shall try a different method. It will be too late to get them their warm spell out of doors, so I shall sow the seed in boxes and give them six weeks in the propagator at about seventy degrees, then put the boxes out of doors for the winter, and then bring them in and put them back in the propagator in, say, February.

Another small discovery we have made is that seeds of hybrids —we are growing several, notably Olympics, Clarion, Green Mountain, Hearts Desire—germinate more freely and the seedlings grow more vigorously than in the case with species, except *L. regale* and *L. tenuifolium*. The contrast is very striking, but unless this is a simple case of the phenomenon known as 'hybrid vigour', I have no explanation to suggest. The thing is most striking in the case of two directly comparable lots of seed, both from the same source: *L. formosanum*, the one species with which I have some experience; *L. formosanum* × *L. longiflorum*. The cross grows much faster and stouter than the species. These two are doing well in pots this year, while last year's *L. formosanum* bulbs, planted out in a specially prepared place in the shrubbery, are growing healthily and vigorously after their winter out of doors, and are obviously going to flower in September.

Of the lilies which have flowered this year, three kinds have given us particular pleasure: *L. pyrenaicum*, *L. martagon* var. *album* and *L. bulbiferum* var. *croceum*. The Pyrenaean lily is a martagon, that is a turk's cap lily, with spotted yellow flowers: ours are still very small, but the stems, covered with fine foliage topped by the charming little flowers, are delightful and incidentally the earliest lily we had yet had in the garden. Apparently, although I have never seen this for myself, this lily has naturalised itself in parts of Devonshire, increasing by self-sown seed. The white martagon looks like settling down here, is as graceful as its commoner dark maroon or brown congener, and, with its white turk's cap flowers, even more distinguished-looking.

L. bulbiferum var. *croceum* appears in most catalogues I have looked at as *L. croceum*. Its perfectly formed brilliant orange bell-flowers, held stiffly upwards and—I find this a very pleasant detail —the petals so gracefully 'waisted' towards the base as to provide drainage slots to let the rain out, last an extraordinarily long time and are so vivid that even three or four inflorescences make a spectacular flash of colour. This lily is very old in cultivation here, and is a European native. It is said to increase so rapidly by bulb offsets that the clumps have to be dug up and the new bulbs distributed as often as every third year. It is indifferent to soil, chalk-tolerant, stands up splendidly to wind and, is, in short, a most valuable lily.

Among the many kinds of lily seeds which I planted in a specially prepared seed-bed were two which I did not expect to germinate until they had been there for a full year or eighteen months: *L. martagon*, with which I already had experience using seed collected from wild plants, which germinated fifteen months after planting in some cases, in others only after two years; and *Cardiocrinum giganteum*, formerly, and in some catalogues still, *L. giganteum*. The latter have behaved according to the book and have not shown a sign of life yet. But about half the martagon seed has germinated within seven months. Why? I have no idea.

One disappointment has been with bulbils of *L. tigrinum*. According to Woodcock and Stearn, the lily grower's bible: 'The great advantage of propagation from bulbils is the rapidity with which they grow into flowering bulbs: bulbils from *L. tigrinum* var. *splendens* will sometimes flower in the first year after planting and most bulbs so produced will flower in the second year.'* Well, at ten months from planting my tiger lily bulbil plantlets are very far indeed from flowering size, being, in fact, no larger than seedlings would be. As the 'germination', if that is the word, was very good, in fact 100 per cent, I sacrificed one or two to curiosity last week and dug them up: the bulbs are not yet as large as a sixpence.

By far the oldest lily in cultivation is the Madonna lily. It was grown in Greek villa gardens, in the great Roman gardens which derived from them, and in the gardens of all medieval Europe, including Britain. Yet, curiously, it is a lily with which even the cleverest gardeners, who succeed with many other species of this genus, repeatedly fail.

THE MADONNA LILY
April 15, 1961

It might be a gardener's proverb that you can plant a Madonna

* 'Lilies of the World.'

lily but you can't make it grow. For it is a horticultural commonplace that although some lilies, and almost without question the oldest in cultivation, *Lilium candidum*, may flourish for a man's lifetime among the leeks and cabbages of a cottage garden, they will fail to respond to the loving and careful treatment of the most expert leiriophil. My own recent experience with this lily promises very well: for having only just planted a number of new Madonna lily bulbs in our Kentish garden when the decision to move west was taken, I decided that while I must leave most of these for our successor, I would take three with me. Now Madonna lilies, because they make their first growth of the season in autumn and are showing leaf throughout the winter, should be planted and left undisturbed in August. Our move was for December, and by that time the lilies were, therefore, in leaf. The three to be moved were lifted bodily, with the minimum of disturbance to the roots, into large polythene bags, transported to the new garden, and so planted. They were checked for a week or two, and then began to grow. By the end of March they were over a foot tall and growing well. It looks as if they have decided to settle down here.

Whence came this lily which has been one of the loveliest ornaments of civilisation for so long? We might suppose the biblical poets to have been familiar with it if we could trust the translators: but we cannot: they translated the Hebrew *susannath* (*susan*) by lily, which was better than the *rose* of the earliest translations, including Luther's. Sometimes they, too rendered this word *rose*, as in 'rose of Sharon' which should be 'lily of Sharon'. But even when they used lily for the Hebrew word, perhaps with the Madonna lily in mind, they were not necessarily right: this word *susan* probably refers to a coloured lily, and Victor Heyn the great philologist suggests that it may have been some kind of spectacular fritillary, perhaps a crown-imperial. The Greek word for *susan* is *krinon*; but the Greek word for the white lily is *leirion*. It would therefore seem that the Greeks did not have this lily from a Hebrew source; for it is usual to import and introduce, with a plant, its native name.

Victor Heyn, in *The Wanderings of Plants and Animals*, says that the Greek leirion (*Λειριον*) is a corruption of the Persian *lâleh*. Since the word for lily was Iranic, then, it is probable that the plant itself came from Media, reaching Greece by way of

Armenia and Phyrgia. In Greece it became Juno's flower, *Rosa Junonis*, and was said to have been made of Hera's milk as she suckled Herakles in her sleep. The lily, having settled among the Greeks, was by them taken to Italy when they sent colonies to that country. It will have reached Italy, then, some time between 700 and 500 B.C., possibly a little earlier. And from Italy, like so many of the good things we enjoy as ancient right, it came to us. And just as the Greeks had changed the name from *lâleh* to *leirion* to suit their tongues, and had attributed the flower to Hera instead of to the angel Horvadad as did the Iranians,* so in the West *leirion* became *lilium*, lily; and Our Lady was in due course appointed its patron.

The Madonna lily was already firmly established here by the thirteenth century; and in Chaucer's time both its purity of whiteness, and its Heavenly association, were proverbial; and proverbs grow slowly. The reader will recall, in the Second Nun's Tale:

> First wol I you the name of Seinte Cecilie
> Expoune, as men may in hire storie see:
> It is to sayn in English, Heven's lilie.

In the Knight's Tale Emilie's fairness is compared to 'the lilie on hire stalke grene'. And again, in the same tale,

> Upon his hand he bore for his delyt
> An eagle tame, as any lily whyte.

Now, while it is true that poets are quick to seize upon any new introduction to give freshness and a modern touch to their analogues, still I think this is evidence that these comparisons were in the vernacular. It is quite likely then that *L. candidum* was a Roman introduction; the other alternative is that it came to use with the establishment of monasteries by the gallicised Saxon clergy or by the Normans. These monastic gardeners did not plant species which were of no culinary or medicinal use: but the Madonna lily had been a medicinal, as well as a sacred, plant for a very long time, since it was used by Egyptian physicians to prepare essences and ointments. According to Woodcock and Stearn's *Lilies of the World* the Cretans also valued it as medicine; and it may have

* *The Būndahisn*, by E. W. West, Pahlavi Texts. *Sacred Books of the East*, Vol. V.

been by way of Crete that the bulbs and the name first reached the Greek mainland. The same book tells me that *L. candidum* was simply known as the White Lily until the second half of the nineteenth century, and only called the Madonna lily then because of the introduction of other white species; yet, as we have seen, Chaucer was calling it Heaven's lily, and earlier cultures had associated it with the Queen of Heaven.

No rules whatsoever can be given for success with this lily. Because it does well in a given soil and situation in one place, it does not follow that it will do so in the same conditions elsewhere. It seems likely that a south-westerly exposure is to be preferred to a south-easterly, and that, while the stalk and flowers should be in full sun, the bulbs and roots should be in shade, which means planting it among herbaceous perennials or low shrubs. Where it does decide to behave nicely, it is very hardy and reliable, coming up and flowering in beauty, year after year. Seeds are never, or at least very rarely, set. But it is very easy indeed to increase stock by lifting one bulb, breaking it up into its component scales, and planting the scales in a seed tray of John Innes No. 2 compost. Bulblets develop at the base of each scale, and as soon as they have reached a reasonable size, they can be planted where they are to remain for years. It is my own practice, when I buy *L. candidum* or any lily bulbs, to remove one or two scales from each new bulb before I plant it: this does no harm, and within a couple of years you have perhaps a dozen bulbs for every one you have paid for. The scales should be planted to about half their depth in the compost, which should be kept moist but not wet, and there is no need to lift the scales to see if bulblets have developed; simply leave the tray alone until the little lily leaves appear next to them within two or three months of planting the scales, or less.

The Madonna lily is a chalk-lover, though it will grow perfectly well in neutral and acid soils. That it is a chalk lover is well established and I am not denying it: the fact remains that we had a very curious experience with these lilies, and one which seems to cast some doubt on its calcicole nature: we had a group of Madonna lily bulbs in a very chalky part of the garden in Kent and they had always been miserable-looking, unhealthy creatures, with poor, twisted foliage and few if any flowers. I assumed that they were infected with virus disease and dug them up with the idea of burning them. My wife, however, suggested that we try them elsewhere in the garden and planted them, with a fine contempt for the pundits, in the peat 'bath' where she grew dwarf azaleas, *Thalictrum dipterocarpum* and some heathers. Well, those Madonna lilies grew away at once, produced fine healthy stalks and foliage, and flowered splendidly. I daresay that they will do so again this year. Rum.

The ordinary, sturdy cottage type of this lily is apparently still the best, but there are some other varieties. *L. candidum* var. *cernuum* has narrower petals than the type, which gives it a more graceful, starry look: it has been cultivated in England since the sixteenth century but remains uncommon. The Oregon Bulb Farms, source of so many good hybrid lilies, have given us the Cascade Strain of madonnas: they set and ripen seed and have flower stalks only about eighteen inches tall, and some other good novelties. *L. c.* var. *aureo-marginatum* has yellow edges to its leaves which merely makes it look sick. The variety *purpureum* denies the whole nature of the species by having its flowers streaked with purple. Finally, there is the Salonika variety: it flowers about ten or twelve days earlier than the type, has even wavier basal leaves, and opens its flowers so widely that they are, as it were, saucers instead of cups. What is more interesting, this alone of the older Madonna lilies sets seed freely in England, without hand pollination.

LILIES THEN PROSPER
July 29, 1961

Many lilies are among the plants which will either grow for you or which will not: I mean that, with many species, even if you have everything which your own experience or expert advice can suggest to prepare a suitable place for the lilies, it does not follow that they will succeed. I have dealt with the extreme case *L. candidum*, which *may* grow very well with you but which, if it fails, no expert in the world can help you to grow. The new, and not so new, hybrids are, on the whole, easier than the species, I find, and as I am growing some of them I shall report on them in due course. But I don't think that any real gardener is likely to fail with *all* the numerous species of this noble genus. For there are certain species which are at the same time among the easiest and the best of garden plants. Moreover, their propagation is easy; and since all lily bulbs are rather dear to very dear indeed, and lilies in the open are much better massed than in ones or twos, growing one's own bulbs from seed, bulbils or bulblets is very rewarding.

L. regale was first flowered in England by Messrs Veitch and Son in 1905, from bulbs sent home by Wilson from Szechwan in 1903. This lily is hardy practically everywhere in Britain, will prosper in poor soil or in rich loam, and is tolerant of chalk. Its bulbs produce numerous bulblets round the top of the mother-bulb, so that increase is easy. A good, mature specimen of this lily will have a bulb six inches in diameter, a strong, windproof stem up to six feet tall, and carrying upwards of twenty flowers. The one thing which *L. regale* demands is good drainage, and that, after all, is easy to arrange for locally, even if your garden is generally unsatisfactory in that particular. The flowers set and ripen seed in great quantity, and this, sown in the following spring, germinates well and will yield you flowering-size bulbs in from two to three years. Really, it is difficult to see why this lily is not to be met with in every garden. The bulbs, by the way, should be planted deep; have at least eight inches of soil between the top of the bulb, and the surface of the soil, for *L. regale*, like many other lilies, produce roots from the stem above the bulb, as well as from the base of the bulb itself. As for manure, it needs none; a top-dressing of leaf mould will be appreciated, but *farmyard manure will poison it.*

If you have farmyard manure, keep it for tiger lilies, which like it. *L. tigrinum* has been cultivated for food for many centuries in Japan and China, whence it was introduced to our gardens, by way of Kew, exactly one century before *L. regale*. The bulbs should be planted eight or nine inches deep in a richer soil than *L. regale* will flourish in, and *L. tigrinum* will not tolerate chalk or any soluble limestone. The farmyard manure must not be used under the bulbs or round them, but only as a top-dressing or mulch, and it should be well-rotted. The variety to plant is *splendens*, which, from mature bulbs, will give you upwards of a dozen fire-red, handsomely marked flowers, scentless but with beautifully recurved petals, per five-foot stem. The stem, which is almost black and marked at the top with a sort of spider-web of fine silvery down, is as resistant to wind as iron wire.

Propagation of *L. tigrinum* is very easy. All varieties produce, in the axils of every leaf, from one to three bulbils, which are small, almost black or dark purple objects the size and shape of an under-sized pea. These are ripe for use, and become so loose that they fall at a touch, at or a little before flowering time, which is early August. (I collected bulbils this year on July 9.) A single stem will yield scores of bulbils, perhaps hundreds. Now whether you are using bulbils, bulblets (baby bulbs produced under ground) or seeds, it is, in my experience, wise to arrange things so the young plants can be left undisturbed for years, instead of sowing thick and then pricking-out. However careful I am, I find that pricking-out minute lily bulbs, seedlings or from bulbils entails heavy losses and severe checking. My way with bulbils or seeds is as follows: first, use a really deep box, at least a foot deep. Fill this, above a layer of clinker or crocks, with sterilised John Innes No. 3 compost. Then place the bulbils or seeds in position, in rows two inches apart and two inches apart in the rows. Press them lightly into the soil so that they will not shift when you sprinkle the covering soil over them. That should be about half an inch, or less. Press firm with a piece of wood, and water thoroughly, using a fine rose. Place the box in shade or half-shade. Thereafter, but for watering so as to keep the soil always moist but never sodden, leave it alone for two years, more in some cases, This simply means that by the time you come to deal with your young lilies again, you will be handling bulbs at least as big as a walnut and quite able to cope with their environment if planted out into a border or a shrubbery or a wild garden. The tiger lily bulbils, treated as seed in this way, turn into bulblets and grow as such.

L. amabile is an easy lily to grow for the front of a border, or shrubbery, or in the rock-garden, for it flowers at about twelve to fifteen inches. Old bulbs may produce longer stems, perhaps up to a yard tall, but they can then be moved. This lily will grow in grass or among low scrubby shrubs. Each stem will carry from one to half a dozen of the flaming orange flowers, which are delicately shaped, recurved and elegant, sometimes a true red, and spotted black. The small bulbs should be planted with six inches of soil on top of them, above good drainage. Seeds will set and are easy to germinate and grow, but it seems to take quite a long time for the seedlings to reach flowering size, which is not surprising since this lily is a martagon. There is a yellow form of this lily but I have not yet grown it. The species will tolerate limestone, but perhaps not pure chalk. It is a Korean plant and was introduced to Britain just before the First World War.

L. bulbiferum var. *croceum* is the correct name of the *L. aurantiacum*, the orange lily of our old gardens. It is a European plant and it has been in cultivation for several centuries. It does very well in what is usually referred to as 'ordinary garden soil', but it demands good drainage. The cup-shaped flowers are not pendent but erect, and there will be from one to fifty per stem, depending on the age and strength of the bulb. The bulbs, which should be under six inches of soil at least, for this is a stem-rooter, increase very rapidly of their own accord, so that propagation is automatic. Clumps of bulbs will require breaking up and replanting every three or four years. I have not grown this lily more than three feet tall, but it can grow much taller, and the variety *giganteum* may exceed six feet. I do not recommend it: the whole point of this lily is being able to look down into the open cups and it is the pendent-flowered lilies, not the erect-flowered ones, which gain beauty from great height.

Nineteen sixty-one was very much a lily year for me. I had become absorbed in the task of succeeding with as many kinds as possible. I had started with the species but very soon became interested in the hybrids.

SOME HYBRID LILIES
September 9, 1961

If I am writing rather a lot about lilies it is for a good reason. It seems to me that the new and even not so new hybrid lilies raised in quantity from seed will be *the* bulb flowers of the next two decades or so. I am, on the whole a 'species' man; that is, I usually find myself preferring the species plant to the complex hybrids. But it cannot be denied that the lily breeders are creating a whole race of very beautiful new lilies and we are, moreover, at the stage of their work when the improvements on nature have not yet gone too far. A time will probably come when the lily hybrids become too large, overwhelmingly floriferous, and excessively highly coloured. But we are not there yet.

With the exception of half a dozen species, lilies as nature made them are not very easy to grow. I have written about a few which are, and shall have something to say later on about one or two other easy species and also about some of the difficult ones. But meanwhile I shall also devote several articles to an attempt to sort out some of the hybrid strains, which I have started to grow here and which, as I have already discovered, are much easier to deal with than the species.

Most of the hybrid lilies are of United States, Canadian, New Zealand or Australian origin, although some very good ones have been started in this country. Most of them are stem-rooting and something must be said about this. If, in any but the lightest, spongiest, almost flaky soil you follow the planting depth instructions in that admirable book *Lilies of the World* by Woodcock and Stearn, you will be, as I was, in trouble. The stem-rooting lilies produce roots from three or four inches of the flower stem just above the bulb. It would, therefore, seem that the bulbs should be planted with six or seven or more inches of soil on top of them, so that these roots find themselves in soil and not in the air as it were. But I have found that if you *do* plant deep, the roots start but will not grow properly. Now the greatest lily nursery in England, is, I believe, Messrs Wallace and Barr's at Tunbridge Wells. This firm, in their lily catalogue, do not advise deep planting of stem-rooting lilies; and, again from my own experience, and despite what I may have written in the past under the influence of *Lilies of the World*, they are right. In most soils there ought not to be more than three, at most four inches of soil between the nose of the lily bulb and the surface. If more is needed it is easy to mulch the growing lilies with leaf-mould; in fact that is precisely what they like.*

BACKHOUSE HYBRIDS. This strain arose from crossing *L. martagon* var. *album* with *L. hansonii*. It has, therefore, the charming martagon candelabra habit. The flower stalks grow about five feet tall and each one carries from fifteen to thirty turks' cap flowers symmetrically arranged in tiers and varying in colour from pale cream through pink-shot-yellow and buff, to rich orange, all spotted with purple or brown. These stately and beautiful lilies are not difficult to grow among low shrubs which shade the bulbs. They are not cheap: a single bulb costs about 12*s* 6*d*. But, as I

* *Lilies of the World* does give this as an alternative to deep planting.

have said, we are at the beginning of the hybrid lily age. Most lilies are self-increasing. Plant three and if conditions suit them you will ultimately have a large clump. Moreover, they are quite easily increased from seed and the reasonably skilful gardener can, by this means, have thousands of bulbs within a few years.

OLYMPIC HYBRIDS. This is a strain of trumpet lilies in which the inflorescence has the tiered, candelabra arrangement of martagons or auratums, that is, the flowers are set up the stem in a spiral and not all opposite each other, as in *L. regale*. My own, from Alexander Best's Greenock Lily Farm in Ontario, have turned out all yellows, but the range of colours is wider and you may get yellows, whites, creams or cyclamen pinks. Moreover, the shape of flower varies from pure trumpet to open auratum like bowls. The outside of the petals is shot with brown or burgundy red.

GOLDEN CLARION STRAIN. The flowers, many to a stem, are long trumpets in various shades of yellow to a rich gold, some unmarked, others with a burgundy-red stripe on the reverse of the petals. These lilies flower at about forty inches tall when the bulbs are mature, are as easy or easier than *regale*, and very beautiful. This strain will, however, be displaced by:

THE AURELIAN STRAIN. The flowering stalks are from five to six feet tall and the inflorescence has up to twelve perfect trumpet flowers of translucent gold. They are strongly fragrant. I do not know whether they are yet obtainable in England.* In the United States good bulbs of this strain cost about four dollars each. There is another aurelian strain called 'Dawn Pink' with colour variation from pale rose to deep pink.

MID-CENTURY HYBRIDS. Why the lilies under this head are grouped under one name, I have no idea. At least four species have been used to produce them and they are so various, not only in height, form and colour, but in the bearing of the flowers, in some cases erect, in others outward-facing, that not much is to be gained by considering them as a group at all. Outstanding among the lilies of this group are 'Fireflame', which is a relatively short lily with very large, beautifully arranged and held crimson flowers which open very wide; and 'Harmony' which has a great umbel of upward-facing apricot-coloured flowers on two-foot stems.

* These and all other de Graaff lilies are obtainable in Britain now.

CREELMAN HYBRIDS. Seedling descendants of the original Creelman (*imperiale*) lily. This was, and is, a six-footer with as many as thirty flowers to the stem, the trumpets being very long and substantial. A stately and magnificent lily. American growers claim that they have found it immune to disease. Its seedling offspring have much the same substance and sturdiness with much variation of colour-marking.

Perhaps the most beautiful of all the new hybrids are the *auratum* × *speciosum* derivatives. Auratum species can be bought for 4*s* a good bulb; and the *L. auratum* var. *platyphyllum* form, which is finer, for half a guinea when the bulbs come from New Zealand, and less when they are Japanese. I gather that New Zealand bulbs are worth the extra money as being certainly free from virus disease. But when we come to the hybrids, the story is different. The two best I have yet seen—I have not got them myself, alas—are 'Excelsior' and 'Crimson Queen'. The latter has huge bowl-flowers striped and shot crimson held to admiration on four-foot stalks. A bulb will cost about £2 10*s*, and an 'Excelsior' bulb £4 10*s*, for which you will get five-foot stalks bearing a number of huge crimson-scarlet bowl-flowers beautifully outward-facing, and with a fine fillet of pure white round each petal.*

American and Canadian lily nurseries have an excellent practice which might be adopted here. They offer not only full-size bulbs, but younger, smaller bulbs, which while they are of flowering size will not, in the first year or two, produce the full length of stem or the full inflorescence of numerous flowers; for these you have to wait until the bulbs grow larger, but on the other hand the practice enables those who cannot afford the stiff price of the new lilies, to buy bulbs more cheaply and make up for poverty with patience.

FLOWERING SEQUENCE
August 18, 1962

I have planted so many different kinds of lilies, each kind in small number, in order to discover which will do here and which will not, that it would not be a good idea to wait until the end of the lily year, late October, after the *L. formosanum* have gone over, and then report on them; I should need half a dozen pages, not one.

* Newer, better ones have since been produced by de Graaff and, of course, these prices no longer apply.

On the other hand, everyone seems uncommonly interested in this garden subject nowadays; hence, interim reports from time to time.

By far the earliest lily to bloom here this year, apparently quite out of its proper season, but I naturally hope it will do the same thing next year, was *L. mackliniae*. I bought six bulbs, small ones which I should not have thought of flowering size, last autumn, and as this lily is relatively short, planted it near the front of a peaty border, in the shade of some dwarf rhododendrons which will keep the sun off the bulbs and roots but allow the lilies to grow through. As I anticipated, the plants were small, to match the bulbs, attaining only about nine inches; with mature bulbs, one can expect this lily to reach about two feet, or even more; when the late Kingdon-Ward found it, there were very dwarf ones in poor soil, but in richer soil some specimens reached three feet; the dwarf ones carried only one flower, the taller ones several. Two of my plants flowered, each carrying a single flower; but this was enough to captivate me and everyone who saw the *mackliniae* in flower. The flower is neither erect nor pendent, but faces outwards; it is a wide open, roughly saucer-shaped flower, neither a trumpet nor a bell, and the colour is a soft pink without mark or blemish. I think I am right in saying that this lily, named for his wife, was Kingdon-Ward's last contribution to our gardens; what a crown to a splendid career. It is a great beauty, it does not appear to be at all difficult, and from several accounts it readily settles down and establishes itself in gardens where it finds the right conditions, an open, fairly gritty soil and good drainage.

I come next to some of the hybrid lilies I have been trying. *L. mackliniae* flowered late in May. Next, but at the very end of June, was *L.* × 'Ruby'. This lily has behaved in the most encouraging way, for last year it had only two flowers in the clump, whereas this year it has, to my amazement, produced no less than fourteen flowering stems, a fine mass of colour. In this garden the stalks are thirty inches tall, very thick and sturdy. The average number of flowers per stalk is five, they are held erect so that they look up at you, and the colour is a deep mahogany red; this (and quite a number of the new hybrid lilies), is too 'hot' in colour for my taste, but provided there are plenty of white lilies in the border or shrubbery, to tone down the general effect, these are spectacular beauties. The constitution of this hybrid seems exceedingly robust.

'Ruby' was followed by another hybrid on July 9; by the way, I fix the dates by recording the variety as 'in flower' not when a single flower opens, but when more than half the buds on the last plant in the group, are open. This second hybrid, then, was *L.* × 'Paprika', a de Graaff lily from Oregon. It is, in my garden, a short lily, the stalks very sturdy and stiff, the foliage bright and clean, the whole about twenty-seven inches tall. In this lily there were, on average, eight flowers per stalk, they faced outwards, and the form was starry with very pointed petals clearly separate from each other; the colour is light mahogany red, or perhaps ox-blood red.

Two days later, there were two more lily kinds in flower: one was *L. amabile* var. *luteum.* It was very undersized, and markedly chlorotic in a border which grows good, healthy *Gentiana sino-ornata*, so that the chlorosis can have had nothing to do with chalk or limestone. I do not think this lily is going to 'do' here; it was equally debile last year. But it is a pretty little martagon if you can grow it. With it flowered the de Graaff hybrid *L.* × 'Prosperity'. This lily was planted in a position where it was shaded until about 2 p.m. whereafter it received some sun. It reached an average of thirty-six inches tall, very straight and sturdy. Incidentally, no lily, not even the much taller ones yet to be dealt with, seemed to have any trouble in standing, unstaked, against quite strong wind. 'Prosperity' had an average of eleven outward-facing flowers per stalk: the fully open flowers are a deep gamboge yellow, a really vivid colour, lightly flecked with mahogany brown dashes rather than spots. If I were to star my lilies for beauty only, I should give *L. mackliniae*, in this list, five stars, 'Ruby' two, 'Paprika' three, 'Prosperity' four. I strongly recommend this last lily.

I should say here that most of the lilies I am reporting on, and shall report on, were planted in two places, from two to six of each kind in each site: the first site was the shrubbery where, according to the books, conditions here for lilies are nearly ideal; the second site was deliberately chosen to try the lilies hard. This is a narrow border beside a lawn and backed by an old mixed hedge; such borders have been long robbed of their goodness and they get very dry. The lilies received no help whatever; no manures, no fertiliser, and, in a season of drought until July 8, no watering, whereas the hoses had been going hard in all the rest of the garden barring the vineyard for seven weeks. They received their first real rain on

July 13. They were, in short, grown as they might be by an amateur with hardly any time to work in the garden and no money to spend on coddling plants. They survived and they prospered.

A day after 'Prosperity', we had *L. bulbiferum* var. *croceum* in full flower: of the species this must be the easiest of all lilies to grow, and, in fact, it has been for centuries. It increases at an almost alarming rate: our own, planted too close to a *Romneya coulteri* which would, we thought, be too much for the lily, grew through it, and its brilliant orange, erect cup flowers look charming among the glaucous foliage of the Californian poppy.

Next in time, flowering with *Lilium regale*, another very easy species, was the de Graaff hybrid *L.* × 'Enchantment'. This is a five star lily if ever I saw one—though I wonder if I shall not have to go up to seven stars when the *L. auratum* reach flowering size here? 'Enchantment' was planted among azaleas in a place where it received only tree-filtered glances of sunshine until late afternoon. It seems to love this, for it grew straight as a rod and very stout from the beginning; another group of it, in the lily ordeal-border, did well but, like the rest in this border, leaned gracefully away from the hedge. 'Enchantment' has very handsome foliage, the leaves rather broader than most, a very bright green and shining. The average height of plants was forty-four inches. The flowers, eight or more to a stalk, are semi-erect, open, starry, a clear light orange handsomely flecked with brown.

It occurs to me that my order of flowering is probably not one from which any general rule can be taken; I suppose that some of the lilies planted in shade would have flowered much earlier in sunshine, and those in sunshine later had they been in shade.

A few hours later than 'Enchantment' came the Bellingham hybrids; they are in full sun from 11 a.m. This group of hybrids was raised by the United States Department of Agriculture. They are 'Turks Cap' lilies, varying in colour, but generally speaking orange or flame red, well-reflexed, and with attractive anthers. My own seem to have too few flowers per stem, the average being eight, whereas thirty is said to be not uncommon. The average height in my clump of these hybrids is sixty inches.

Newly planted Madonna lilies were coming in to flower at about the same time as the Bellinghams, that is mid-July. I take it that all these lilies, like most plants, are late this year, so perhaps the whole time scale should be moved forward in order to give a fair idea of the season for hybrid lilies.

The conclusion, up to date, would seem to be that the new hybrid lilies are good garden plants, easy to grow; for apart from the ones named on this page, I have about fifteen more varieties, not quite in flower at the time of writing, but all doing extremely well. There has been not a sign of the trouble, dreaded by lily growers, botrytis; but then, the season until mid-July was uncommonly dry.

TRUMPETS AND TURK'S CAPS
September 1, 1962

Among the new hybrid lilies there are a number of varieties which have certain characters in common and vary only in detail. I refer to the class of tall, robust trumpet lilies, with more or less white trumpets, strong, fleshy petals, a fragrance which is sometimes overwhelming, and a very good constitution. The first of these to flower here was 'Green Dragon'. The average height of stems was forty inches but I believe they grow taller as they become established. The huge trumpets, three to a stem from my first year bulbs, face outwards and they were seven inches in diameter when fully open; their white is faintly tinged with green, and their foliage not quite so handsome as in other varieties. A four star lily. 'Sentinel' stems were also about forty inches but there were five flowers per stem, average, and these hung slightly and very gracefully downwards. The flowers are heavily scented, their outside is satiny white, their inside stained with golden-yellow. I liked this lily better than 'Green Dragon', if only for its stately bearing. It looks very beautiful among shrubs. The leaves are narrow without being grass-like, and of a good, bright green. Another in the same class is 'Emerald Strain'—'strain' because these are seedlings of a group with some variation from individual to individual. The average stem was sixty inches tall and they flowered on July 31. There were six flowers per stem, very large trumpets, fragrant, white shot with green and gold. Beautifully healthy dark green foliage. Five stars for this one.

'Limelight' turned out to be a pale golden trumpet lily with four flowers per stem, the stems being on average thirty-seven inches tall; the outside of the trumpets is faintly marked with greeny-brown along the 'spines' of the segments. The foliage consists of fine, relatively broad, bright green leaves. A fine lily.

For size and substance of the trumpets, the outstanding trumpet lily to flower here this year, on August 3, was 'Moonlight'. The flowers, three per stem, are lemon yellow but on the outside of each segment, along its spine as it were, is a broad green stripe fading into the base colour. The flowers were enormous but in this garden, and in a position in full sun after 11 a.m., the stalks, though stout enough to hold the flowers up even in a sou'westerly gale, were too short, about thirty-six inches. They may be longer if the bulbs settle down and establish. Despite the grandeur of this lily, I found that I preferred among the yellow trumpets, 'Golden Clarion', which flowered on July 30. The stems were fifty-six inches tall, and an odd thing was that the tallest flowered last, the shortest first; this was quite marked. The dark green leaves clothing the stem neatly, were four inches long and half an inch wide. To each stem there were, on an average, five glorious golden trumpet flowers, pure yellow inside, but with a reddish-brown stripe on the outside of each segment. This lily is fragrant. If I were allowed only one trumpet lily in my garden, this would be the one; if two, I would add 'Sentinel'. (I am not taking species lilies into account here, for if I did I should still give the preference to *L. formosanum* for late flowering, although in the case of the earlier lilies, I think that several of these de Graaff hybrids now supersede *L. regale*.)

I come now to a form of lily which I like better than the trumpet lilies, for I think that they have more grace though less magnificence, and certainly for semi-wild planting among shrubs and in woodlands, they look, to me eye, more in place. These are the Turk's Cap lilies with the general look of a martagon though the flowers, without being as big as those of *L. tigrinum* var. *splendens*, are bigger than those of the wild martagon. The first to flower here, on July 30, in deep shade, was 'Burgundy' which among its many qualities, is very long lasting. Average stems were fifty inches tall, average number of flowers per stem in the first year, twelve. The delightfully reflexed Turk's Cap flowers are scarlet, lightly speckled with a darker colour, and shading to a darker red at the centre. A very beautiful lily, and flowering with it, and very suitable for planting with it *en masse*, was 'Citronella' which is like it in every respect excepting that the flowers are a bright lemon yellow. I have a feeling that these two lilies must be a selection from the 'Fiesta' strain of Turk's Cap lilies, although I may be quite wrong about that. At all events, my 'Fiesta' lilies turned out to be the same height as the other two, flowered at the same time, and varied in colour from pale yellow to a deep orange-red. The whole strain will be admirable for naturalising among open woodland if it proves to be prolific.

Finally, what I consider to be the very best of the new lilies which we have yet flowered here—but please remember that there have as yet been no *auratums* and *auratum* × *speciosums* and we are, in fact, having more trouble with them—is 'Bright Star'. This is quite different from all the others: the stems were on the average forty-eight inches tall and they were in full flower in a not very favourable position on August 1. The outward-facing flowers are flat saucers but with the petals slightly reflexed; there were six flowers to each stalk, and they were fragrant. The base colour is white, but on the inside each segment is marked with a broad triangle of golden-orange, so that the heart of each flower has a starfish marking which is most attractive, a sort of truncated version of the 'ray' of an auratum. The plant and flowers have the look of an aurelian lily. This is a great beauty: six stars.

LILIES IN JULY
August 17, 1963

Last year I gave a good deal of attention to the subject of the new invasion of British horticulture by American hybrid lilies; I did so because not only did it seem likely that they would add something new and very fine to our mid-summer garden display, but because these lilies have become the subject of controversy in that exalted sphere where the lily specialists dwell in bliss. These mandarins cast doubts on the new lilies; they were sure, in advance, that they would not 'do' here, meaning that they would not establish themselves and increase to form the impressive clumps of fine healthy plants which we can more or less rely upon from certain species of, mainly, Asiatic lilies. The American lilies would, it was said, probably be as difficult in their new hybrid avatar, as they had, for the most part, been as species, even though many of the hybrids were of Asiatic parentage. They would be attacked by botrytis and debilitated by virus disease.

When Mr Jan de Graaff stayed for a few days at our house, he answered these doubts not with extravagant claims, nor with indignation; perhaps, he said, the mandarins would turn out to be right. True, his lilies were raised by the million in hard field conditions and put through the mill of a trying ordeal by weather before they were released into commerce. But still, English and Scottish conditions were different and who was he to raise his voice in the presence of the head-shaking great men? The answer, mine and not spoken in so many words, was, and is, that he is the scion of a great Dutch family with more experience, during three centuries, of turning bulbous species into good garden plants, than any other in the world. Mr de Graaff's own answer to all the doubts was simply, 'Why not *try*?'

With a couple of exceptions more likely due to my own carelessness than to the bulbs, the Oregon lilies, as they are now generally called (the de Graaff lilies are raised at the Oregon Bulb Farms near Gresham), planted here have (*a*) increased very rapidly into large clumps, in some cases so rapidly that they will need strict control; (*b*) increased surprisingly in stature; (*c*) flowered as freely right under trees and in quite deep shade, as in full sun; (*d*) shown no sign of disease and none of susceptibility to botrytis. Now, of course, I have stuck my neck out: quite possibly, in the years to come, awful things will happen to these lilies. I can only, as they say, speak as I find: and what I find up to now is that the Oregon lilies are neither more nor less difficult than, say, *L. regale* and quite as adaptable.

I cannot here deal with all, or even many, of them. But the following notes may be of use to gardeners who would like some of these lilies. I have chosen those which seem to be particularly robust and easy:

'Enchantment'. One of the class called Mid-Century hybrids. It grows between two and three feet tall, each stem carrying many outward and upward facing flowers of a vivid, clear orange known as nasturtium-red. Clumps form rapidly. Foliage, medium-green and wonderfully healthy. Flowers (here) late June or early July or, in shade, mid-July. It produces bulbils in the leaf axils which affords a means of propagation easier and quicker than from seed.

The Mid-Century hybrids have all the same general character but vary in colour.

'Fiesta Hybrids'. I am, as they say, crazy about these. They are derivatives of *L. amabile* and *L. davidii*. They are all about a yard tall, with strong wiry stems remarkably resistant to wind. Each stem bears up to a score of reflexed flowers in candelabra arrangement, the colours ranging from pale yellow, through the oranges, to deep maroon-red. Although de Graaff recommends that this lily be planted in full sun so that one should do that if possible, the fact remains that I have seven good clumps of Fiesta in semi-shade and they are doing perfectly well up to now. The flowers are very long-lasting. A great virtue is that, of naturally erect stance, they do not, like so many trumpet lilies, demand staking; they seem never to lean, let alone fall over.

CHINESE TRUMPET LILY STRAINS. Of those which de Graaff places under this head, the most impressive in our garden, up to now, are:

'Black Dragon'. Our plants have not yet exceeded five feet but their vigour is such that I expect them to go to eight feet when clumps are well established. The stout stems, with a tendency to lean away from shade which must be checked by staking, bear fine, healthy leaves and up to a dozen enormous trumpet flowers of magnificent, fleshy substance, pure white inside, purple on the outside. The buds, deep blackish-purple before opening, are very handsome. A superlative lily.

'Green Dragon'. With all the merits of size and strength of the above, the mighty bowl-shaped trumpets are white-shaded chartreuse-green.

TRUMPET LILIES DERIVED IN PART FROM *L. Henryi*. Of this (de Graaff's Division 10) I have as yet tried only three out of about two score thoroughly, and am starting with one or two more. I think that possibly the finest all-round lily in the garden, though not as magnificent as the great auratums, is 'Golden Clarion'. This is a strain of lilies of which the best is the eponymous one. Or, at least, one seems to be offered as *the* 'Golden Clarion'. Height about five to six feet, upright, remarkably rigid stalks, foliage glossy and healthy, flowers up to eight per stem, large, perfectly shaped, rich golden-yellow inside, and outside, but striped with a deep maroon-red. First flowers open here, in full sun, in mid-July, but they are at their best in late July.

'Moonlight'. Height from four to five feet, maybe taller. General qualities as for the above, but the flowers are yellow-with-a-tinge-of-green, as it were, very pure and clear.

'Heart's Desire'. Height up to six feet; the flowers are too shallow, wide and almost bowl shaped to be called trumpets. They are white with an orange centre.

AURATUMS AND SPECIOSUMS. These are the most stately and imposing of all, of course, but I have as yet only tried very few. I have a collection of the lilies bred by Dr Yeats in New Zealand, but for a reason which I will write about in due course, I shall not be able to describe these until next year. Meanwhile of the de Graaff lilies in this class, I have grown two, 'Imperial Gold' and 'Imperial Silver'. Both are strains, that is there are small variations from plant to plant. They are *auratum* × *speciosum* hybrids, with huge, bowl-shaped white flowers which, in the former strain have the typical golden ray and also maroon or crimson speckles, and in the second, no ray but crimson speckles. Their scent, by the way, is very strong and sweet. For the latest and finest of the de Graaff auratum hybrids, I shall have to wait until the price comes down as stocks increase; at the moment these, e.g., 'Empress of India' and 'Empress of Japan' with all the auratum character but richly coloured petals and flowers up to ten inches across, still cost about £20 a bulb.

To sum up: as far as my own small experience goes, the Oregon lilies combine the qualities of 'Show' flowers with the robust resistance to the amateur gardener's conditions which make them good garden plants.

DE GRAAFF IMPERIALS

September 26, 1964

The lily season has been very good: it is by no means over as I write, for the latest, *speciosum* and *formosanum* have yet to flower; the summer trumpets and aurelians are over, but *auratum* and its derivatives are in full season. It is gratifying that the botanical species *auratum* seem to like it here: our best specimen has just been measured with great care: its topmost flower is nine feet from the ground and there are fourteen flowers on this great stem. No derivatives of this species has reached such a size in this garden, but nevertheless the three I want to write about are of imposing stature at their best. They are the de Graaff lilies 'Imperial Gold', 'Imperial Silver' and 'Imperial Crimson'. In our garden they are from three years old to only one year, by which I mean they have been in their present positions for those times; they were planted as mature bulbs, of course, though we have young ones coming on.

'Imperial Silver' flowers, for some reason, ahead of its relatives here, although not by much. It varies in stature from two feet in poor specimens, to four in good ones, with from four to eight flower heads. These are what is rather misleadingly called 'bowl-shaped', six fully open petals which have inherited from their *speciosum* var. *rubrum* parent a remarked reflexing of the petal tips. When fully open the average diameter of the flower is eight inches, but now and again I have had flowers nearly a foot across, usually on plants which for some reason, confined themselves to one or two flowers. The base colour is pure white but this is heavily speckled with crimson dots and dashes, as it were. I have planted this lily in two different positions: in one it has morning shade but afternoon sun, and is shielded by evergreens from north-west; in the other it has morning sun and afternoon shade and a little broken shade overhead. I cannot see any difference in the behaviour of the two clumps.

'Imperial Gold' seems to me to be, at least in my garden, an even more vigorous lily than the above. I have none less than three feet tall and one or two measure six feet from the top-most flower to the ground; most stems carry from four to six flowers and these are larger than in the case of 'Imperial Silver', being for the most part about nine inches in diameter. The base colour of the petals is faintly creamy rather than pure white, and each petal bears the median golden ray of the *auratum* parent. Over the rest of the petals is a stippling of deep crimson dots and dashes. This is an astonishingly beautiful lily, of imposing stature at its best, and of most satisfying substance, with a stem of such toughness that even the gales which we had in early July made no impression on these robust plants.

The most spectacular of the three Imperials is undoubtedly 'Imperial Crimson'. In the now familiar colour folder of de Graaff hybrid lilies the representation of this one is, in my opinion, not as satisfactory as many of the others. On looking at it as I write I am reminded of Queen Victoria's complaint to her portrait painter: 'Sir, we are redder than that.' The stems here are from three to four feet in height, very tough and firm against wind; each bears from three to five flowers, the largest individual flowers being on the stems with fewer in number. The flowers are from six to seven inches across when open and of massive substance. The median line of each petal is a ray of solid crimson and this has, as it were, 'run', so that on each side of the ray is an area of stain, crimson but not quite so dense; this, again, tapers off into a zone of deep crimson spots on a white stained-crimson ground; and finally there is an edge or zone to each petal which is clear unstained white.

I should add that in all three Imperial lilies the flowers are held out from the stem on stiff, tough, wiry stalks which ensure a perfect display; other points are the rich and sweet fragrance on mild, still evenings particularly, only less in its carrying power than that of the most fragrant lily I have yet grown. De Graaff's 'Pink Perfection' which, for some reason, is far more powerfully fragrant than even the other trumpet lilies, so that its sweetness was perfectly apparent up to twenty yards away.

We have, I think, given these lilies only ordinary care. In most cases they are planted in a mixture of lightish clay and leaf-mould enriched with peat, and annually top-dressed with leaf-mould composted with farmyard manure. The best specimens stand on a slight eminence which ensures drainage so sharp that drought is a problem with most of the plants at that point and, for example, meconopses just die there. I have come, after a few years' experience, to the conclusion that these lilies and other hybrid lilies and some species too prefer a dry summer to a wet one, and can stand quite serious drought without turning a hair. The places where lily clumps 'go back' and tend to die out are all on the flat and all in rich, moist soils where rhododendrons grow fast. I have found few lilies to grow in shade; it may be true enough that they like shade for the bulbs, but there is no doubt that they like plenty of exposure to sun and wind for the stems and foliage. I no longer believe in making special local drainage arrangements for lilies. If drainage is bad then the whole lily border, however large, must be raised to get it above the surrounding level. It is easy to do this on a small scale. I find, also, that lilies enjoy a lot of grit in the soil. If I have new bulbs to plant and no special site in mind for them, then I put them in one particular bit of the garden where, when you drive in a spade, there is a nice grating, gritty noise from fragmented slate.

A final point: Imperial lilies do not need staking; they have stems like steel rods. But nevertheless we often have to stake them, and the reason is that unless the degree of light is equal all round them, which is almost never the case, they take a slant away from the shade, however light, the stems growing in a gentle curve.* In many cases this is fine; but in others it proves necessary to use stakes to pull them upright.

* This attribute is so marked in *L. Speciosum* even where fully exposed that I take it to be inherited from that species.

Rosa lutea flore simplici.

Chapter 13

Roses

Looking over everything I have ever written about roses, I find a *leitmotiv.* I am against hybrid teas, hybrid perpetuals and floribundas, as garden plants. The flowers are very beautiful; but the bushes they grow on are ugly, either stiff and without grace if healthy, and even worse if not. In the West Country the incidence of Black Spot is such that these bushes are often defoliated; the disease is either uncontrollable or controllable only with such difficulty that it is not worth the labour. And supposing you do succeed with these plants, unless you are very careful to grow the right variety you are apt to get, in the floribundas, a clotted mass of screaming colour because of the mania for orange and yellow flowers; or, in the hybrid tea class, something in ice-cream pink like 'Peace'. I should, I think, always plant a few hybrid tea roses —in the kitchen garden, for cutting. But no floribundas. There are so many roses which are so much better.

The first article I ever wrote on roses was on this theme.

FIVE GOOD SINGLES

August 15, 1959

Whatever qualities may be attributed to the modern roses, the hybrid tea, the floribundas, and so forth, it seems to me useless to deny that they have, as plants, no beauty of form. Far too much of our newer garden material has this fault. We look to the shape and colour of the individual flowers, to the free production of flowers, but hardly ever to the form of the shrub itself. Even the cleverest pruning can only make the hybrid teas more or less tidy; nothing on earth can make them shapely. It is in this respect that the old shrub roses, and the species roses or simply hybrids of species, have an enormous advantage. It is an advantage which no gardener with eyes in his head can deny; and one which, indeed, has in the last decade, restored these sorts to favour, a restoration achieved, to some extent, at the expense of the modern kinds.

For my part I would go much further; I love a good hybrid tea rose, but, if I had room, I would grow it in the kitchen garden, behind the stout, rectangular quick-hedge which we are growing to hide the merely utilitarian part of the garden, and for the same reason that I grow cauliflowers there. As *produce*, both are delightful; as *plants*, neither lends itself to what I think of as good garden design. As for the floribundas, they have exactly the same fault as the flowering cherries: they produce too much flower, giving a sort of clotted colour effect which is distressing and without grace. But I am still not at the end of my reactionary opinions in the matter of roses. The brilliant work of rose-breeders and the beautifully-folded forms of their blooms have made us forget the beauty of perfectly simple forms. If you ask a child to draw a flower, it draws a circle for the centre and adds petals spokewise: in short a daisy. This simplicity has great charm. So has the element of design we call the 'Tudor' rose. Well, to finish my confession, roses which look like Tudor roses, that is the lovely single flowers, please me better than the wonderful hybrids. And after them, the flowers of the bush roses of the Bourbon section, so strongly sweet-scented and with their 'thousand leaves' arranged in such pleasing symmetry. Last of all, the moderns, so many of which, for example 'Peace' have the vulgar look of pastrycook's work, and the colours of ice-cream.

Of the quite numerous shrub and species kinds which I have grown or tried to grow, there are five which I should like to write about this week, now that they are nearly all over for this year, all five singles. That will leave me free to come back to shrub roses later.

Rosa hugonis is widely planted nowadays, and no wonder. My own specimen is, I think, six years old. It stands eight feet tall at its highest point, and is nearly as large in diameter through the bush. Its stalks fall in graceful fronds, as if the art of careless elegance had been used to display the flowers to advantage. These are numerous, single, primrose yellow, and about the size of an English wild rose. Without any help from me, the whole shrub grows naturally into a graceful form. It never gives the slightest trouble; aphis may attack the other roses, but I have never seen them on *hugonis*. Black Spot scourges such fragile beauties as 'Austrian copper' and 'Austrian (or, if you like, Persian) gold' and makes even the maintenance of the moss roses, especially 'Napoleon's Hat', expensive in captan spraying. But it leaves *hugonis* alone. The plant has one fault: whole branches die back and have to be cut out. But so vigorous is the growth that even this does not much matter, there is always ample replacement wood.

My specimen of *R. omeiensis* var. *pteracantha* is too young to be judged, and the one I have in mind as I write and which inspired my affection for its kind is in the Withersdane garden belonging to Wye College, one of the most perfect small gardens in England. It is again a big, graceful, 'natural' looking shrub with splendidly healthy foliage, and the flowers are about the size of *hugonis* flowers; but they are dead papery-white with a purplish or crimson marking in the form of a lacing on the inside of the petals. The stems are bright red.

Of the rose called *R. ecae* I have two specimens. They form 'fountains' of very slender, spiny, reddish stems which rise, curve over, and then fall, like water, and carry an only moderately free flowering of shiny, buttercup-yellow roses about the size of a half-penny, beautifully displayed among the minute, delicate foliage. These two plants are now between four and five feet tall, open, graceful shrubs well filled from a little above the ground. One, in a border which is kept hoed, is markedly more vigorous than the other, which stands in grass not always as close-mown as it might be. The minute flowers, which seem to radiate light rather than merely to reflect it, enchant everyone who sees them. Like so many other fine plants, I first saw this one at Sissinghurst Castle; but I believe that the better of my two is now finer than the Sissinghurst specimen, a triumph if ever there was one.

'Canary Bird': this, again, is a yellow rose, but the flowers not only larger than those of *hugonis*, but of a much deeper yellow—not, indeed, the Devonshire butter colour of *ecae*, but still, a rich colour, further enriched by the still depeer chrome centres. The flowers open almost flat in the sun and, moreover, they are extremely early: my own was in full flower in the first week in May (true, a May such as we are seldom vouchsafed), four days before *hugonis*. As a plant, it is healthy, disease-resistant (excepting for a little dieback) and grows naturally into an agreeable shrub form without much, or indeed any, help from pruning.

The giants among species roses of this kind are the *R. moyesii*.

We have four, and they seem to be of two different strains, varieties, even, perhaps, species. One sort grows to (up till now at six years of age) twelve feet tall, the individual stems being great, stout, woody growths which in youth, carry the most murderous prickles. From the five or six of these arise the bearing shoots, strong but gracefully curved, and rather sparsely flowering, at least when compared with, say, *hugonis*. But what flowers! From about one and a half to two inches in diameter, with bright yellow centres, the petals are an indescribable, blood red—ruby, indeed, but with no surface sheen, so that they look rather like very good chalk drawings. These flowers, as is well known, are succeeded by enormous, elongated hips which turn bright orange or scarlet when ripe, and are almost as decorative as the flowers.

The other *moyesii* is a shorter and shrubbier plant, on the whole less impressive, but more free-flowering. The flowers, however, have not the unique blood-red colour of the first form, and are best described by the name given to this strain of the species at Wisley, where it was raised, 'Geranium'. Another variety of the species (or is it a separate species?) is *R. kingdon-wardii*,* with the same habit of growth as the tall *moyesii*, but white flowers which are smaller, and laced with crimson or even a sort of purplish brown.

Since we go to so much trouble to gather in species roses from all over the world, it seems a pity to make no garden use of our own species. Even the Burnet rose, *R. spinosissima*, for all it is rather an awkward little plant, might find a place for the sake of its flowers and despite its shape. The wild ones known to me are rarely more than ten inches tall. All the flowers I have seen were primrose yellow, but in some places this species has pink flowers.

One of the pleasures of putting this book together has been watching the progress of my own growth as a gardener. From one article to the next corrections based on closer observation or longer experience appear. This has entailed what appear to be inconsistencies—for example between the reference to *R. spinosissima* in 1959 and that which follows, in June 1960. Very often the inconsistency represents the growth of a new interest, a change not in the description of the plant but, subjective, in my attitude to it.

I do not think I have often misled my readers touching the

* I have not since been able to find this rose in any list. E.H. 1966.

quality of a plant; but I have sometimes changed my own attitude to it in a way which has, I suppose, sometimes been disconcerting.

A JUNE NOSEGAY

June 25, 1960

On the evening of June 1, the weather being warm and clear, as if June were promising to be as glorious as May, I walked round the garden and made a small nosegay of roses. All were of the form which I prefer—the perfectly simple single with four or five petals only. Of these species roses, which flourish here, the earliest were already over—namely, *R. xanthina* 'Canary Bird', of which I wrote in praise just a year ago; and *R. hugonis*, which, at seven years of age, is an immense bush about eight feet tall and nearly as wide and deep. But others were in full flower, or not yet at their best; and some had not even started to open their buds.

When I had finished there were six roses in the nosegay, only one of each kind. As it seems to me that everyone who has room for them would want to plant these May-flowering or very early June species, here they are.

First, what I think is the most perfectly formed of all single roses, shapely, pure and simple, the flower of our native *R. spinosissima*, the Burnet rose. My specimen was 'collected' as a tiny plant from the thousands which grow in the rough of the Royal St David's golf course, as well as in other sandy parts of Wales. It is now a prostrate shrub covering about one square foot of ground and growing strongly. Its flowers are pure white, pearly in the evening light and almost translucent in the gloaming, and of such beauty that it is difficult to move on to something else. It was, by the way, very difficult to include in the nosegay as the flower-stalks are not much more than a quarter of an inch long. It is my ambition to find the pink variety of this lovely species in such plenty that I can collect a specimen with a clear conscience.

The second presents a difficulty of nomenclature: when I first saw it in someone else's garden it was introduced to me as *R. kingdon-wardii*; as such, I ordered it from the only nurseryman in England likely to have it; as such I received it. But no such rose appears in the list of species in the R.H.S. *Dictionary of Gardening*. At all events, it is of the *R. moyesii* kind in habit of growth, shape and size of leaves, and perhaps, in vigour, though my plant has been difficult to nurse into growing, whereas all our *moyesiis* have grown enormously since they were first planted. The flowers of *R. kingdon-wardii* are cup-shaped singles about one and a quarter to one and a half inches in diameter, with a burgundy red centre surrounded by a fringe of bright yellow stamens. This centre gives the flower an 'eye' which makes it very striking and charming. The flowers are gracefully carried on long, sweetly-curving sprays, as in *R. moyesii.*

The third rose I picked was a *moyesii* of the type that is about two inches in diameter or a shade less, and an incomparable blood-red in colour. The largest of our *moyesiis* stands something like thirteen feet tall now, and carries its flowers nicely distributed, not too crowded, so that every one can be seen individually. If, at evening, you stand between the tree and the declining sun so that the light shines through the petals, then the colour is exactly that of a pigeon-blood ruby. When *moyesii* is referred to in catalogues and handbooks there is often a note to say that the Wisley form, called 'Geranium', is a good garden form; well, it is bushier, not so tree-like, but the flower colour, that of a scarlet, or perhaps vermilion, geranium, is neither so unusual nor so beautiful as that of the type. Incidentally, in our garden, 'Geranium' is much later to flower than the type.

'Canary Bird' being over, I had nevertheless two good yellows to choose from, and took a flower of each: they were *R. ecae* and *R. foetida* in the form called 'Austrian Gold'. I have praised *R. ecae* before but I have since looked up a note on it by Mr F. P. Knight, F.L.S., published in the R.H.S. *Journal* for January 1953. The rose is a native of Afghanistan, from which country it was introduced by Dr Aitchison (on Lord Roberts's staff in the Afghan War) in 1880. Mr Knight says that the species does best in a light, sandy soil and sunny position: of my two, both are in rather heavy brick-earth, one is in a sunny position and one in partial shade. Both do well, the larger being now about five feet tall and its thin, graceful red stems well covered with the tiny golden flowers. I have not succeeded in growing this rose from cuttings, but it can be done.

'Austrian Gold' is a thin-stemmed briar growing up to five or six feet, light and graceful in habit, subject to dieback and carrying its vividly dark lemon-yellow flowers in drooping sprays. It should be isolated, or well forward among other species of roses, for it rarely makes a substantial plant. As to 'Austrian Copper', I am puzzled by the description of it in works of reference, where it is said to be a sport of 'Austrian Gold', and is called var. *bicolor* on the grounds that the petals are 'scarlet within, yellow without'. In mine the colour must have run, for flowers are a lemony-orange without and a very rich orange within, the combined effect being so much the colour of really well-polished copper that the plant is well-named. The habit of the bush is exactly that of 'Austrian Gold'. By the way, 'Austrian Gold' is not the same as 'Persian Gold', with which it seemed sometimes to be confused: in the latter the flowers are double.

The last flower to be added to the nosegay was a pearly-white specimen of another *spinosissima*, var. *hispida*, which comes from Siberia. This bush, standing isolated on a lawn, is six feet tall and three feet through. It is, as I write in the first week of June, literally covered with its two-inch wide flowers, the form of which only falls short of those produced by its British type. In the mass, they are pale yellow or cream, but a fully mature flower has a curious opalescent luminescence which, as it were, whitens the colour.

I should have liked to add one of our native 'Alexandra' roses, *R. canina*, to the bunch, but none was yet in bloom. These are fairly easy to introduce into a suitable part of the garden, from cuttings, and it is worth doing this when a really good form of a species notoriously variable is found, notably one of the deeper pinks which are almost red. These are rare, at least in my experience; I have only once seen a very deep pink specimen, and it was not at the time convenient to take cuttings, so that I am still searching.

Not only have the species and old bush roses been—for that matter still are—exceptionally fine this year, but the vigour and bud of the hybrid teas and other garden kinds are equally fine. I can only suppose that last year's very hot summer suited them well. There is, too an exceptional amount of bud and flower on the *rugosa* and *rubiginosa* varieties. But best of all is 'Hidcote Yellow', or 'Lawrence Johnston'. Our specimen of this magnificent *foetida* hybrid has been grown in a rather unusual way which has been a great success and is, for that reason, worth describing.

'Hidcote Yellow', for those who do not know it, is a very vigorous climber which readily grows to twenty-five or thirty feet; its clusters of large, cup-shaped flowers are semi-double and a warm, non-metallic yellow; it has produced them, this year, in very great plenty. Now a climbing rose of the vigour of 'Hidcote Yellow' makes a very stout trunk, the wood of which is flexible, however, so that it will not stand upright un-supported. We grew our plant vertically tied to a strong, well-planted chestnut stake until it was five feet tall, and then stopped it and forced it to make branches. What we now have is a very graceful little *tree*, with a trunk clear of growth and a head of branches, many of them well over eight feet, rising, curving over, dropping and then tending to turn up again at the tips, so that the whole effect, with the flowering shoots rising from these branches vertically, is that of an enormous candelabrum. The 'Hidcote Yellow' tree is backed by a tall, mixed hedge, so that as the plant grows, as grow it must, and so loses its tree form, which I doubt being able to maintain by pruning in the case of so aggressive a doer, it will be able to scramble along the hedge. I am now trying the same method with other varieties of similar habit, but I have a feeling that a result which has been as much accidental as deliberate can never be repeated.

Just to show I am not hopelessly bigoted about hybrid roses:
'STERLING SILVER' AND OTHER HYBRID TEAS
July 8, 1961
What I want to write about this week is roses. It was, I think, after visiting last year's autumn show of the National Rose Society that I raved, on this page, about the 'blue' rose 'Sterling Silver'. Several gardening friends, and others with posts in academic horticulture, shook their heads. One man said that if he planted these 'unnatural' looking roses, his wife would leave him. The general opinion seemed to be that this was a rose quite difficult to grow well and of delicate constitution. I am now in a position to say, 'nothing of the kind'. I have flowered 'Sterling Silver' on two bushes, and it is a magnificent rose. First, although not a record-breaker for growth, it is sufficiently vigorous, not one of those puny varieties unable to support the weight of their own flowers and refusing to make any sound wood. It is, in short, a 'good garden plant'. As to the flowers, I cannot praise them too

highly: of course, the colour is a matter of taste; personally I find this silvery lavender enchanting and it is years since I grew a rose which I have returned so often to contemplate. In the second place, the shapeliness and substance of the bloom are perfection in their class. Thirdly, and I did not notice this at the show so that it came as a pleasant surprise, 'Sterling Silver' is not only a scented rose, but it has the delicious fragrance of the old deep crimson roses, the scent which, to me, is the 'real' rose scent.

In order to test this variety severely none of the bushes was given any fertiliser at all. We have a mixture of our own, or rather one recommended to us years ago by a famous rose specialist. 'Sterling Silver' received no such help and it has still done well. With the normal treatment, it should be perfectly satisfactory. One other test we made: three bushes received the usual occasional spray of captan against Black Spot; one did not. The unsprayed one has developed Black Spot, and remarkably early in the season, and that in a drought period, although overhead watering with a rainer has probably provided the moisture the fungus requires. The other three, with normal spraying, show no sign of trouble.

The rose garden we are constructing, with blue slate flagstone paths and round a water-lily pool, has four L-shaped beds. It is in these that we shall grow the only tea-roses in the garden. No floribundas: they have, no doubt, their merits, but they cannot be fitted into our scheme. At all events, one of these beds will be devoted to 'Sterling Silver' planted with the only white tea-rose I know which is really white, produces valid flowers, and is reasonably vigorous: 'Virgo'. I know that 'Frau Karl Druschki' is a fine old white, but the variety invariably tries to climb a tree and it suffers very badly from troubles when in the bud stage. The best way of using this, and the fragrant old crimson 'Hugh Dixon' which has the same heaven-aspiring habit of sending up enormously long, stout shoots, is by arching the longest shoots down, bow-shaped, to the ground at the end of the season, pegging the end, firmly, and forming a more or less symmetrical pattern with the arches. In the following season you get a forest of flowering stems from these arches, of a particularly good length for cutting. Hoeing and weeding under them is very awkward, of course.

Each of the other beds in the rose-garden will also have a bi-colour scheme; cream with crimson, gold with scarlet, and one of the subtler colours, to allow us to plant that lovely single hybrid tea, 'Ellen Wilmott'.

The back of the rose-garden will be defined by a very low wall of granite—old kerb stones set on edge—containing a higher piece of ground behind it. The border in front of this terrace will be rather narrow, but it is to be planted with shrub roses. These all propagated last year in Kent and planted in temporary quarters when we moved, are a selection of our favourites either budded or grown from cuttings or bought from a nursery. When I planted them in their temporary quarters I unwisely gave them some of our rose fertiliser (one part sulphate of ammonia; one part sulphate, *not* muriate, of potash; one part bone-meal); as a result I shall have larger plants to move than we anticipated. The tallest in the new shrub border will be *R. moyesii*, with its blood-red single flowers; the smallest, *R. ecae*, with its cloud of buttercup-like flowers in May. The sun sets behind this terrace, so that a good place will be allotted to *R. omeinsis* var. *pteracantha* for its great translucent, rose-pink prickles. There will also be a clump of 'Roseraie de l'Hay' and 'Blanc double de Coubert' with their bright green briar leaves, the rich purple flowers of the former and the latter's fragrant white ones. Finally, some *R.* × 'Nevada' for its abundance of big single white flowers turning slightly pink as they fade, and some 'Frühlingsmorgen' with its flowers like outsize Alexandra roses.

In building the rose garden we are managing to work round, instead of uprooting, two old apple trees. The fruit they produce will do for cider, but their principal purpose will be to provide support for climbing roses of the *moschata* group. Somewhere, too, we shall find room for an 'Albertine', despite the sneers of our friends among the horticultural highbrows; it is a plant which delights by its sheer vigour and the generosity of its flowering.

Our experience in trying to grow many varieties from cuttings, for transplanting here, may be of interest. Of the species, all but three succeeded: the three failures are *R. moyesii*, *R. xanthina* 'Canary Bird'—annoying, this, as it is supposed to be easy and I want a whole hedge of it—and *R. ecae*, one 'take' out of twenty cuttings. Old shrub roses and climbing roses all rooted well, but the *moschatas* all failed. As for self-rooted hybrid teas, they are always poor doers.

Why did I not take my own advice and confine the hybrid tea roses to the kitchen garden? The answer is that I not only cultivate a garden, I write about it. And the rose is, beyond all comparison, the most important English garden plant. I am bound to compromise, a little, with the taste of others.

A SELECTED LIST

March 31, 1962

There has long been controversy about when to prune tea-roses and other complex hybrid roses; some gardeners wait until March; others prune in December or even November. Those who did this winter will, no doubt, change their ways in future. Their early pruned plants were doubtless safe enough during the Christmas cold spell, but I noticed in many gardens that the warm weather in late January and early February started a lot or roses into growth; this growth has been, in most gardens, killed by the atrocious weather at the end of February. As a rule, of course, there are some dormant buds at the very base of the stems, but there is no doubt that a lot of damage has been done and many hard-pruned hybrid tea roses which were cut to three buds in December may have been left with no buds to replace the frost-killed shoots. No, even in the mild counties it is safer to wait until March so that any premature growth takes place at the top of the old stems and the lower buds, which will be wanted for the coming season, remain dormant and safe until hard frosts are over.

The other way is to grow roses which need no pruning but the removal, from time to time, of excess old wood and an occasional touch of the secateurs to improve the shape of the plant. I have this year planted a number of roses whose desirability as garden plants I had noted in my garden diary over a period of years. They are as follows:

'Maiden's Blush' forms a handsome shrub, about six feet tall and five feet through. The foliage is glaucous, and the flowers are in clusters; they are pale pink, roundly, fully double and they are fragrant. 'Coralie' is a very good moss rose which also makes a handsome, shapely bush, bearing an enormous number of flowers with a delightful silvery tint in the colour. A charming old rose which you should plant if you have room is *R. damascena* var. *versicolor*: this is the true York and Lancaster rose; the flowers are either pale pink or white, and in either case they are striped with carmine.

Among the so-called Scotch roses and their hybrids there are two which I have already praised. 'Frühlingsmorgen' and 'Frühlingsgold'; now here is another which at last I have found room for, 'Glory of Edzell'; in May this rose produces a great number of its small, single flowers on the short laterals which have developed all along each main branch, usually one per lateral but sometimes more. Thus the flowers are very gracefully displayed, not bunched; their colour is old rose, with richly yellow centres and soft yellow veins. An exquisite rose.

Many gardeners are talking enthusiastically about their hybrid musk roses, which they find exceptionally robust and disease-resistant, as well as very shapely plants. These are bushes, well furnished, not leggy, about four to five feet tall at maturity; they all have at least a touch of the musk scent, and they can be planted to form hedges to a rose garden or a walk. But they can also be planted as specimens. A good representative one, very handsome in autumn, with semi-double, shell-pink saffron-tinted flowers, is 'Penelope'. Another group of very hardy and robust roses which is popular with gardeners is that of the Penzance Briars. These are hybrid sweet briars with characteristic scent. Left unpruned they grow into very tall, open plants, as if they could not quite make up their minds whether they are, or are not, climbers. They therefore need either a stout post, or an old tree trunk not so much for support as to keep them reasonably tidy. They start flowering in early June and may easily attain ten or eleven feet. Of this group my favourites are 'Amy Robsart', a very floriferous briar with flowers of a deep rose-pink; and 'Lord Penzance', which has flowers of buff tinted with gold and rose.

The term 'species' roses has come to be very widely abused, for a number of the varieties which appear in lists so headed are, in fact, hybrids. Nevertheless we must use the term since nurserymen do so and a pedantic purism at this stage would merely cause confusion. It would be true to say that all species roses are good, and certainly I wish I had room for the lot. Those I have actually planted this year, in addition to the ones, like *R. moyesii*, planted as soon as we got possession of the garden, are five in number:

'Arthur Hillier': This is for large gardens, only, since in time it attains a height of twelve feet and a spread of quite as much, a huge fountain of graceful branches which bear a vast number of pale crimson flowers succeeded by scarlet hips. This rose is a cross between *R. macrophylla* and *R. moyesii* and a very great beauty when well grown. A much smaller, bushier and very different shrub rose is the species *R. sinensis* var. *mutabilis*; as its name implies, the flowers change colour in the course of their life; they are single, and they begin as yellow buds flushed with copper; they open buff shading to carmine, and are about three inches in diameter when fully open; as the flowers age towards their decline they become first rose-pink, and finally crimson. An astonishing performance.

I have remarked before on the extraordinary colour of *moyesii* flowers, that deep but chalky crimson; well, there is a rose bearing the specific name *hillieri*, though in fact a hybrid between *moyesii* and *willmottiae*, which has flowers of similar form and colour, but the colour darkened by several shades. Hilliers, who raised this hybrid some forty odd years ago, claim, I think rightly, that it is the darkest of all single roses. The shrub grow about nine feet tall and needs a good deal of side room, too.

Now some climbers. Last year I planted a yellow Banksian rose on the south-east wall of the house. It has behaved like an evergreen although it is not so listed. It made very fast growth, attaining about eight feet with four main stems in one season and in rather poor soil. It did ultimately drop about half its leaves, but not until new shoots had appeared in literally every leaf axil; clearly, it is going to be an enormous plant; by the way, the two spells of cold weather did not harm the young shoots, although this rose is not regarded as perfectly hardy. I gather that we cannot expect it to flower for several, perhaps, many years.* This is not so with another favourite climber of mine, *R. moschata* var. *grandiflora*; this can really only be planted effectively if you have an old, large, rather gaunt tree to cover, for it is a colossal rose, producing masses of creamy-white flowers of musk fragrance. Even lovelier and in the same class for growth and size, is *R. odorata* var. *gigantea* Cooper's Variety: it comes from Burma but it is hardy; the flowers are three-inch singles, pure white, with big

* In fact it flowered the following year.

golden centres. Its very large leaves are exceptionally shiny, and it is altogether a most beautiful rose.

I am not sure that my favourite rose is not the common Burnet rose, the *R. spinosissima* of Scotland and Wales. I have planted it here, but I cannot get the form I want, it insists on growing vertically, whereas the one which I collected years ago on St David's golf-links made a prostrate plant whose flowers, of the most perfect form, thus looked up at you from the ground. Plants of this species bought from nurserymen form, instead, a round bush about three feet tall, which is very nice but not what I want. It may be that ordinary garden soil is too good for it; the one I so regret leaving behind in Kent was growing in absolutely pure peat; and at St David's it had been in pure sand.

If you like the old Austrian Gold or Austrian Yellow rose, do not plant it but instead have *R. lutea* var. *maxima* which has exactly the same flowers, that is single gold ones of an uniquely glowing colour, but which grows into a decent-looking healthy bush. The Austrian briars are a nuisance in any garden; they not only suffer badly from Black Spot which they convey to other roses, they grow leggy and shapeless and they die very young. *Lutea* var. *maxima* has none of these faults.

Here are two species, much neglected, for very mild gardens in the south and west, admittedly far from hardy in most of Britain but it would be nice to see them planted where they certainly would survive and flourish, for example in the southern littorals of the western peninsulas, probably the Isle of Wight, and in other places with soft winter climates and plenty of summer sunshine. The better of the two is *R. bracteata*, one of the relatively few roses which is a true evergreen. It was, perhaps, the only practical benefit this country received (excepting Sir John Saunders' admirable book) from the famous Macartney embassy to the Emperor of China in 1791. Lord Macartney, despite the gout which afflicted the poor man, must have been a gardener, for he brought this rose home with him. It is something between a bush and a climber; that is, it produces shoots so long, perhaps twenty feet on a warm south wall or over a tree in a sheltered place, that they are 'climbing' shoots. The leaves, with up to eleven bright, shining green leaflets which attain two inches of length in vigorous specimens, are very handsome. They appear to be able to stand about ten degrees of frost without harm, but really low temperatures scorch them horribly without actually killing the plant once it is well established. The flowers, on independent stalks surrounded by downy bracts, are white, beautifully 'cupped', very substantial, subtended by stout, green bracts, begin to open in June and go on doing so until October; they are up to four inches across, and fragrant.

I confess that I have never seen the next one in Britain, only in places like Teneriffe, but it has been and can be grown here where there are (*a*) plenty of space, (*b*) mild winters and (*c*) ample summer sunshine. This is the fabulous *R. gigantea*, a plant which can apparently climb to eighty feet and which makes new shoots of twenty feet long and an inch in thickness in one season of growth. The point is that the flowers—white in the two specimens I have seen but apparently they can be yellow or pink in the Shan Hills whence this species hails—are six inches in diameter. However, unless the plant is so placed as to receive every minute of sunshine there is, it will not flower at all. Obviously this is something for the enthusiast, not for the average gardener.

Now here is a short note on the *Rosa banksiae* written two years and three months after my first reference to planting it, in 1962.

ROSA BANKSIAE

June 13, 1964

Perhaps the plant which has exceeded our most optimistic expectation in this garden has been the *Rosa banksiae* of which I wrote two years ago. Whenever I look at it I can, as it were, hardly believe my eyes. We had never grown it before we planted it here on a wall of the house which faces east of south. That was in the autumn of 1961 when the plant was a rooted cutting about eighteen inches tall. We were told that (*a*) the species was difficult and (*b*) it never flowered when young. In three years it has attained the eaves of the house which, I suppose, must be about twenty-five to thirty feet and has quite covered the wall between two lots of windows; it has to be cut back from obscuring the windows. It first flowered in 1963. This year the flowering has been such that some sprays were completely yellow with blossom, hiding the foliage. In the bitter winter of 1962–63 the plant lost its leaves; it is supposed to be deciduous anyway. But in ordinary winters here, like the last one, it isn't, it's half evergreen.

There are several forms of this plant and in that respect too we have been lucky, for ours has perfectly double flowers and they are a clear sulphur yellow. Cuttings root easily and furthermore these cuttings flower. That rule, 'does not flower young', must relate to seedlings only; for, come to think of it, a cutting from a part of the plant which has already flowered is, surely, physiologically no 'younger' than the parent plant?

This same plant has continued in its flourishing course and has now sent some immense shoots over the roof of the house. Tying its higher growths is a major operation with tall ladders; it flowers with regularity and gratifying freedom. There are very few objects whether of art or nature, which have given me more pleasure than this magnificent Chinese rose.

Index